THE HAMILTON LETTERS

John A. Davis is Emiliana Pasca Noether Chair in Modern Italian History at the University of Connecticut and Editor of the Journal of Modern Italian Studies. His most recent book, *Naples and Napoleon: Southern Italy and the European Revolutions 1780–1860*, was published in 2006. His previous publications include *Gramsci and Italy's Passive Revolution, Conflict and Control: Law and Order in 19th Century Italy,* and *Merchants, Monopolists and Contractors: Economy and Society in Bourbon Naples 1815–60.*

Giovanni Capuano is a teacher and translator. His previous publications include *Naples and its Environs* and *William Hamilton e la Rivoluzione Napoletana del 1799.*

THE
HAMILTON
LETTERS

The Naples Dispatches of Sir William Hamilton

Edited by JOHN A. DAVIS and GIOVANNI CAPUANO

I.B.TAURIS

LONDON · NEW YORK

Published in 2008 by I.B.Tauris & Co Ltd
6 Salem Road, London W2 4BU
175 Fifth Avenue, New York NY 10010
www.ibtauris.com

In the United States of America and Canada distributed by Palgrave Macmillan, a division
of St. Martin's Press, 175 Fifth Avenue, New York NY 10010

ISBN: 978 1 84511 611 8

A full CIP record for this book is available from the British Library
A full CIP record is available from the Library of Congress

Library of Congress Catalog Card Number: available

Printed and bound in Great Britain by TJ International Ltd, Padstow, Cornwall
from camera-ready copy edited and supplied by the author

CONTENTS

Introduction by John A. Davis   1

The Dispatches   31
  January–December 1797   36
  January–December 1798   71
  January–December 1799   146

Conclusion   221

Appendix: An unpublished letter from Ferdinand IV to Cardinal Ruffo   231

Notes
  Introduction   237
  The Dispatches   241

Bibliography
  Introduction   255
  The Dispatches   258

Index of Names   259

This book is the result of research promoted by the Istituto Italiano per gli Studi Filosofici of Naples that resulted in a previous publication in Italian under the title *Sir William Hamilton. Dispacci da Napoli (1797-1799)* a cura di Giovanni Capuano (Istituto Italiano per gli Studi Filosofici, Napoli 2006).

INTRODUCTION

John A. Davis

Sir William Hamilton, Lord Nelson and the Neapolitan Jacobins

Sir William Hamilton served for 36 years (between 1764 and 1800) as the minister of King George III of England at the court of the Bourbon rulers of Naples. The correspondence published in this volume and edited by Giovanni Capuano relates only to the final years of his mission (from January 1797 to December 1799), and consists mainly of the reports sent by the British minister to the Foreign Secretary in London. Nonetheless these give a very clear sense of the tumultuous nature of the events in which Sir William Hamilton played a significant part.

For most of his career – by no means an arduous or exacting one – his principal brief had been to improve commercial relations between Britain and the Kingdom of the Two Sicilies. But Sir William's efforts in this direction were never as energetic as his pursuit of antiquities and great masters, nor were they as successful as his growing reputation as a host and guide to a city whose mysteries had by the end of the eighteenth century made Naples one of the most sought after stations on the itineraries of the European Grand tour. In the aftermath of the French Revolution, however, Sir William's role would change dramatically. From the dispatches published here we can easily understand how it was that what Sir William liked to refer to as 'this remote corner of the world' unexpectedly found itself at the epicentre of the conflicts that after half a century of peace once again engulfed Europe[1].

Sir William needs little introduction since the events that followed would make him one of the most notoriously deceived husbands in history. Following the death of his first wife Catherine Barlow in 1782, in 1792 Hamilton married Emma Lyons, the former mistress of his nephew Charles Francis Greville who adopted the name Emma Hart for propriety's sake when she became Hamilton's mistress in 1787. Renowned for her beauty, Lady Hamilton was of course destined also to become the lover of Horatio Nelson and it was the resulting and bizarre *ménage à trois* that made Sir William one of the lampooned cuckolds of his day[2].

The notoriety of Sir William's very public private life was compounded, however, by the sinister although still far from clear role that the Hamiltons played in the final act of the Neapolitan Republic in June 1799. It was this that makes his correspondence of special interest, since both he and Lady Hamilton were caught up in what proved to be the most controversial and fiercely debated episode in the career of Britain's most admired and respected national hero, Admiral Horatio Nelson.

In November 1798 the king of Naples, Ferdinand IV, under strong pressure from the English government, Sir William and Rear Admiral Lord Nelson in Naples, had embarked on what proved to be a disastrous offensive against the small French army that had occupied Rome earlier in the year and set up a Republic. The Bourbon army suffered an unexpected and catastrophic defeat. With the French in hot pursuit the king fled, abandoned his capital, Naples to its fate and on 21 December he, together with the royal family and its courtiers, were carried on Nelson's men-o'war to the safety of Palermo.

A month later a Republic was declared in Naples, which after fierce popular resistance was occupied on 22 January by a French army led by general Championnet. In the months that followed, however, a violent royalist counter-revolution spread through the mainland provinces, and on 13 June the royalist irregulars – organized in what their leader, Cardinal Fabrizio Ruffo called his *Most Christian Army of the Holy Faith* (known for short as the *Santafede*[3]) – supported by troops provided by the king's Russian and Turkish allies, entered Naples and gained control of the lower part of the city.

A terrible massacre followed as royalist mobs – described simply as '*lazzaroni*'[4] – sought out and killed all those they suspected of supporting the Republic. Ruffo and his officers were horrified by the scenes they witnessed, but did not have the means to impose order or to control the Sanfedist irregulars. The situation was especially dangerous because the Republicans still controlled the forts, while from the St Elmo castle a well equipped French garrison of 800 men commanded by Colonel Joseph Méjean threatened to bombard the lower districts of the city held by the Sanfedists. The Royalist leaders also believed that a French fleet was in the Mediterranean and feared that it might appear off the Bay of Naples at any moment. For that reason, on 19 June they offered terms of capitulation to the patriots in the forts and to the French garrison. The armistice was counter-signed on 22 June by Captain Foote[5], the senior British naval officer present in the Bay of Naples at the time, and by Baillie and Acmet, the commanders respectively of the Russian and Turkish troops that had joined forces with Ruffo for the final assault on Naples[6].

When two days later on 24 June Rear Admiral Lord Nelson's squadron of no fewer than 14 British warships entered the Bay of Naples, Nelson immediately declared the armistice to be null and void. On board HMS *Foudroyant* with Nelson were Sir William and Lady Hamilton. As well as being the envoy of the king of England, Sir William and his wife had become trusted advisers of the Bourbon rulers (who were still in Palermo) and in the days that followed they acted as interpreters for Nelson during the difficult negotiations that ensued between the British Admiral and the royalist leaders, Cardinal Fabrizio Ruffo and Cavaliere Antoine Micheroux[7].

Ruffo was still concerned about the anarchy in the city and eager to move the patriots to the *polacche*[8] waiting in the harbour as quickly as possible, partly for their own safety and partly for fear of the anticipated imminent arrival of a French war fleet. Hence the urgency of the negotiations and parleys that followed Nelson's and the long controversy that began with Nelson's peremptory order that the armistice be revoked. On the 25th a heated encounter between Ruffo and Nelson took place on board the *Foudroyant*. Nelson claimed in exasperation that 'an Admiral is no match in talking with a Cardinal'[9]. But then he apparently changed his mind and on the 26th this decision was allegedly communicated to Ruffo by Captains Troubridge and Ball. As a result, the patriots agreed to leave the fortresses and embark on the *polacche* that would carry them to Toulon. In recognition of Nelson's concession, Ruffo celebrated a *Te Deum* on the 27th in the Carmine church, while the patriots quitted the forts with full military honours and for their safety were taken under the escort of the Turkish and Russian regular troops through the hostile city and embarked with their families on the transports in the harbour. Ruffo also agreed to surrender to Nelson prominent rebels who had been captured, including Francesco Caracciolo, commander of the fleet of the Neapolitan Republic. Since these prisoners were not in the forts, they were not included in the terms of the capitulation.

A day later – 28 June – Lady Hamilton received a letter from Palermo in which the queen, Maria Carolina, denounced the armistice. Similar instructions from Palermo also arrived for Sir William from the queen's closest advisor and minister, Sir John Acton. In the afternoon Nelson's ships suddenly changed position, bringing the *polacche* under their guns and making the patriots prisoners once again. A detachment of British marines went ashore to pick out the most prominent among them, while at Nelson's request Hamilton wrote to the king requesting further instructions and adding the comment that the patriots now seemed to be in his hands[10].

On the same afternoon Nelson gave orders for the captured Francesco Caracciolo to be brought on board the *Foudroyant*, where on the following day a court martial of Neapolitan officers presided by a senior Austrian officer, Commodore Count de Thurn, sentenced Caracciolo to death for the High Treason committed when he ordered his ships to fire on the Neapolitan frigate the *Minerva.* Nelson endorsed the sentence and Caracciolo was transferred that afternoon to the Sicilian warship *Minerva* where the sentence was carried out. Still on the same afternoon Nelson also rejected a final plea from Micheroux that the *polacche* be allowed to sail for Toulon under the terms of the capitulation. Instead, the rebels (termed 'patriots' by their defenders, including Ruffo and Micheroux, 'Jacobins' by their opponents including Nelson and his officers) were held on the *polacche* and on Nelson's own ships until the King returned to Naples on 10 July on board the *Sirena.*

The patriots were subsequently transferred back to the same fortresses they had voluntarily left shortly before to await trial by the special tribunal (the *Giunta di Stato*) that was set up to punish the supporters of the former Republic Between July 1799 and the royal amnesty of 30 May 1800, of the estimated 3,000 suspected patriots who were arrested in the capital alone, including those who left the fortresses in June under promise of safe-conduct, 99 were executed, 222 sentenced to life imprisonment, 322 to shorter prison terms, 288 to deportation and 67 to permanent exile. For the Kingdom as the whole Mario Battaglini has estimated that 168 executions were carried out and 3,712 individuals were tried for participating in the rebellion[11].

Sir William and the 'Nelson Wars'

The debate over Nelson's conduct in the Bay of Naples in June 1799 has focused primarily on Nelson's role and specifically whether a senior British naval officer and national hero deliberately broke his word of honour when he first agreed to the armistice and then violated its terms. That in turn focuses the issue on whether Nelson did, or did not, agree on 26 June that the armistice should be honoured. Much of the debate hangs on timing, and is complicated by the slowness of communications at the time as well as the variances between standard time, local time and nautical time. For that reason circumstantial evidence also becomes relevant since the attitude of the Bourbon rulers towards the Republican rebels had been stated very clearly long before Nelson arrived on the scene. Both the queen Maria Carolina and her closest advisor, Sir John Acton, had given clear instructions to Cardinal Ruffo early in April not to make concessions to the rebels in Naples, the queen stipulating in particular that 'absolutely no terms should be offered to rebellious Naples and its ingrate citizens. Order will be re-established in that monstrous city by rewarding those who have been loyal and by making an example of the wicked. Your task is to restore order and our throne so that from this atrocious disaster may follow a happy and tranquil future'[12]. A further letter to Ruffo from the queen dated 17 May was even more specific, and named the Republican leaders who were to be brought to justice: Francesco Caracciolo, the Prince of Moliterno, Lucio Caracciolo, the Duca di Roccaromana and General Federici[13].

Acton's instructions to Sir William Hamilton (dated Palermo 26 June, but received by Hamilton on 28 June) were also unambiguous:

'My dear sir, we have received at last the infamous convention for the Jacobins at Naples under the pretext of capitulation for the rendition of the castles. His Majesty is to have ship freighted immediately to send a person to relieve the Cardinal and order him to give account for his disobeying so openly the commands and instructions of his own sovereign'[14].

Nelson did not receive these instructions until the 28th, however, so why – given his initial hostility to the armistice – had he agreed on the 26th to honour it? That remains the key question. Nelson's critics insisted that the only explanation was that Nelson – who had only a limited number of marines on board his ships – deliberately chose to trick the patriots into leaving the safety of the forts, from which they could not have been dislodged by force and where they were safe. But if the decision had been made in good faith why then was it reversed on 28 June when Hamilton received Acton's letter – was Nelson not bound by honour to maintain his promise to the patriots? Should he not have challenged an order from a foreign ruler that forced him to break his word, or at very least have consulted first with his commanding officer Lord Keith? Or, finally, had Nelson never changed his mind, and had the release of the prisoners been done at the initiative of Sir William Hamilton, as many have claimed, or at that of Cardinal Ruffo who literally took the law into his own hands?

The case has all the makings of a thriller and it has now run for two centuries without reaching a clear ending – although the previously unedited letter from the king to Cardinal Ruffo which has been found by Giovanni Capuano in the National Archive in Kew may perhaps finally offer a solution to this long running controversy[15]. There can be no doubt, however, that had the Republicans in the Castel Nuovo and Castel dell'Ovo been allowed to leave under safe conduct, many victims of the royal Terror that followed might have been saved, although for the remaining supporters of the Republic in Naples who were not in the forts and for those elsewhere in the Kingdom these would have been little chance of escape.

Revulsion at the repression that followed the fall of the Republic quickly brought these events and Nelson's role in them to international attention. From the start a variety of different motives and prejudices came to bear on the polemic. There were the jealousies that Nelson inspired especially amongst his superiors, as well as broader considerations of national honour and pride[16]. Admiral Lord Keith, who succeeded Earl St Vincent as the senior naval commander in the Mediterranean and hence became Nelson's commanding officer in July 1799, shared that feeling of revulsion and played a part in focusing responsibility on Nelson – although many believed that Keith was motivated also by personal jealousy[17]. There was also a class connotation – in period when common rebels were shot out of hand, Nelson's honour was doubly stained by the noble status of many of the victims of the royal terror in Naples.

The historical debate on Nelson's personal conduct has as a result taken on a life of its own that at times has become separated from the issues immediately at stake in the Republic of 1799. The controversy offers a text book example of the intricacies of historical evidence, documentation and interpretation, since the issues hang as much on the intentions of the different actors as on what they said or wrote, or were reported to have said, or saw fit later to record. As has also been recognaized, the controversy also throws interesting light on the inter-connections between heroism, honour and national identities[18].

The controversy was immediate as well as historical. The charge that the British admiral had deliberately deceived the patriots into surrendering on the assurance that they would receive safe-conducts was taken up by the survivors, notably by those who reached Paris, and by Vincenzo Cuoco and Pietro Colletta[19]. These charges were endorsed later by the Italian historian Benedetto Croce, for whom Nelson was the evil genius of the counter-revolution: 'he came to defend only what was out-dated and corrupt in our society and he drowned in blood the new forces of nobility and generosity that were at that moment coming into being'[20]

Nelson's conduct in the Bay of Naples was first publicly questioned in England in a speech made by Charles James Fox in the House of Commons on 3 February 1800. Denouncing atrocities committed by British forces in general, Fox referred explicitly to the events in Naples in 1799:

'Naples, for example, has been among other what is called 'delivered': and yet, if I am rightly informed, it has been stained and polluted by murders so ferocious and by cruelties of every kind so abhorrent that the heart shudders at the recital'.

Fox went on to claim that a British armistice signed with the Republicans in the Castel dell'Ovo and the Castel Nuovo had been violated[21].

In his *Life of Nelson* published in 1806, Harrison rejected these charges, but accused Captain Foote of signing a dishonourable armistice without authority. That charge provoked a vigorous response from an outraged Foote, who in a published vindication of his own conduct denied the claim made by Nelson himself (in a letter to Lord Spencer) that Foote had been party to an 'infamous armistice'[22]. Foote claimed that he had been calumnied, but also that he had been persuaded by the Board of the Admiralty not to make a formal protest against Nelson's action in overthrowing the Capitulation. He repeated the charge of treachery:

'I believe it is but too true that the garrisons of Uovo and Nuovo were taken out of those castles under the pretence of putting the Capitulations I had signed into execution...and that some of those unfortunate people were treated with very great severity: none of them suffered death on board the British ships, but Caracciolo was tried on board the *Foudroyant*, bearing Lord Nelson's flag, by Neapolitan officers.'

Foote added a further insinuation, however, that gave the controversy new heat:

'Be assured, dear sir, that the less is said about Lord Nelson's conduct in the Bay of Naples, the better: for however great and noble on most occasions, his Lordship at the time was absolutely infatuated'[23].

The suggestion that Nelson's judgment was at the time impaired by his infatuation with Emma Hamilton would subsequently gain greater prominence. But the claim that Nelson deliberately deceived the patriots into leaving the fortresses and giving up their considerable stocks of guns, ammunition and food, also featured in the first English language account of the revolution in Naples published abroad. This was the detailed account of the Neapolitan Republic that appeared in the *Sketches of the State of manners and opinions in the French Republic* published in Paris and London in 1801 and written by Helen Maria Williams – an English woman who had been settled in Paris in 1792, and whose initial enthusiasms for the Jacobin cause had not survived the Terror[24].

In her account, Helen Williams agreed that Nelson had acted dishonourably, although she strenuously defended the efforts made by his officers to protect the patriots. In support of her claim she also published the text of the act of capitulation with the patriots in the forts which had been given to her in Paris by the Bishop of Canosa, Monsignore Forges D'Avanzati, a former member of the legislative assembly of the Neapolitan Republic and by Omodeo Ricciardi who had been commissar for the Neapolitan provinces[25].

The most damaging and memorable indictment of Nelson's conduct, however, came in the passage in Robert Southey's *Life of Nelson* published in 1813 that described the imprisonment of the Neapolitan patriots as:

'a deplorable transaction, a stain on the memory of Nelson and upon the honour of England. To palliate it would be vain: to justify it would be wicked. There is no alternative for one who will not make himself a participant in guilt but to record the shameful story with sorrow and shame'[26].

It was this ringing indictment that spurred Nelson's defenders into action in defence of Nelson's honour, that of the Royal Navy and indeed of Britain itself. The first strenuous denial of the charges levelled against Nelson was made by Commander Jefferson Miles in a short 'Vindication' published in 1843[27]. A more heavily documented defence followed with the publication of Nelson's letters and dispatches by Sir Nicholas Harris Nicholas in 1845[28].

The controversy was only just beginning, and it was not only the honour of the man who had become England's greatest national hero that was at stake but by extension that of Great Britain and the British Navy. On the British side a steady flow of publications designed to exculpate Nelson followed, while in Italy Neapolitan historians were equally busy searching for documents that would demonstrate Nelson's guilt.

The 'Nelson wars' came to a peak as the first centenary of 1799 approached, in preparation for which numerous previously unedited documents were published, particularly in one of the leading scholarly reviews in Italy, the *Archivio Storico per le Provincie Napoletane*. An article published in 1899 in the prestigious *English Historical Review* by the British historian F.P. Bradham then gave the controversy a new and bitter focus. Reviewing all the documentation that had become available, Badham concluded that Southey had been correct and that the new documents published by the Neapolitan historian Antonio Maresca showed conclusively that Nelson had deliberately tricked the patriots. Bradham concluded his article by citing verbatim Southey's earlier denunciation[29].

This provoked a withering riposte from the American naval historian, Captain A.T. Mahan, a leading expert on British naval history who was writing a biography of Nelson. Mahan utterly rejected the claim that Nelson was guilty of breaking his word and violating the armistice, citing the letters from the king and from the Bourbon minister, John Acton, that were delivered to Nelson on board the *Foudroyant* on 28 June and which instructed him to annul immediately an armistice that the Bourbon authorities denied Ruffo had authority to negotiate. On the other charge leveled against Nelson – that the British admiral had unlawfully permitted a Neapolitan courts martial to convene on a British warship and had then, without the authorization of his superior officers, intervened to insist that the death sentence passed on Francesco *Carracciolo* be carried out immediately – Mahan was prepared to agree that Nelson has acted incorrectly but not, he claimed, without justification. Above all, however, Captain Mahan vented his fury and anger on Professor Bradham, whose accusations against Nelson demonstrated, he believed, a lamentable lack of patriotism[30].

Two more publications followed. The first was commissioned by the *Navy Record Society*, not a body that was likely to publish anything derogatory about Britain's most admired naval leader. The volume was published in 1903, and its editor, H.C.Gutteridge, brought together for the first time in translation virtually all the records and documents available at the time. Gutteridge not unexpectedly endorsed Mahan's conclusions, and absolved Nelson of the charge of deception, although he too censored Nelson's conduct in the trial and execution of Caracciolo[31]. In the same year Constance H.D. Giglioli, an English woman who was married to a Neapolitan and lived in Naples, published another account in which she also marshaled the now immense documentation that had been accumulated. Rejecting the claims made by Mahan and Gutteridge that the decision to arrest the patriots in the transports was the result of the orders received from Palermo on 28 June, Giglioli made Sir William Hamilton the villain of the piece, claiming that he had deliberately deceived Ruffo and Micheroux into believing that Nelson would honour the armistice[32].

With much less heat and nationalist passion now than at the time of the first centenary, the controversy still rumbles on. In his recent biography of Nelson, David Vincent repeats the arguments raised by Mahan and Gutteridge without adding any fresh evidence[33]. Mr. Carlo Knight, on the other hand, has provided additional albeit circumstantial evidence to substantiate the claim that Hamilton was the guilty party[34]. In the meantime, the 'Nelson wars' have also entered the realm of literature. Barry Unsworth has written an outstanding novel (*Losing Naples*) that takes the controversy surrounding Nelson's behaviour in the Bay of Naples as the central theme for a brilliant exploration of the construction of national identities around images of national heroes[35]. Both Nelson and Hamilton also feature prominently in Susan Sontag's *The Volcano Lover*, another novel that explores themes that historians would only later follow up on – especially the ways in which portrayals of Emma Hamilton reveal a whole series of contemporary and later prejudices and stereotypes inflected by gender. Susan Sontag was also amongst the first to draw attention to the wider significance of Sir William Hamilton's career as a collector of antiquities[36].

Sir William, Bourbon Naples and British Diplomacy 1764-92

Sir William Hamilton's dispatches published in this volume do not resolve these long running controversies. Those that relate directly to the events of June and July 1799 have long been known to historians, represent only a small part of Hamilton's correspondence in this period and in any case need to be set in the context of the wider documentation mentioned above. Nonetheless, the dispatches published here do offer an opportunity to reflect again on Britain's role in the events that led up to the Republic of 1799 and in the tragic events that surrounded its collapse in June 1799.

They also tell us a great deal about their author, about diplomacy, about courtly life and ritual, and also more generally about European society in the closing years of the Ancien Regime. As Brian Fothergill and David Constantine have shown in their excellent biographies, Sir William Hamilton was very much a man of his age. A collector and connoisseur, an amateur scientist, self-taught vulcanologist, occasional anthropologist, art dealer and at times fraudster, Hamilton reflected many different aspects of a European gentleman of taste and intellectual curiosity in the age of the Enlightenment. By the end of the century that fashion had passed, and there was no more savage caricature of Sir William than James Gillray's 1801 depiction of him as "A *Cognoscenti* contemplating ye Beauties of ye Antique' (British Museum, London). Yet it was Sir William's broad curiosity, his passion for collecting great masters and the remarkable Greek and Roman vases that had been discovered during the early excavations at Herculaneum and Pompeii that made his residence at the Palazzo Sessa an obligatory port of call for the numerous foreign visitors that in the second half of the Eighteenth Century made Naples an eagerly sought after station on the itineraries of the European Grand Tour[37].

These wealthy foreign visitors were unwitting harbingers of the profound economic changes that were taking place as yet in the distant north western corners of Europe. Well before what later became known as the Industrial Revolution, the growth in European trade, especially with the growing numbers of colonies and plantations across the Atlantic, had brought unprecedented wealth to the elites in many parts of Europe – and especially Britain and France. It was that wealth that gave rise to Europe's first great consumer revolution in the eighteenth century, which found expression in an unprecedented capacity for luxury consumption, for foreign travel, for buying and collecting art and antiquities. Indeed, the ways in which artistic taste came to be considered an essential accoutrement of a person of 'quality' also revealed how ideals of nobility were also being redefined in the closing years of the European Ancien Regime[38].

Naples, of course, was involved in this new consumer economy only as an object of curiosity. With the accession of the Bourbon monarchy in 1734, the ancient Kingdom of the Two Sicilies had finally regained the status of an independent dynastic principality after two centuries of colonial subordination first to Spain and then more recently and briefly to Austria. The experiments in absolutist reform that took on new vigour in the second half of the century reflected the rulers' desire to assert the independence of their new kingdom, and above all to acquire the material resources needed to realize the monarchy's aspirations to dynastic grandeur[39].

Massive obstacles lay in the path of that project, however, of which the most challenging was the poverty of the kingdom's natural resources, a subject that by the 1780s had become one of the principal subject of the remarkable generation of writers and reformers whose work would give Naples an important place in the Italian and European Enlightenment. The target of the reformers was feudalism, which was also the principal object of the monarchy's reforms. But the Bourbon experiments in absolutism provoked fierce resistance from sections of the nobility and the church[40].

On the eve of the Revolution in France, the monarchy's reform project was in tatters. But the social and political tensions that were becoming more evident had deeper roots. Those wealthy northern travelers who flocked to admire the kingdom's remarkable artistic and natural treasures were visible signs of the economic and commercial changes whose epicentres although far distant deeply affected the Kingdom. As the consumption of goods and prime necessities of every sort began to increase in Britain, France and the Low Countries, so did the demand for Mediterranean staple products – for grain, olive oil, silk, citrus fruits, spices. Merchant ships from northern Europe became increasingly frequent visitors in the ports of the eastern and central Mediterranean and one of Sir William Hamilton's few official tasks – that characteristically he failed to complete – was to negotiate a new commercial treaty between England and the Two Sicilies[41].

There was a marked increase, nonetheless, in the Kingdom's exports in the final quarter of the eighteenth century, in particular to France and Britain, and this created incentives for commercial production that had far-reaching effects on the Kingdom's primary economic sector, agriculture. The development of new markets in particular speeded up the processes of enclosure and privatization of land that were taking place throughout Europe. In southern Italy, where feudal monopolies were extensive and where agriculture was carried on in close partnership with transhumant grazing, the impact of enclosures was particularly explosive.

All of this would contribute to the violence that overwhelmed the Kingdom in the closing years of the century. But although Sir William Hamilton's curiosity led him to travel far and wide – to the mainland provinces of Isernia, Molise, the Abruzzi and Calabria, and to Sicily – and although his interest extended beyond vases, volcanic eruptions, and the consequences of earthquakes to popular religious traditions[42], neither in the dispatches published here nor in the earlier parts of his copious correspondence does he make reference to the deeper changes taking place in the economic fabric of southern Italy in these years, although he did frequently bemoan the Kingdom's backwardness:

'Effeminacy and idleness are the favourite inclinations of its inhabitants... What an immensely rich Country this would be if Industry, arts, sciences, navigation, Husbandry, freedom of trade, toleration, natural liberty and the circulation of money were encouraged and protected'! And Injustice, the Despotism of the Powerful and arbitrary laws for ever abolished!'[43]

Nor did Sit William believe that prospects for increasing trade – the main purpose of his mission – were promising:

'The trade of this island with Great Britain is not very considerable: Brimstone, Barilla Shumaco, oil, and Silk are the principal materials which our manufactures import from Sicily: Cantharide and Manna by our druggists: raisins, almonds, figs, currents, and green fruit by our Grocers – All kinds of cotton, woollen, and linen cloths, heardware (sic), Lead, tin Earthenware are imported in this island from England. It is true the imports in England exceed the exports, but considering that the freight and primage is paid to British Subjects, that the materials are purchased at the first hand: and that our Manufactures have a recompense for their industry, I think that on the last Analysis, the trade is not unprofitable to our Country.

The wheat of this Island is in general of a very hard kind, and not for the English Markets – The superfluous is exported to Italy, Spain, and Portugal: The most profitable trade of Sicily is with Marseilles.

Our Government has prohibited the exportation of Brimstone to England, notwithstanding that a permission is easily granted for France. The Prohibition does not proceed from bad will, but is repugnant to our Principles[44].

Nor indeed did the British minister have much to say on the political and diplomatic developments that well before the Revolution in France were recasting the balances of European power. Rather than end the rivalries between Britain and France, the loss of the American colonies but had simply transposed them to other theatres – including the Indian sub-Continent. The Kingdom of Naples had ceased to be a 'remote corner of the world', however, and now found itself at the centre of a region that had acquired a new strategic importance to both Britain and France. Those developments were accentuated by changes taking place in Eastern and South-Eastern Europe, where Ottoman domination was now challenged by the expansionist policies of Catherine the Great of Russia that were challenging Ottoman domination in the Balkans and creating a new sense of political uncertainty throughout the Adriatic region.

This was a situation that the Bourbon rulers in Naples believed they could turn to their own advantage, and the idea that they could punch above their weight in European diplomacy was strengthened by their close dynastic and

diplomatic ties with the Habsburg imperial family. The key to that alliance
had been the marriage in 1768 of the young king Ferdinand IV of Naples to
the Arch-Duchess Maria Carolina, daughter of the Empress Maria Theresa of
Austria, sister of the Emperor Joseph II, of Grand Duke Peter Leopold of
Tuscany and of the young queen of France, Marie Antoinette. Still part of the
Bourbon family alliance, Naples was now also a client of Vienna. While carefully preserving its neutrality between the Bourbon and Habsburgs, the
Neapolitan government's diplomatic ventures became increasingly ambi-
tious, and a new commercial treaty with St Petersburg signed in 1787 was a
major diplomatic coups, opening the way to closer relations with Tsarist
Russia. The treaty had been negotiated by Sir John Acton, the son of an
exiled English Jacobite who had previously served the Grand Duke of Tuscany and who by 1790 had risen to become the most powerful minister in
Naples and was widely reputed to be the lover of Queen Maria Carolina.
Acton would also be a key player in the events of 1799[45].

The diplomatic and dynastic aspirations of the Bourbon rulers far
exceeded their diplomatic, military or naval resources, but were boosted by
the long period of peace that had followed the end of the Seven Years Wars.
The war suspended the rivalries between France and Austria that for decades
had kept Europe in an almost constant state of war. The partition of Poland
between Austria, Russia and Prussia demonstrated that dynastic imperialism
had not been put on hold, but the prolonged period of peace did provide the
opportunity for many European rulers – including the Neapolitan Bourbons
– to turn their minds to domestic reform[46].

Sir William Hamilton, Naples and the French Revolution

To say that the events that followed the Revolution in France in 1789 caught
the Neapolitan rulers off guard would be an understatement, yet their difficulties were shared by every other Italian ruler and indeed by the rulers of
Europe as a whole. It quickly became clear, however, that the relatively long
peace that had preceded the Revolution had been little more than the suspension of hostilities. In 1792 hostilities resumed along familiar dynastic
lines and the new French Republic was faced by an imposing coalition of
enemies led by its old foe the Austrian emperor, in alliance with Prussia,
Great Britain and initially also Spain.

The new conflicts had more to do with longstanding enmities than with
the Revolution. They were driven by Prussia's suspicion of Austria, by
Spain's concern to divert British threats to its Atlantic trade and colonies, by
Russia's ambitions to play a greater role in European (and for that matter

non-European) affairs. As Patrick O'Brien has persuasively argued, what are termed the revolutionary wars were no more than the final round in an unfinished Two Hundred Year War between Britain and France[47].

With the defeat of France first in North America and then in India, in 1792 the epicentre of the struggle switched back to Europe itself. When in 1793 the Allies prepared to attack the southern French port of Toulon it seemed that the Mediterranean would become a major theatre of conflict. In fact, the Mediterranean was never more than a diversionary tactic for the British, whose aim was to force the French to reduce their forces in the much closer and more threatening Low Countries – always the key to Britain's strategic interests in Continental Europe.

This was not something that the king of Naples had understood, and the alliance with Britain in 1793 broke with a long tradition of Neapolitan neutrality that had been carefully preserved since the founding of the Bourbon monarchy in 1734. Bernardo Tanucci, the minister of Carlo III and then head of the regency government during the minority of the new king Ferdinand IV, understood that the Kingdom was too weak to risk engagement in any major international conflict. His successors had followed the same policy, and in this they were favoured by the long peace in Europe that followed the Seven Years War between France and Austria. It was during this period of peace that the Bourbon rulers in Naples had looked to reorganize and strengthen their army and to create a navy, both tasks entrusted to Sir John Acton.

When news of the revolution in France first reached Naples in 1789 it did not initially cause much stir. But matters took a different turn after the arrest of Louis XVI and Marie Antoinette (the sister of Maria Carolina of Naples). Suspecting that the Neapolitan government might be tempted to join the coalition of France's enemies, a French naval squadron commanded by Rear Admiral Louis Latouche-Tréville took up station off the Bay of Naples for two months (December 1792-January 1793) as a warning. But Naples was now coming under enormous pressure from London and Vienna to join the coalition against France, which it did in July 1793[48].

The Toulon expedition that followed was a disaster for the Allies in every respect. It caused Spain to withdraw from the coalition against France, and when in 1795 Spain and France became allies France no longer had to fear an attack on her southern land frontiers. This new sense of security made it possible for the French Directory to reopen the Continental war in 1796, launching offensives against Austria simultaneously in the Rhineland and in northern Italy.

The failure of the Toulon expedition had also revealed that the British navy was as yet incapable of maintaining prolonged operations in the

Mediterranean. East of Gibraltar it had no naval stations where its fleet could rely on finding supplies and provision or carry out repairs. This was one reason for Britain's eagerness to recruit the king of Naples for the Toulon expedition. But this had caused heavy losses and needlessly exposed Naples to the threat of French reprisals which, as Neapolitan critics of the war were quick to point out, left the Kingdom of the Two Sicilies dangerously dependent on the protection of the British navy. Despite the huge sums that had been spent on its own army and the navy in the previous decade, the brief campaign of 1793 had shown that the Kingdom's armed forces were ineffective and its homeland defenses unprepared.

To make matters worse, the war in the Mediterranean had brought Neapolitan trade to a standstill and was causing immense hardship and unemployment. In the capital there were fears of a famine, and emergency measures were taken to purchase grain abroad – but food prices rose, and with them popular unrest. Then in 1794 the government discovered what it described as a Jacobin conspiracy in the capital. The repression the followed marked the definitive break with the monarchy's former reform projects. It began to persecute all those who had been associated with the former reform movement and abandoned its former hostility to Rome, instead calling on the clergy to mobilize against the Revolution[49].

The Hamiltons and the Neapolitan Crisis

When in 1796 a French army led by the young Corsican general Napoleon Bonaparte invaded northern Italy and quickly defeated the Austrians, the Neapolitan rulers were in an extremely dangerous position. Their government quickly sued for an armistice, which Bonaparte was willing to concede in return for hefty indemnities and the promise that the Kingdom would observe strict neutrality and close its ports to British naval and commercial shipping. France's ally Spain agreed to mediate and advised Naples to declare its neutrality and hence move out of harm's way[50].

This the Neapolitan government failed to do, in part, as Sir William Hamilton's dispatches show, because the government was now deeply divided. There were already major differences between the queen, Maria Carolina, and her former favourite, Sir John Acton, while as Sir William's dispatches vividly illustrate, king Ferdinand IV played little part in this and spent most of his time hunting and slaughtering vast quarries of birds and animals. But the queen and her advisers – amongst whom Emma Hart, Lady Hamilton, had become prominent to the point that her enemies had it rumoured that there was also a sexual relationship between the two women

– had more ambitious projects. In the summer of 1797 the Neapolitan envoy at the court of Vienna, the marchese di Gallo, was given the task of negotiating on Austria's behalf the peace treaty with France that was concluded at Campoformio. The expectation was that the Kingdom of the Two Sicilies would in return receive some territorial compensation in northern Italy – a clear sign that the old Bourbon dream of recovering the Medici and Farnese lands in northern Italy as a step towards creating a Kingdom that would reach to the Po Valley had not yet died.

Such dreams were not only unrealistic but dangerous. In the meantime, as Sir William Hamilton's dispatches in 1797 reveal, the Kingdom was coming under growing pressure to take sides. Through indecision and inaction the Neapolitan government avoided committing itself, but Sir William's dispatches reveal how the pressures on it to act grew. The situation became increasingly tense from the moment that the French occupied Rome in February 1798, bringing French troops for the first time to the Kingdom's frontiers.

In response, the Neapolitan government put its army on a war footing and began raising reserve militias[51]. Sir William's dispatch to Lord St Vincent (Document 20:15 April 1798) set out the 'miserable Situation to which this Country is reduced by having, as Your Lordship well knows, follow'd *mezzi termini* or half measures, which seldom or ever succeed. Notwithstanding it's (sic) apparent Peace with the french Republic, this Monarchy is threaten'd with immediate destruction. The last message from the french Directory at Paris is exactly the language of our Highway men – Deliver your money or we will blow your brains out'.

Bonaparte's Egyptian expedition in May 1798 marked the beginning of the next phase in the crisis. When he left Italy after signing the Treaty of Campoformio (17 October 1797) Bonaparte had returned to France where he was now considered to be one of the most influential supporters of the directory. Initially his plan had been to invade England, but this was now deferred in favour of an alternative project he had first outlined in a letter to the French foreign minister, Talleyrand, written in 1796 shortly after his armies had occupied the papal port of Ancona on the Adriatic: 'Let us now concentrate all our activities on the navy and destroy England. That done, Europe is at our feet'[52].

In May 1798 Napoleon set out from Toulon with a large expedition headed for an undisclosed destination that was in fact Egypt. There was great alarm in Naples when the French fleet was first sighted off Sicily in May, but without stopping it sailed on to Malta, which was occupied in June. On 1 July Alexandria was stormed and the French made their way inland. But Bonaparte's failure to settle scores first with the British navy proved costly.

On 1 August Admiral Nelson's ships finally caught up with the French fleet anchored off Aboukir Bay. In what even by the standards of the time was a remarkably bloody naval engagement, the French fleet was destroyed. Although Bonaparte remained in the Middle East for another year and pressed as far East as the crusader fortress of St John of Acre, without naval support the expedition was doomed.

The governors of the East India Company had no doubt of the wider significance of Nelson's victory when they voted him a bounty of £10,000 in recognition of his services to them[53]. The victory also earned Nelson a baronetcy. But although some interpreted the Egyptian expedition as an attempt to extend the struggle for European hegemony to Asia, this was not the government's view. From India, Arthur Wellesley (the future Duke of Wellington) argued that the expedition had had no clear strategic objectives, and had in any case enabled the British to drive the French out of India and decimated France's Mediterranean fleet[54]. And indeed the defeat of the sultan Tipoo Sahib of Mysore a year later would bring France's imperial ambitions in India to end (as was mentioned also by Sir William in his dispatch of 14 October 1799, Document N. 46).

Sir William's dispatches reveal the deep alarm that these events caused in Naples, as well as the extreme difficulty of obtaining accurate information until well afterwards (news of Nelson's victory on 1 August reached Naples only on 4 September). They also vividly depict how Nelson was greeted as the saviour of the Kingdom when he returned to Naples. While his ships were being repaired, the Hamilton's took charge of the British admiral's convalescence and it was in these months that the love affair between Nelson and Emma Hamilton came to its peak. As a result Nelson became a key player in the alliance – described in the dispatches that follow – between the queen, Lady Hamilton and Sir William – whose aim was to persuade the king to launch an offensive against the small French army that still occupied the Eternal City and had carried pope Pius VI off into captivity.

Leaning on Naples

Sir William's reports provide a wealth of information on the rituals of court life, the open and clandestine struggles for precedence and the ear of powerful people, the frequent galas at the newly refurbished San Carlo Opera House and the royal receptions that are quaintly anglicized as *Bacio Manos*. They also include some amusing lampoons of the representatives of the French Republic, whose refusal to conform to either Court procedures or etiquette in Naples made them a laughing stock and in whose discomfort Sir

William took the greatest of pleasure. But they also indicate that as the crisis deepened Sir William Hamilton was increasingly out of his depth in the troubled political, diplomatic and military shoals that he unexpectedly found himself trying to navigate.

Nonetheless, his dispatches also reveal the often brutal terms on which Britain did business with its allies. Together with the queen and Nelson, the Hamiltons were the leading players in the war party in Naples, although the main pressure came from London where Bonaparte's Egyptian campaign was considered a disastrous blunder that had unexpectedly played right into Britain's hands. A large French army was uselessly tied down in the Middle East, while the expedition had brought two important rulers into the alliance against France. The first was the Ottoman sultan, and the second the Russian Tsar. The Ottoman Porte was incensed both by the French attack on Egypt and by France's acquisition in 1797 of the former Venetian islands of Corfu, Zante and Cephalonia in the Adriatic. The Tsar, on the other hand, was drawn into the alliance because of the French occupation of Malta, whose rulers – the Knights of the Order of St John of Jerusalem – were under his protection.

With a French army and France's most brilliant general tied down in the Middle East, and with a significant part of France's Mediterranean fleet destroyed, this was an ideal opportunity for the allies to counter-attack. The problem was how to mobilize Austria, since the emperor had just signed a treaty of peace with France. A possible way of persuading Austria to intervene, it seemed, was to use the king of Naples as a pawn. The plan was for Ferdinand to attack the French forces in Rome, in coordination with a naval operation commanded by Nelson whose ships would carry 5,000 Neapolitan infantry to Livorno, from where they could cut the French army's line of retreat. The trap would then be closed by the Austrian emperor, whose forces would descend on northern Italy and seize the fortress of Mantua to make it impossible for the French armies to escape.

The instructions sent to Hamilton from London as early as April 1798 revealed the ruthless game that the British government now played a with its potential Neapolitan ally. It encouraged the king of Naples to take the offensive, but refused to commit either financial or naval support. (see dispatch 1798/12 - 20 April 1798). As in 1793, Naples was to bear the full cost of maintaining the British fleet sent to protect it, and in addition provide 3,000 seamen not just for the campaign but for the duration of the war.

Hamilton's dispatch of 5 June shows how London turned the French invasion of Rome to its own advantage, playing on Neapolitan fears of invasion to threaten withdrawal of the protection of the British fleet if the king did not launch an offensive. In his dispatch of 4 August Hamilton did not hide his irritation that Nelson had not received everything he had demanded and expressed the hope that this would not be the case when his fleet entered the port of Siracusa prior to setting off in pursuit of Napoleon. To London, Hamilton also expressed his impatience with the Neapolitan government for failing to exploit the revolts attempted by the 'peasants of Rome' following the French occupation, while acknowledging that unless the Austrian emperor was willing to resume hostilities in northern Italy the Neapolitan government would remain wary of taking offensive action against the French in Rome.

Hamilton's dispatch of 28 September 1798 shows that it was Nelson's victory at the Battle of the Nile on 1 August that finally tipped the Neapolitan government in favour of war. The British government now also had it own reasons for resuming the war in the central Mediterranean, but to do so it needed the provisions and supplies that the Neapolitan ports could offer. The Neapolitan government agreed, even though it was in direct violation of the Franco-Neapolitan armistice of 1796. The reservations of the two principal opponents of war, Acton and the Marquis di Gallo (who had recently been appointed Foreign Minister) were now over-ridden by the war party – the queen, the Hamiltons and Nelson – who were pressing for a pre-emptive strike against the French regardless of the Austrian emperor's intentions. The Neapolitan envoy in London, the marchese Circello, was accordingly instructed to negotiate an alliance along the lines that London had set.

Although not mentioned by Sir William, the central concern of the British government in 1798 still focused on the Low Countries, which under the terms of the Treaty of Campoformio in 1797 had passed from Austria to France. As in 1793, a Mediterranean campaign offered trhe opportunity to force the French forces to divert their forces towards the Mediterranean and hence create opportunities for the British to regain the Netherlands. This time Bonaparte's expedition had created the opportunity the British needed. But since Britain's power in the Mediterranean relied on its navy, to engage also in land operations it desperately needed allies. And if the campaign was to have any lasting impact, the participation of Austria was essential.

Hamilton's reports also reveal the massive financial pressures that the preparations for war were placing on the rickety Bourbon monarchy. He had noted in the previous year that 'the discontent that prevails in this Kingdom has likewise in some degree infected the Army.' (Document 1797/ 16: 6 June 1797).He also knew that militarily the situation hung on the Austrian emperor. Nonetheless he was prepared to adopt ruthless measures to press-gang king Ferdinand into going to war, including raising hopes that the British government would provide financial assistance, despite knowing full well that it would not. (3 October).

The dispatches also chart the growing difficulties facing the Neapolitan government, not least that of paying for an army that had been on a war footing for over a year (Naples 24 September 1798). Hence Neapolitan government's continuing uncertainty and the wariness, which also reflected anawareness that it was caught between more than one irresistible force and that inaction was frequently the best strategy. The foreign minister, the Marchese di Gallo, remained firmly opposed to an offensive, knowing full well that the French would not voluntarily risk moving South from Rome since this would leave their lines of communications dangerously extended in the case of an Austrian counter-attack. Di Gallo also understood that the British were using the Neapolitan king as a lever to bring the Austrians back into the war.

Nelson and Hamilton were well aware that Ferdinand IV could not mount an offensive without substantial cash support from Britain, but they both nonetheless insisted that the Neapolitan army was likely to defeat the smaller French force in Rome without difficulty. Despite his earlier doubts about the loyalty of the army, Sir William gave a very positive account of the its commander, the Ausrtrian General Mack, and its preparedness:

'General Mack after having made the Tour of all the Confines, and out Posts, returned here last Week for a few hours to make his report and to settle with His Sicilian Majesty the Plan of Operations that the Neapolitan Army might immediately go on and Secure the most advantageous Posts in the Roman State. The General told me that he had been much pleased with the appearance of His Sicilian Majesty's Troops and which he found greatly beyond what he had Expected. His Sicilian Majesty is determin'd to put Himself at the head of His own Army, and proposes going from hence with General Acton, to join the Army on Thursday Next, so that I flatter myself that No time will be lost in putting into Execution the Salutary Plan this Government seems at length to have realy (sic) adopted. A very few days must make this Matter clear.

According to the Accounts received here of the Enemy's Force in Italy at this Moment counting, french, Poles, Romans, Cisalpines etc. it amounts to no more than twenty six Thousand Men. The King of Naples's Army ready to march is said to Consist of Sixty eight Battallions of Infantry and thirty two Squadrons of Cavalry, in all upwards of Thirty thousand men, and according to the late Treaty between the Courts of Vienna and Naples When Naples furnishes Thirty the Emperor is to furnish Sixty Thousand men.

Every, and most necessary precaution, is taking here that the Neapolitan Army going into an exhausted Country may be well supplied with Provisions from hence. We hear from Rome that the french force is there diminishing daily, and it appears that Ancona will be their Fortress, as they have already errected (sic) strong Batteries to Command that Port'[55].

Nelson gave a similarly approvingly account and commented that General Mack says it is "la plus belle armée d'Europe" and as far as my judgement goes in those matters I agree that a finer army cannot be'[56].

King Ferdinand continued to be sceptical about the enterprise, but Nelson irritably commented that the king had only two choices:

'Either to advance, trusting to God for his blessing on a just cause or to die *l'épée à la main*, or to remain quiet and be kicked out of his Kingdom'[57].

The Neapolitan Defeat

The king had good reason to be hesitant, particularly since the assurances of support from his allies proved far from forthcoming. In fact the Russian and Albanian troops promised by St Petersburg and the Sublime Porte would not materialize until May of the following year, while Austria refused to move.

Nonetheless on 24 November king Ferdinand set off at the head of an army of 50,000 men, reaching Rome on the 29th. General MacDonald, the commander of the French forces, at first made a feinted retreat, then regrouped his forces and counter-attacked, throwing the Neapolitan army into confusion. As one contemporary quipped: 'Ferdinand came, saw and fled' – abandoning his army he hurried to Naples where he paused only to empty what little remained in the bank deposits before leaving with his family and courtiers for the safety of Parlermo on board Nelson's ships. The Hamiltons sailed with them[58].

Before leaving for Sicily, Sir William's reports vividly captured the horror and disbelief that greeted the news of the defeat of the Bourbon army in Rome. In his last dispatch before embarking for the safety of Palermo Hamilton simply noted: 'The fine army of His Sicilian Majesty from Treachery and Cowardice, is dwindling away without resisting' (Doc.1798/52; Naples 19 December 1798). His following dispatch contains a detailed account of the events in Naples immediately prior to the flight of the king and his courtiers on 23 December to Sicily on board HMS *Vanguard* and its escorts.

Nelson's advice had caused Ferdinand to be 'kicked out of his Kingdom', exactly what the Admiral had predicted would happen if the king did nothing. Contemporaries blamed the British for the disaster and in an essay published in Milan in 1806 Vincenzo Cuoco (who had been a member of the Republican government in Naples in 1799) would claim that Britain was the real enemy of Italian independence and liberty, and that its aim was to subordinate Italy to its economic power:

'The English are the enemies of every people on earth. Their trade and their industry is what the English seek to take away from all other nations. ...and this is what makes them the cruelest enemies of all'.

There was no clearer example of the law that 'If you are not strong you will be lost'. Naples, Cuoco claimed, was a prime example: its trade had been ruined by the monarchy's friendship with England'[59].

In his later *Storia del Reame di Napoli* Pietro Colletta made similar claims and also, denounced the damaging impact of British 'thessalocrazia' on the Kingdom of Naples for which he held Maria Carolina's favoured minister, John Acton, primarily responsible[60].

Those denunciations attribute coherence to British policy that in 1799 simply did not exist, however. As the debates over the value of Mediterranean trade for Great Britain following the Peace of Amiens in 1802 indicated, there was no strong feeling as yet that this was a region of major commercial or strategic importance for Great Britain. That realization would come only later, and was always closely related to the strategic importance of the Mediterranean in relation to the communications between Britain and its empire. As Sir William's dispatches clearly show, in 1799 British concerns were tactical rather than strategic.

The Republic and the Counter-Revolution

News reached Palermo only on 29 January that a Republic had been set up in Naples on the 21st and that a French army led by General Championnet, after overcoming fierce popular resistance, had occupied the city on the following day. In his dispatches from Palermo in early January.

Sir William' was quick to blame the Neapolitan government for the disaster. On 17 January he wrote:

'Alas! I have long experienced that there is nothing like Energy or decision in this Government, and it will probably end in the Nobility of Naples calling the french Army into Naples to quell the populace and save their persons, and the Revolution will be hasten'd by an Event which well Conducted might have rescued the Kingdom of Naples from its impending Ruin'. (Document 1799/5 16 January 1799).

He feared that the revolution would spread to Sicily:' All I can say as to the Security of this Island is that the French are in general detested by the Sicilians, yet there are discontents here also, and Extreme poverty and Misery among the common people and therefore in my Opinion the best and only Security wou'd be keeping the french at a distance. Shou'd they get possession of the Calabrias, this Island wou'd be in great danger, Notwithstanding the powerfull protection afforded it by His Majesty's Squadron under the Command of our Brave Lord Nelson' (Document 1799/ 10: 7 February Palermo).

A week later he refers to a letter from Cardinal Ruffo (now in Calabria) reporting that the Tree of Liberty had been erected everywhere: The Whole Kingdom of Naples will very soon be compleately Republicanized, some sort of Change of Government may naturally be expected to take place in this Island. (Document 1799/11; 13 February)

Cardinal Ruffo had in the meantime landed in Calabria in February with the task of raising royalist revolts against the Republic. After Calabria, the royalists quickly gained control of the Cilento, Basilicata, Apulia and Molise between March and May before marching on Naples in June[61]. Ruffo's expedition had begun with little expectation of success, however, and even less support from the Court in Palermo. Acton in particular was highly jealous of Ruffo, which may explain why neither Nelson nor Hamilton showed much interest in the developments in Calabria. Hamilton showed little enthusiasm and Nelson painted a similarly black picture, writing on 13 February to Earl St Vincent in very pessimistic terms and like Hamilton expressing concern that the revolutionary upheavals would most likely soon spread to Sicily:

'Our news from Calabria is very bad, as most of the Towns have planted the Tree of Liberty, and the madness approaches the coast towards Sicily. In this Island are many discontented people who have shown themselves in various places in manner contrary to the law and nearly approaching rebellion...In short, my dear Lord, everything makes me sick, to see things go to the Devil and not have the means of prevention'[62].

The constant refrain of Nelson's bulletins was that the French could only be driven out of Italy through the intervention of the Austrians, blaming the defeat of the Bourbon army in December 1798 entirely on the failure of the Austrians to intervene; '... all must be a Republic if the Emperor does not act with expedition and vigour'[63]. The Rear Admiral therefore saw no possibility of change in Italy until the joint Austrian and Russian offensive against the French was finally launched in northern Italy at the end of March 1799. On 18 February he again warned Earl St Vincent that the revolution was likely to spread to Messina.

It was not until the beginning of March that Nelson made any reference to Ruffo's expedition, and then only in typically cursory and dismissive terms:

'The situation of affairs in Naples and Tuscany is, from what we hear, no better than when I last wrote...In Calabria and the Provinces the French have not dared to advance: although the Nobles that have remained at Naples, have wrote to their vassals to erect the Tree of Liberty, which has been done and cut down again in many places. A Cardinal is Vicar-General in those provinces, and by preaching and money, has collected a number of people. Still, nothing can be said whether all is lost or saved or may yet be saved: that must depend on the Emperor'[64].

Hamilton was more optimistic about Ruffo's prospects but he shared Nelson's broader interpretation of events. He had told Lord Grenville in London that the revolution in Naples was led by the nobility: 'the Neapolitan Nobility has shown no loyalty to the Bourbons but the People appears to be violently anti-French and loyal to their Sovereign'[65]. Shortly after Captain Troubridge had seized the islands of Procida and Ischia Nelson made a very similar point when he reported to the Duke of Clarence that arrangements were being made to bring the Jacobins captured on Procida and Ischia to trial and execution: but he also added that :'all the lower orders are loyal and attached to their Sovereigns, and indeed so are they in the Provinces: for this war presents the very extraordinary circumstances of the rich taking the road for the destruction of property and the poor to protecting it'[66].

The fact that the Republic was headed by dissident noblemen who should have been the most loyal supporters of the monarchy compounded their crime in Nelson's eyes, and exacerbated what was clearly already his fiercely anti-Jacobin feelings[67]. In this his views reflected the growing strength of popular anti-Jacobin ideologies in England, which had not been present at the start of the Revolutionary wars. Even after the execution of Louis XVI, Pitt the Younger had continued to argue that the war against France was a continuation of those differences that had made the two countries enemies for most of the eighteenth and indeed much of the seventeenth century too. Pitt refused to accept that the conflict with France was an ideological war between Legitimism and Republicanism, insisting that French internal politics were a matter for the French alone: if they weakened France so much the better for Britain. The issues that brought the two countries to war were not ideological but material: the struggle for commercial and strategic hegemony in the Atlantic in particular[68].

That view had been challenged by Edmund Burke, whose *Reflection on the Revolution in France of 1790* had insisted on the ideological challenges that Republicanism posed to legitimist monarchy. But even after the start of the conflicts with revolutionary France the government continued to insist on the conventional nature of the struggle: the need to guarantee the neutrality of the Low Countries, to maintain a European balance of power and to protect British commercial and strategic interests. Nor was this insistence on the non-ideological character of the war surprising since Britain lacked the military and material means to embark on a prolonged land-war on the European Continent, hence its heavy reliance on changing coalitions of European allies throughout the struggles first with the French Republic and then with Napoleon[69].

Anti-Jacobin sentiment in Britain was fueled by revulsion at the Jacobin Terror, however, which disillusioned many early supporters of the Republican experiment in France (including Helen Maria Williams[70]) and provided Pitt's government with a convenient excuse for energetic measures against sympathizers with the Jacobin cause in England, Scotland and Ireland. The repressive measures against radical associations reached a peak between 1793-5, and had been accompanied by the rapid expansion of popular royalist associations. Through the writings of Hannah Moore and others, popular support for the monarchy grew and was infused with the often crude and scatological hatred of all things French that was evident in the satirical cartoons of Gillray and Rowlandson. The war against France was as a result transformed into a war in defence of British liberties, the British Crown and the British Constitution against the tyranny of the Revolution[71].

The first wave of popular royalism in England peaked in 1795 following the collapse of the Terror, but then revived again strongly as internal tensions in Britain itself brought new threat of revolution at home. Particular concern was caused by the situation in Scotland, but above all in Ireland where General Hock had unsuccessfully attempted to provide naval support for what was planned as a major rising against British rule in 1796. Hock's expedition was destroyed by a storm, and was followed by one of the most savage repressions in Ireland's history. But although the situation was contained, the British government remained convinced that France was still seeking to foment unrest in Ireland. When in 1797 preparations began for what would in the following year become Bonaparte's expedition to Egypt, British observers were convinced that Ireland was the most likely destiny of the battle fleet. Although the rebellion in Ireland had been brutally silenced, signs of popular opposition at home were a continuing cause of alarm, not least when mutinies spread through the fleets at anchor off Spithead and the Nore in 1797[72].

As a career naval officer, Nelson was necessarily mindful of both these examples of rebellion which he equated with the denial of the principles of order, authority and hierarchy on which he assumed civilization to depend. It was not by chance that in June Maria Carolina should have advised Nelson (through Emma Hamilton) to treat Naples like a rebel Irish town[73].

Yet despite the fierce hostility towards the Jacobins shared by both Nelson and his officers (Troubridge, Ball and Foote seem indistinguishable in this respect), they showed no interest in exploiting the popular support for the monarchy to which Nelson's dispatches frequently refer. Nelson's references to Ruffo's expedition in his dispatches are cursory and dismissive. Until news broke in March of the Russo-Austrian ultimatum to France, Nelson could see no way to defeat the French in Italy. However, the onset of the Russian and Austrian offensive in April signalled the rapid withdrawal of the French forces from Italy and the crisis of the Italian Republics. In Naples General MacDonald ordered his troops to begin their withdrawal in April, leaving behind only small garrisons in the St.Elmo castle in Naples and in Capua and Gaeta, the principal fortified towns north of the city[74]. But as the French retreat began, Nelson's main concern was that the regular troops promised by the Russian Tsar and Ottoman Sultan should join Ruffo as soon as possible in order to prevent any popular disorder, even if it was pro-royalist.

The original plan had been for the Hereditary Prince to act as nominal leader of a naval expedition to regain Naples that would in fact have been under Nelson's command. This would have reached Naples early in April, long before Ruffo's forces were near the city. In his instruction to Nelson dated 30 March the king ordered the former judge of the Vicaria prison[75], Michele De Curtis, to accompany the admiral and act as is political adviser. But the king also warned Nelson against advancing too rapidly in the Bay of Naples for fear this might provoke a popular royalist rising in the city, for which no ground support could be provided.

In the event, this expedition was entrusted to Troubridge who took possession of Ischia and Procida at the beginning of April[76]. Preparations for the expedition headed by the Hereditary Prince were again interrupted early in May when Nelson received news from Earl St Vincent that the French fleet in Brest had slipped Admiral Bridport's blockade and was heading for the Mediterranean. On 12 May the news was confirmed and Nelson took up station with his squadron off Palermo, preparing to rebuff an anticipated French attack on Sicily. At the same time, Nelson recalled Troubridge and his squadron from the Bay of Naples, leaving behind Foote as the senior officer[77].

Despite repeated attempts by Maria Carolina and the Court to persuade him to accompany the Hereditary Prince to Naples with his squadron, Nelson was obliged to wait off Palermo for orders from Earl St Vincent to attack the French and Spanish fleets which were seeking to join forces. The arrival of Admiral Duckworth's squadron in Palermo finally made the expedition against Naples possible, and on 10 June king Ferdinand begged Nelson to prevent the city falling prey to anarchy. Nelson was now already embarked and ready to sail for Naples but on 13 June – the day Ruffo's Sanfedisti gained control of the Ponte della Maddelena and entered Naples – he received orders from the new commander in the Mediterranean, Lord Keith, informing him that the French fleet seemed to be headed for Naples. To protect Sicily and the Bourbon sovereigns, Nelson was instructed to stand off the island of Marittimo with his squadron, where he remained until returning to Palermo on 21 June[78].

As a result, during the week preceding Ruffo's entry into Naples on 13 June and the dramatic 11 days that followed before Nelson's squadron finally arrived in the Bay of Naples on 24 June, the British naval presence in the Bay of Naples amounted to a small flotilla consisting of 'one sloop of war, two Neapolitan frigates and some smaller vessels' commanded by Captain Foote. This small force had the task of bombarding the coastal fortresses held by the patriots, while at the same time keep an alert watch for the French and Spanish fleet that was expected at any moment to enter the Bay of Naples[79].

Foote's dispatches during this period emphasize above all the risk of popular anarchy, which seemed to him as dangerous in royalist as in Jacobin colours. On 24 May he warned Nelson that the desperate shortage of food on Procida threatened to cause a revolt. On 2 June he reported approvingly that 13 Jacobins had been hanged in Procida, while three 'renegade priests [had been] sent to Palermo for execution'. On 4 June he reported that the Jacobins now held only Naples and some 20 miles of surrounding country, but that Ruffo was advancing too fast and leaving his left flank dangerously exposed and he urgently requested additional regular troops – 2,000 men, ammunition and guns – to avoid anarchy in Naples when the Royalist irregulars recaptured the city.

'There is no saying what pillage and disorder would ensue, as few if any of these people [i.e. the Royalist irregulars] receive any pay and are consequently obliged to subsist by rapine and plunder which I fear has given the Country people much cause to complain their conduct'[80].

Despite a dispatch from Nelson ordering him to send more of his ships to join the flotilla off Marittimo, on 11 June Foote renewed his appeal for reinforcements, in particular of marines, so that he could attack Castellamare and strengthen Ruffo's exposed left flank. On 16 June Foote reported that his ships had taken the surrender of the Granatella fort near Portici and of the Rivigliano fortified headland off Castellamare[81].

Foote's concern about the need to prevent the disorder in Naples increased after Ruffo's followers entered the city on 13 June, which was why he agreed to accept the terms of the capitulation that Ruffo and Micheroux offered the patriots in the Castel Nuovo and the Castle dell'Ovo on the 22nd. Foote had already negotiated the surrender of the small garrisons of Rivigliano and the Granatelle fort, and in his dispatch to Nelson dated 4 June he stated:' With

all Submission to the better judgment of my superiors, I beg leave to recommend a free pardon because animosities, jealousies and every trifling
object should be disregarded'[82].

Conclusions

Sir William Hamilton's last dispatch from Palermo was dated 16 June and
reported that Nelson had set sail from Palermo for Naples, but had then been
recalled by Lord Keith (who replaced Lord St Vincent as commander of the
Mediterranean fleet) in order to await the French fleet that had slipped the
blockade off Brest and was already in the Mediterranean, where it had joined
forces with the Spanish. When we next hear from him, he and Lady Hamilton were on board the *Foudroyant* in the Bay of Naples, bringing us back to
where we started, and to the last of the documents that follow.

These include a draft letter written by Nelson to his superior office Lord
Keith on 27 June, in which he states his firm opposition to the armistice. A
second letter from Nelson dated 30 June simply states that the patriots had
come out of the forts and been arrested by his marines, and reports the execution of Caracciolo. This is followed by a statement made later by Captain
Foote setting out for Nelson the reasons why he had agreed to be a signatory
to the armistice with the patriots. Among the remaining documents the
most important is Hamilton's letter of 14 July which is generally recognized
to be full of errors of fact and reads like an *ex post facto* justification by the
British minister of what had taken place. It was Hamilton's letter to Acton
dated 28 June that led Constance Giglioli and Mr. Knight to conclude that
Sir William had been responsible for tricking the patriots into leaving the
forts on 27 June[83].

These documents offer only fragmentary clues to a more complex story
that will probably never be fully told. However, after two centuries of close
analysis there is still nothing that reveals incontrovertibly the guilt of either
or both Nelson and Sir William. The king's letter to Ruffo reasserting his
explict instruction that there be no negotiations with the patriots and no
pardons published in the Appendix to this volume is not conclusive, but it
does add further and incontrovertible evidence that would exonerate both
Nelson and Hamilton and instead place the blame for what happened instead
on Ruffo.

Taken together, however, these documents have a wider interest. They
vividly recall the immediacy and uncertainty of the events as they were seen
at the time. They also reveal the means and methods of diplomacy, and
despite all Sir William's self-pleading expose the duplicity of an envoy whose

whose part in the persuading the king of Naples to embark on the disastrous royal offensive of November 1799 was less than honest and whose close relations with the increasingly insubordinate Admiral Nelson in the following months led to his dismissal and disgrace.

There is something else that these dispatches record, albeit indirectly. The overwhelming diplomatic pressures that came to bear on the Neapolitan Kingdom in these years were a sure sign that the aspirations to autonomy that had begun with the accession of Carlo III in 1734 had come to an end. The presence of British and French warships, of Russian, Turkish and French troops on Neapolitan soil were clear signs that Naples and its Kingdom was no longer a 'remote corner of the world'. Since 1743 the world had shrunk and had also become a more dangerous and threatening place. The independence of the new Bourbon Kingdom in southern Italy had always been precarious, and its fragile foundations were now brutally exposed. The causes for this have to be sought well beyond the confines of this Mediterranean kingdom and was part of the geo-political forces driving the rivalries between Britain and France, the expansion of Britain's new empire on the Indian sub-continent, and the changes taking place in South-Eastern Europe where Russia was pressing it challenge to Ottoman power with growing insistence. The struggles to control the Adriatic islands, and above all the critical conflicts that centred on Malta were all signs that the Mediterranean had acquired a new strategic sensitivity. The winner in this contest would be Great Britain, and one of the most durable outcomes of the events that drew the kingdom of Naples into disaster in 1799 was Britain's acquisition of Malta. This would be why the most serious attempt to restore peace in Europe that followed – the Peace of Amiens (1802-3) – collapsed. When the revolutionary and Napoleonic wars ended in 1815, Malta remained firmly in British hands and would down to the late 20th century remain critical for sustaining Britain's naval supremacy in the Mediterranean, the sea route to India and the British empire.

Once Malta was under British control, the British navy had no further need for the ports of southern Italy and Sicily. Yet the events of 1799 foreshadowed the future of the Bourbon kingdom – restored by a foreign power in 1799, the Bourbon rulers would never again rule as independent sovereigns. In 1806 the mainland became a French colony in Napoleon's imperial system, while the Bourbons again fled to Palermo and the protection of the British navy. In 1815 they were finally restored to their throne by an Austrian army and by the British navy. Following the revolutions of 1820-1 in Sicily and Naples, Ferdinand IV (now Ferdinand I of the unified Kingdom of the Two Sicilies) was restored to power once more by an Austrian army ('this is the third time the king of Naples has fallen off his throne: let's hope

this time he stays there' Metternich commented without much optimism).
Nominally independent, the Bourbon rulers were puppets of the Habsburg
monarchy, and once that monarchy began to show signs of weakening in the
decade after the revolutions of 1848, the Bourbon rulers' aspiration to autonomy became impossible to sustain. Even before 1860 the kingdom was in
effect a colony of its powerful foreign protectors, a transition that the events
of 1799 had made irreversible.

Editorial Note

For reasons of accuracy and authenticity we have not attempted to interfere
with or 'improve' the text of Sir William's correspondence which is tran-
scribed in its original form with all its inconsistencies of grammar and
spelling and other idiosyncrasies. To have attempted to change or 'modernize'
Sir William's use of English would transform the dispatches into something
different and at the same time deprive the modern reader of the opportunity
to engage with how Sir William actually wrote. The footnotes serve to explain
the references to people and events in the text.

THE DISPATCHES

GIOVANNI CAPUANO

The documents that follow this brief foreword and which make up the essential part of the present work are mostly the dispatches sent by the British plenipotentiary minister at the Bourbon court of Naples, Sir William Hamilton, to the British Secretary of State in London, Lord Grenville, during the so-called Jacobin triennium, i.e. from January 1797 to December 1799, when Hamilton was forced to leave his post to Arthur Paget after thirty-six years' service.

The dispatches, whose originals are to be found at The National Archives in Kew, London[1], have, to all appearances, generally been neglected up to now, or rather only partially used, and from a different point of view, by Acton in his *The Bourbons of Naples* and Constantine in his biography of Hamilton, *Fields of Fire*. It is therefore hoped that the texts may shed some light on the history of the relations between Great Britain and Naples in the last years of the 18th century and provide an insight into the role that Britain played in the events which preceded and followed the proclamation of the Neapolitan Republic in 1799. As well as practical considerations of economy, this particular three-year period was chosen, because Hamilton's dispatches for these years appear to provide a wealth of historical data that are still controversial today and which may draw attention to the Neapolitan Revolution of 1799 once again.

In fact, from the very beginning of the French Revoluion and the subsequent French revolutionary Wars, Hamilton and the Kingdom of Naples had ceased to live on the fringes of the European political scene and were forced to take centre-stage. But there is no denying that it was the Jacobin triennium which was characterized by a swift succession of momentous events culminating in the Revolution and a bloody counter-revolution; and Hamilton did not fail to record them in his dispatches.

As John Davis writes, it was in this period that Britain for the first time took a direct and decisive part in the political destiny of the Italian peninsula, and this marked the beginning of a British involvement, both direct

and indirect, in the domestic policy of Italy which was to last well into the
Napoleonic era and beyond with long-standing consequences for the country's political history in the age of the Risorgimento[2].

In this regard, it is beyond question that Nelson's personality has taken
the lion's share in the historical debate on the part played by Great Britain
in the Neapolitan Revolution, whereas Hamilton's role, which would seem
to be as important, has not been adequately highlighted. Yet Hamilton went
a long way in improving relations between Naples and London by greatly
curtailing the traditional subjection of the kingdom to the Spanish and Austrian courts ruled by Ferdinand IV's brother and daughter, and, moreover, he
was instrumental in persuading the Neapolitan king make his short-sighted,
ruinous decision to attack the French in November 1798.

Hamilton's following dispatches are best analysed in terms of communication factors (sender, addressee and context) and functions (emotive, directive and referential), which are normally interlinked. In reporting events
(referential), Hamilton hardly ever missed the opportunity to emphasize, and
boast of, his crucial role he had played in them (emotive) with the obvious
purpose of gaining favour with the Foreign Office and being given credit for
his diplomatic skills, and in the hope of being rewarded with wealth and
glory (directive)[3].

It is also worth noting that Hamilton did not just record events but, on
more than one occasion, was also able to influence them by acting of his own
accord as did Nelson too, who, for example, did not hesitate to disobey Lord
St. Vincent's orders when he thought it fit. As the means of transport and
communication of the time were still rudimentary and consequently rather
slow, people in high offices were sometimes forced, or rather free, to make
momentous decisions without waiting for their superiors' instructions[4].

Some background information on Hamiton will therefore be useful in
gaining an insight into the sender's personality and into the nature of the
intelligence he was supposed to trasmit to the addressee (Lord Grenville)[5].

Brought up at the court of the Prince of Wales almost as a foster-brother to
the future George III, at the age of sixteen, Hamilton joined the Third Regiment of Foot Guards taking part in the last two years of the War of the Austrian Succession and in the first two of the Seven Years War against France,
who remained the arch-enemy throughout his life. A violinist, lover of pictures
and member of the Society of Arts, Hamilton married Catherine Barlow in
1758 and in May left the Army, her fortune relieving him of the need to soldier for a living. In 1761 he was elected MP to serve the court party but, being
discontented in his situation, he took advantage of Sir James Gray's moving to
the post in Madrid[6] and managed to be sent to Naples as Envoy Extraordinary
thanks to the King's protection and Lord Grenville's benevolence.

Hamilton was pleased with his new post because Naples climate would be good for his wife's poor health while, as a lover of the arts, he would be sure to enjoy a land that, had he been wealthier, he would have toured when he was a soldier. During his first year in Naples he became deeply interested in Vesuvius whose volcanic action had been already mentioned in Gray's correspondence. By a curious coincidence, the volcano was more active than it had ever been after the eruptions of 79 A.D. and 1631, thus giving him an opportunity to send interesting reports to the Royal Society in London which earned him a reputation as a new Pliny.

Hamilton's only predecessor in the post had been James Gray, who was appointed in 1753. Prior to that, British trade interests had been looked after by a consul and Gray's appointment as ambassador had therefore been a mark of their growing importance. As remarked by Venturi[7] and reiterated by Giura and De Divitiis[8], the English government took a deep interest in what was going on in the kingdom of Naples for political and military reasons since the Neapolitan ports could give assistance to the British fleet, and even more for economic reasons concerning the trade balance between the two countries. Britain was concerned about its commercial relations with Naples for a variety of reasons, ranging from the development of the Neapolitan manufactures, to the great number of bankruptcies, to the great difficulty in recovering credit and, last but not least, to the ever increasing import of French textiles and other goods from Spain.

Before leaving for Naples, Hamilton "prepared himself by reading through Gray's correspondence. He learned what kind of reports he would be expected to write, and in ten handy notebooks made extracts and notes to take with him to Naples"[9]. His main task was the regulation of trade between Britain and Naples, but also that of receiving, entertaining and helping the numberless travelling fellow-countryment who flocked to visit Naples[10]. The only existing trade treaty dated from 1667 but Neapolitans often ignored it or modified it and wanted a new one. As a result, Hamilton would be continually pestered with complaints and claims by English captains arriving, and English merchants resident in Naples throughout his time in the capital[11]. His first important job was to gather accurate information on the Kingdom, on the army and the marine, on the population, on the public order and the lack of it, on the finances, according to the instructions received from the Secretary of State, Halifax. "It was the Envoy's job to report to his Secretary of State, and this Hamilton did, except when on leave, every ten days or so and in some periods more often than that, for thirty five years. He wrote his letters in draft, then in fair copy. Often there was not much to report, and he would apologize for it as he was a long way away from the centre of things. The post was slow and unsafe, so, whenever he could, Hamilton entrusted his dispatches to British travellers heading home, as when he used Henry Ellis to carry the old ciphers safely back.

In drafting a letter Hamilton marked any part of it that in fair copy should go into code; or he might write the code in there and then between the lines, for transcription later into his fair copy. He probably suspected his letters would be opened before they left the Kingdom of Naples since the things he put in cipher were often of a kind that might interest or offend the Neapolitans.

Hamilton made a point that he should be shown the same respect as the ministers of France and Spain, and he undoubtedly achieved his aim. After ten years in post the King took to calling him "Paesano Nostro" and his life flowed comfortably between his job as Envoy and his two passions for the arts and sciences, vases and the volcano"[12]. However, his life was to change dramatically after his return from England in 1791 with his second wife, Emy Lyon. The Court of Naples, which Hamilton used to refer to as "a remote corner of the world", had suddenly become politically strategic. The French Revolution, which had first been received favourably in Italy and Britain, was making its impact felt across the Italian peninsula, triggering off several revolutionary plots. The turning point was the foundation of the French Jacobin Republic, the subsequent Terror and the war between France and Austria, the climax being reached with the execution of Louis XVI and Marie Antoinette. Burke's views in his *Reflections on the French Revolution* of 1799 were highly praised in Britain when France declared war on Austria in 1792. Naples, which had been under the influence of Madrid and Vienna for a long time, started improving its relations with London. The Queen of Naples's implacable hatred for the French coincided with Great Britain's urgent need to avail itself of friendly ports for its navy involved in the failed attempt to conquer Toulon. To this purpose the young English commander, Horatio Nelson, came to Naples for the first time and established his close relations with Emma Hamilton and the court of Naples, which were to be of great significant in the years to come[13]. In December 1792 Naples was forced to recognize the French Republic after a French naval squadron had appeared in the bay of Naples, threatening to bombard the city, After France declared war to Great Britain, the Mediterranean became a theatre of operations and the court of Naples a key point. On 12 July Hamilton and Acton signed a treaty of alliance according to which Britain would maintain a fleet in the Mediterranean while Naples was to stop having trade relations with France and not to conclude separate peace without Britain's consent. In June 1794 Hamilton observed a violent eruption of Vesuvius; in July Robespierre was put to death while *habeas corpus* was suspended in Britain. A long war with France was looming large and in 1796 Napoleon started his campaign in Italy promising his soldiers to take them into the most fertile plains in Europe where they would be able to conquer rich provinces and large cities. After the French conquest of Northern Italy, the kingdom of Naples, on British advice, began negotiating for peace. The armistice was signed on 5 June and the peace treaty on 10 October. As Queen Carolina wrote to Lady Hamilton, "Naples was nominally neutral, but never in our feelings"[14]. In the meantime, on 5 October, Spain had declared war on Great Britain.

We have reached the year 1797 and below are Hamilton's dispatches during the three-year period of the Jacobin Republics in Italy.

SICILY

Letters and papers from Sir William Hamilton at Caserta, Naples, Persano & Portici; and Consuls Bomeester at Palermo, Jennings at Naples, and Tough at Palermo, to the Secretary of State: with Drafts to Sir William Hamilton

From January 3rd 1797 to December 22nd 1797

1) Caserta January 3d 1797

My Lord

His Majesty's Frigates the Romulus and Pallas sail'd last week from the Port of Naples on a Cruize, and the Dido sailed from the same Port on Friday last for Porto Ferraio having under her Convoy two of our Government's Transports loaded with Provisions which had been fortunately embarked before the arrival of the Ratification of the Treaty of Peace with the French Republic. The Hereditary Prince of the Two Sicilies is arrived at Caserta perfectly recovered from his late indisposition.

I have seen a printed Copy of the Orders of His Catholic Majesty published at Madrid with respect to the fitting out and regulating Their Privateers during the present War and which appeared to me to be similar to those issued by the Court of Spain in former Wars.

Accounts have been received by this Court of the Spanish Fleet's having left Toulon and retired into its own Ports.

The Queen told me yesterday that by the last Dispatches from Madrid Her Majesty had been well assured, that there was a remarkable coolness between the Prince of the Peace[15] and the French Minister at the Court of Spain, supposed on account of the French Republic's not having fulfilled its Engagements to the Duke of Parma.

I have the honor to be
My Lord
Your Lordship's
most obedient and
most humble Servant
Wm Hamilton

2) Naples January 12th 1797

My Lord

I have just had notice from General Acton[16] that a Neapolitan Messenger will go off this Night, or early Tomorrow, for London, but I have not been informed of the Object in sending off this Messenger.

Captain Freemantle[17] in His Majesty's Frigate the Inconstant is arrived here to take Sir Gilbert Elliot[18] (who is returned from Rome to this Capital) to Porto Ferraio. Sir Gilbert expects to be able to return home in a very short time. He will inform Your Lordship of the sentiments of this Court and Ministry, having had many conferences with Their Sicilian Majesties, Genl. Acton and the Prince CastelCicala[19] in the most confidential way. They appear to be well aware of the insecurity of the Peace they have been drawn into by various untoward Circumstances notwithstanding it's aspect on paper.

Monsieur Cavelos, who was an officer in the french Service during the Monarchy, is expected here every day as Minister to the Court of Naples from the french Republic.

This day being His Sicilian Majesty's Birthday there will be a Grand Gala and Bacciomano at the Palace, and I am to have a numerous presentation of either The King's travelling Subjects, or french an(d) Corsican Emigrées lately in His Majesty's Service in Corsica.

Tomorrow the King of Naples goes on a Shooting Party to Persano for eight or ten days and has been graciously pleased to invite me to partake of this Chase.

I have the honor to inclose the last Letter which I received from Mr. Drake[20] of the 31st of Dec. and in which your Lordship will see that Coll. Graham[21] has fortunately effectuated his Escape from Mantua, and that We are at the Eve of some great Event in that Quarter.

A discovery has been lately made of a french plan for changing the present Government of Florence into that of a Republic and perhaps the Marquis Circello[22] will be able to give your Lordship the particulars of this discovery.

His Royal Highness Prince Augustus[23] continues to enjoy perfect health at Naples[24].

I have the honor to be
My Lord
Your Lordship's
most obedient and
most humble Servant
Wm Hamilton

3) Persano January 24th 1797

My Lord

An Epidemical Fever[25] which has unfortunately taken place in the Cantoonments of His Sicilian Majesty's Army, both in Puglia and Abruzzo, continues to carry off many men daily, but as every precaution is now taken to stop the progress of this disorder (which is already abated) it is to be hoped that it may soon be entirely removed.

Nothing new has occurred since my last Number, and from hence I can only say that His Sicilian Majesty is in perfect good health and Spirits, having with His Party, consisting of Nine Guns, killed in Eight days five Wolves a great number of Stags Wild Boars, fallow Deer, chevreuils, Foxes, Hares and Woodcocks. To give Your Lordship an idea of the quantity of Game in this Forrest, Yesterday's Chase was by His Majesty reckon'd but very moderate when The Party kill'd Ten Stags, Forty Nine Wild Boars, Two Hundred and twenty four Fallow Deer, a Chevreuil, Eight Foxes, Six Hares and twenty five Woodcocks. When I had the honor to be here twenty eight years ago with the King and the Queen of Naples (who used then to shoot also) I remember the Party, consisting of Eighteen Guns, killed in this Forrest, in one day, Two Thousand four hundred head of fallow Deer, and of which The Queen killed upwards of Sixty.

Having had nothing more material to communicate to Your Lordship at this Moment, I flatter myself You will excuse the liberty I have taken in writing these particulars of the King of Naples's Chase, meerly as a Matter of Curiosity.

His Sicilian Majesty proposes to return Tomorrow to Naples and soon after to Caserta.

Sir Gilbert Elliot sail'd from Naples for Porto Ferraio in the King's Frigate the Inconstant on Tuesday last the 18th instant[26].

I have the honor to be
My Lord
Your Lordship's
most obedient and
most humble Servant
Wm Hamilton

4) Caserta February 7th 1797

My Lord

As it is probable that Your Lordship may not have receiv'd my Dispatch

N. 1 of the 3d of January a party of French having between Florence and Venice robbed the Mail with the Letters of that date, and sent them to Buonaparte at Milan, I here inclose a duplicate of that Number.

The Court is now settled at this Royal Palace and His Sicilian Majesty is following up His Hunting and shooting parties in this Neighbourhood as Usual.

The Epidemical disorder continues to reduce His Sicilian Majesty's Army daily, altho' every precaution is taken to stop its fatal progress. It is evident that this disorder cannot be attributed to bad Air, as the Troops quarter'd in the most healthy situations have suffer'd more than in places where the Air has been always reckon'd dangerous[27]. The true Cause of this disorder is I beleive (I have heard it from good Authority) that the Troops were in general crowded together without being either properly fed, well clothed, or comfortably lodged, altho' Their Sicilian Majesties' intentions and Orders were that this Army shou'd be well provided in every respect. A Lieut. Collonel and two Majors have already been broken for a total neglect of their duty, and perhaps, as examples of severity in this Country have hitherto been very rare indeed, they may now be attended with good Effect. Fourteen thousand men are said to have died already, but I beleive that Number to be rather exaggerated. Mr. Bomeester arrived here yesterday from Palermo with the Account of the death of his Father Daniel Bomeester, His Majesty's late Consul in Sicily whose long and faithfull Services, both in Spain and Italy, may be well ascertain'd by his papers in Your Lordship's Office. Owing to continual Wars the profits of his Office in Sicily cou'd have afforded him but a very scanty maintenance, added to which he had the misfortune to lose all his effects at Messina, his house having been destroy'd by the Earthquake in 1783. Mr. Bomeester has left his second wife with three young children to the care and dependance of His Son by his first wife, but I fear from what I can learn when the late Mr. Bomeester's debts shall have been paid little or nothing will remain towards the maintenance of his distressed family. I flatter myself on this account that your Lordship will excuse the liberty I take (at the earnest desire of Mr. Bomeester) of presenting the inclosed Memorial to your Lordship and of entreating your Lordship to employ your good Offices with The King in favor of this distressed family.

As Mr. Bomeester has assisted his father for many years passed in his Consular business, I have desired him to return to Palermo and do the business there until The King shall have appointed a New Consul for Sicily. I have likewise authorized Don Pietro Anfuso, Vice Consul at Messina, to continue in his office until His Majesty's further pleasure shall be known.

We have as yet no account of the Island of Elba's having been entirely evacuated, but by the last Letters from Porto Ferraio of the 21st of Dec. His

Majesty's Troops had began to embark and the Maremma had already been evacuated[28].

I have the honor to be
My Lord
Your Lordship's
most obedient and
most humble Servant
Wm Hamilton

P.S. I have this moment received a Letter from Genl. De Burgh dated from Porto Ferraio January 29th informing me that Sir Gilbert Elliot left Elba the 28th of January and that Commodore Nelson sailed at the same time, but that he shou'd wait for Orders from England for evacuating that Island.

5) Caserta February 14th 1797

My Lord
General Buonaparte's Invasion of the Pope's State has render'd the common Post between Rome and Venice so insecure that as I have been informed all the Letters from hence of the last Week are still detain'd at Rome.

Altho' We have not received an absolute confirmation of the News of Mantua's having surrendered to the french on the 2[d] instant, it is credited here, and yet does not seem to cause such a lively Sensation at this Court as I shou'd have expected having always thought that the future fate of Italy depended on that Fortress.

As Mr. North and Mr. Goddard[29] are at Rome your Lordship will naturally have in so interesting a Moment more intelligence from thence than I can pretend to give, but I take the liberty of inclosing a Letter which I have just receiv'd from Mr. Denham[30] an English Merchant who has resided at Rome, or in other parts of Italy, upwards of thirty years, and whose information I have in general found to be more exact that that of any of my Correspondents at Rome.

It is whisper'd here that the Pope will soon be at Naples and some say that He is already at Monte Casino (sic), it appears to be more probable if He shou'd quit Rome that He wou'd go to Terracina where He has a Palace and from whence He cou'd remove in two hours time into the Dominions of His Sicilian Majesty.

General Buonaparte's Plan, supposing Mantua taken (of which there can be little doubt) seems to be to raise as much money as he can hastily in the

Pope's and Venetian States, and to push forward with his Army into Germany by the Tyrole to induce the Emperor to make a separate Peace.

The late Peace with the french Republic ensures a Moment's Security to these Kingdoms, but whilst the french remain in possession of Mantua and continue to give the law to the rest of Italy, no one here can reasonably count upon the duration of the present Tranquility.

The Epidemical disorder in His Sicilian Majesty's Army is greatly abated, this Government having taken every precaution to stop it's fatal progress.

I have the honor to be
My Lord
Your Lordship's
most obedient and
most humble servant
Wm Hamilton

6) Naples February 21ˢᵗ 1797

My Lord
The french continuing to intercept the Letters between Rome and Venice at their pleasure it is in vain to write with any degree of certainty by the usual Post, but not to interrupt the Course of my Correspondence with your Lordship I shall continue to write the occurrences of the day here.

The Court is come to pass ten days of the Carnival at Naples and the present confusion at Rome occasion'd by Gen.l Buonaparte's having reduc'd the Romagna and approached the Capital with the confirmation of the fatal News of Mantua's being in the possession of the french (of which your Lordship will have had earlier Notice than I cou'd give from hence) does not seem to affect in the least the usual gaety and diversions of the Naples Carnival.

The Mesdames of France[31] are expected to arrive here at the Palace of Caserta Tomorrow night. The Pope remains at Rome, and it is imagined that a sort of Peace (probably both disgracefull and disadvantageous to Rome) will soon be concluded, however many of His Majesty's Subjects are already arrived at Naples from Rome to avoid the Confusion that the arrival of the french Commissaries might occasion in that City. Lady Berwick[32] with her daughters and Mr. Jenkins[33] are come to Naples.

The News of the arrival of the Archduke Charles with a considerable reinforcement (Thirty thousand men as it is said) to the Austrian Army in Lombardy, which News has been confirmed, may give a new turn to affairs in that quarter, but it is to be lamented that they did not arrive in time to save the important Fortress of Mantua.

(His Majesty's armed Cutter the Rose arrived here this morning from Porto Ferraio and brought me Letters from General De Burgh dated the 17th instant. All well there and the General busily employ'd in putting that Port in the best state of defence.) I have received by this Cutter three more Corsican Emigrants who are upon Sir Gilbert Elliot' List as pension'd by His Majesty.

His Sicilian Majesty has been graciously pleased to allow all the french and the Corsican Emigrants that were recommended to my Care on the Evacuation of Corsica to reside in the Kingdom of Naples as long as it may be convenient to them, and every desired protection is afforded them by this Government.

Mr. Goddard will probably have informed Your Lordp. of his return to Naples on Sunday last in much better health than when he left this City.

I have the honor to be

My Lord

Your Lordship's

most obedient and

most humble Servant

Wm Hamilton

7) Caserta February 28th 1797

My Lord

The Peace between the Pope and the french Republic was Signed at Tolentino the 19th Instant. I have the honor of inclosing a printed Copy thereof which I have just receiv'd from Rome[34].

The Mesdames of France arrived at this Palace from Rome on the 20th instant, where They are for the present lodged and most hospitably Entertained by Their Sicilian Majesties. These Unfortunate Princesses do not appear to have laid aside any part of their former Etiquettes and the same ceremonies are observed in the interiour of Their Appartments here as were formerly at Versailles.

We hear that the Arch Duke Charles is returned to Vienna. It is said that the french Army in Lombardy lately received a reinforcement of thirty two thousand men.

The Grand object of France and Spain appears clearly to be that of driving the Emperor entirely out of Italy and of Shutting out His Majesty's Ships from as many Ports as they possibly can. We Suppose now that the Port of Leghorn will be reoccupied by a french Garrizon.

The Post between Rome and Venice being still at the mercy of the french I only venture to send Your Lordship (until a safer conveyance of my Letters shall present itself) the common occurrences of the day.

I have the honor to be
My Lord
Your Lordship's
most obedient and
most humble Servant.
Wm Hamilton

8) Naples March 21st 1797

My Lord
His Majesty's Armed Sloop the Pelerel[35] arrived here the day before yesterday and Lord Proby brought me Letters from Genl. De Burgh with the Statement of The King's Fleet under the Command of Sir John Jervis and of the Spanish One off Cape St. Vincents[36] on the memorable Fourteenth of February last, and which The Admiral had been pleased to direct might be forwarded to His Royal Highness Prince Augustus and to me, a simple cast of the Eye over that Paper must ever rejoice the heart of a true Briton. I most sincerely congratulate your Lordship on this Signal Victory which can not fail of contributing greatly towards the desired object of humbling the pride of our perfidious Enemies and of restoring a general Peace to Europe.

Two Neapolitan Ships of Seventy four Guns and four Frigates under the Command of Marshal Fortiguerri are to sail to day for Trieste to fetch the Princess Royal of Naples as mentioned in my last. The King and Queen of Naples dined on board the Commodore's Ship yesterday and were pleased to invite H. R. Highness Prince Augustus and also Lord Proby of the Pelerel amd Captain Elphinston of His Majesty's Sloop Speedy both at anchor in this Bay and on the point of returning to Porto Ferraio.

At Rome there is an appearance of general discontent and last Week a very serious conspiracy of the people has been as We hear discovered but just in time to save that City from being plunder'd and burnt.

We cannot yet trust much to the Post between Rome and Venice, but probably the Approach of the Arch Duke Charles with His reinforced Army may draw off the Enemy soon from the Romagna.

All was Well in Porto Ferraio by the last Letters from thence of the 13th instant[37].

I have the honor to be
My Lord

Your Lordship's
most obedient and
Most humble Servant
Wm Hamilton

9) Caserta April 11th 1797

My Lord
The News from Venice of a second defeat of the Austrian Army under the command of the Arch Duke Charles by the French, who were said to be advanced as far as Clagenfurth in their way to Vienna, has thrown this Court into the greatest consternation and deranged the Plans of Their Sicilian Majesties and the Prince Royal Who were on the point of setting out for Manfredonia to receive the Arch Duchess who was to have left Vienna on the first of April and to have embarked at Trieste on board one His Sicilian Majesties Line of Battle Ships.

The last Post brought better News from Venice, and that the french Army had received a considerable check from that of the Emperor, but these accounts are such as can not be depended upon, and probably Their Sicilian Majesties will not move from here until They shall receive certain Accounts of the Arch Duchesse's having left Vienna, which it is not probable She will do in such a moment of confusion.

The Old Palace here is fitting up[38] for the constant Residence of the Mesdames of France, upwards of fifty families having been turned out of it to make room for Their Royal Highnesses, and Their numerous suite.

His Majesty's Sloop the Speedy is arrived at Naples from Porto Ferraio and brought me Letters from General De Burgh of the 3d. instant, when all was well there. The Speedy intends to return immediately to Porto Ferraio and Mr. Goddard intends to take a passage in her to Porto Ferraio from whence he hopes to have an opportunity of getting a passage to Gibraltar or Lisbon in one of the King's Ships.

The Miss Hills are arrived at Naples from Manfredonia and are lodged in my House where they will remain untill they shall receive instructions from their relations as to their return home. The body of the late Lady Berwick has been embalmed and remains at Manfredonia with His Sicilian Majesty's gracious permission to be disposed of as the Family shall here after direct.

Our remote situation and the interruptions the German Post meets with from the french keeps us in the dark as to all sort of News, or we receive it of a very old date.

I have the honor to be
My Lord

Your Lordship's
most obedient and
most humble Servant
Wm Hamilton

10) Naples April 17th 1797

My Lord

I avail myself of the opportunity of Mr. Samuel Ragland, a British Merchant and my banker, going from hence to England with all speed to inform your Lordship Secretly and Confidentially of the present State of this Court and Government to the best of my judgement: the Post between Rome and Venice having been entirely at the mercy of the french for some time past I could not venture anything in my Dispatches but the common Occurrences of the day.

It is plain that General Acton was not fair with me in concealing from me the Conclusion of the Peace with the french Republick even after one of my Colleagues of the Diplomatick Corps having received and communicated to me the most convincing proofs of it's having been not only Signed at Paris but ratified at Naples. The Queen of Naples was I beleive firm to the last, but being deserted by the General was under the necessity of acquiescing and I can not help thinking that General Acton has of late been more inclined to the interest of France and Spain in Italy that to that of the Emperor. Since the Peace was made His Excellency has often said to me that if the French shou'd march the smallest body of Troops into the Pope's State then the Neapolitan Army wou'd march forward immediately and the Peace be at an end, yet when General Buonaparte enter'd the Romagna lately and obliged The Pope to Sign His ruinous and humiliating Peace, it caused the least motion or alarm here, and when Monsieur de Verniac was at Naples lately in his way home from Constantinople General Acton gave him a great Dinner and actually wrote him a Billet to inform him of the french having taken Mantua. My idea then is, that the King of Spain having at last worked upon His Brother the King of Naples to make his Peace, with a view of having His share also, in the intended division of Italy, General Acton may have inclined to the King's opinion, but this is meerely my own conjecture, for altho' I perceive that there is little harmony between the Queen of Naples and Genl. Acton Her Majesty has never open'd to me fully on the Subject[39]. It is clear that a total change of this Ministry is in agitation and what is given out (and I beleive not entirely without foundation) is that the Marquis de Gallo[40], The Neapolitan Minister at Vienna, is to be Vice Roy in Sicilly,

The Marquis Circello the Captain of the King's Guard here in the room of the late Prince Stigliano and in which case either the Prince Castelcicala wou'd return to London or if he continued in his present Situation in the foreign Department under General Acton, then that the Prince Belmonte wou'd be sent to London.

I know for certain that General Acton has His Sicilian Majesty's leave to go for a few months to England to look after his Estate in Shropshire, and that one of His Majesty's Seventy four Gun Ships has orders to be ready in the Month of June to carry him there, yet I don't think his departure to be absolutely determined. He must see that if he does go he can not be sure of enjoying at his return the high offices he has occupied for so many years passed and so much to his honour in this country[41].

The General whose Constitution is much impair'd by constant application to Business, and who is naturally very chilly, even in this Warm Climate, wou'd not I beleive be soon habituated to the damp Climate of Great Britain, and as Ambition is the predominant Passion with him, I can not well conceive His Excellency's philosophy to be sufficient to make him relish the life of a simple Baronet at his Country Seat in Shropshire, to which place he talks of retiring after having for so many years been at the head of every thing great in this Country. My idea then is that this Plan of retirement was formed at the time the french Directory were insisting upon Genl. Acton's dismission as one of the first Articles in their Treaty of Peace with Naples, and no mention of such an Article being now made confirms me in the private opinion I have formed of there being now a good understanding between the Courts of Spain Naples and the French Republick, and that Genl. Acton by having acquiesced to the Views of the King of Naples and gain'd His Confidence and affection, will Continue to Govern this Country supported by the King Himself as He did by having his hold on the Queen of Naples, who has certainly no longer the same irresistable influence over His Sicilian Majesty which Her Majesty has hitherto possessed.

It is certain that His Sicilian Majesty has a predilection for the English which He can not help shewing on all occasions; on the News of Sir John Jervis's glorious Victory over the Spanish Fleet on the 14th February last He cou'd not conceal the joy He felt, and I am sure that His Majesty will on all occasions be happy to give every proof in His power of real friendship for Great Britain, as far as He can consistently with the new Engagements into which I suppose him to have enter'd with the Court of Spain and the french Republick. Without Vanity I may say that my Constant attendance on His Sicilian Majesty for more than Thirty Years has greatly contributed to the evident partiality His Majesty constantly shews to the English in preference to the Individuals of any other Nation, and I am sure that favourable impression will remain with Him as long as He lives. The Queen of Naples has often said to me C'est Vous qui a de 'Bourbonisé' Le Roi et Notre Cour et Vous est içi en effet le seul Ministre de Famille.

The King of Naples's favorite object is to have it in his power to go to England one of these days. I have often heard Him say so. Since I have written the above I have had a private Conversation with the Queen of Naples and find Her Majesty precisely of my opinion that altho' Genl. Acton still talks of his voyage to England yet that She does not think it will take place. Her Majesty very generously said that altho' She has private reasons to be much displeased with him, She shou'd ever respect him and continue to do him every Service in Her power.

I remember the late Lord Pembroke, who, as your Lordship knows, made the Natural History of the female Sex the principal Study and occupation of his Life, told me once that when ever he found it difficult to account for any strange Event by bringing in a Woman the Aenigma was immediately solved. No one surely can have a greater respect than I have for the Queen of Naples. Her talents are certainly very great and your Lordship is possessed of a strong proof of it in the Copy of a Letter Her Majesty wrote to the King of Naples in a moment of great difficulty, and which I had the honor of transmitting to your Lordship. Had the Queen's advice prevailed Italy in all probability might have been saved, but it is well known (and indeed the Emperor Joseph told me so Himself) that all the Daughters of the Empress Maria Theresa had very tender hearts Susceptible to sudden and violent impressions. Now I have reason to believe that such an impression took place lately in the heart of the Queen of Naples; for She shew'd for some time passed a remarkable attention to the Prince of Saxe, Son of the Prince Xavier of Saxony, who is in a Regiment of Cavalry in His Sicilian Majesty's Service, He is a young man of a very good figure and does not want Talents. It is then highly probable that general Acton perceiving this growing attachment, dreading its consequences, and not being able to conquer it, let His Sicilian Majesty into the Secret, who immediately ordered the Prince of Saxe to go to Vienna, and He set out accordingly about a month ago and narrowly escaped being drowned in the Adriatick, the Vessel in which he had taken a passage for Trieste having been cast away.

The strong hold the Queen of Naples has had hitherto upon His Sicilian Majesty was by taking the weight of Affairs of State on her Shoulders, whilst His Majesty diverted Himself on his Sporting Parties, and which, with the assistance of General Acton, She was able to carry on to the King's perfect Satisfaction; but if my conjectures shou'd prove to be well founded and that the General has actually Sided with the King, The Queen's influence wou'd be entirely lost, and indeed from the remarkable coolness in the behaviour of

His Sicilian Majesty to the Queen which I have lately remarked, I shou'd judge it to be so.

His Sicilian Majesty's kindness to me remains Constant and Conspicuous, and the Friendly confidence which the Queen of Naples has long placed in me and Lady Hamilton is very flattering indeed.

As it is now Six Years since I have been in England, and my private Concerns in South Wales suffering greatly from my long absence, may I beg the favor of Your Lordship to lay me at the King's feet and humbly entreat of His Majesty's goodness that I may be permitted to return home for a short time to look after my private affairs and of which gracious permission (shou'd I be so fortunate as to obtain) I do not mean to avail myself of at this moment of confusion, but wait for that in which I shall judge that I may be absent without the smallest prejudice to the King's Service here.

His Royal Highness Prince Augustus Frederick continues to enjoy perfect health in Naples[42].

I have the honor to be
My Lord
Your Lordship's
most obedient and
most humble Servant
Wm Hamilton

11) Caserta April 18th 1797

My Lord
His Sicilian Majesty notwithstanding there being no Tidings of the Arch Duchess (The Princess Royal of Naples) having left Vienna, Went on Saturday last to Foggia and General Acton followed His Majesty the next day. They are now making the Tour of Puglia, and the Queen of Naples talks of going from hence in a few days with the hereditary Prince of the two Sicilies to meet His Majesty and proceed together to Manfredonia, if They shou'd have Notice of the Arch Duchess's being embarked on board a Neapolitan Ship of War which is waiting for Her in a Venetian Port near Trieste, accompanied by two more Neapolitan Ships of the Line and three Frigates. It is most probable from the rapid advance of the french Army towards Vienna (supposing the inclosing bulletin be founded on truth) that the Arch Duchess's departure has been delay'd, and that Their Sicilian Majesties, after having made the Tour of the Provinces of Puglia and Lecce will return to Caserta.

Having wrote fully and without reserve to Your Lordship in my last Number, which Secret Dispatch Mr. Ragland, a British Merchant going from hence to England has been so good as to take the charge of, and which Your Lordship may probably receive as soon as this, I have nothing further to add at present.

As it is now Six Years since I have been in England and my private concerns in South Wales suffering greatly from my long absence, may I beg the favor of Your Lordship to lay me at the King's feet and humbly entreat of His Majesty's goodness that I may be permitted to return home for a short time to look into my private affairs, and of which Gracious permission (shou'd I be so fortunate as to obtain it) I do not mean to avail myself of at this moment of Confusion, but wait for that in which I shall judge I may do so without the least prejudice to the King's Service here.

I have the honor to be
My Lord
Your Lordship's
most obedient and
most humble Servant
Wm Hamilton

12) Naples April 25th 1797

My Lord
The Queen of Naples and The Hereditary Prince of the Two Sicilies set off at four 0' clock Yesterday morning to meet His Sicilian Majesty at Foggia in Puglia, but by the last Accounts brought from Vienna to Caserta by the Count Carinola, Son to the Duke of Montedragone, who left Vienna so late as the 12th instant, The Arch Duchess had not left Vienna, where the greatest preparations were making by general Wallis and Mack for a vigorous defence in case the Negociations for Peace which were then carrying on at the Head Quarters of Genl. Buonaparte near Gratz shou'd not have an happy issue. I have been assured by very good Authority that it is the Emperor's determination to stand all chances rather than to Submit to a Separate and ignominious Peace, and that the proposal of His Majesty's Plenipotentiary is, upon some given Preliminaries, for a Congress to which His Allies my be called in order to settle a general Peace. The Six days' Armistice that was to have terminated the Thirteenth instant was prolonged to the Twentyeth. This is the News brought by the Count to whom I spoke myself on Sunday last at Caserta.

Your Lordship will have heard from Mr. Wyndham that the King's Orders have been obey'd and Porto Ferraio Evacuated on the Sixteenth instant.

The young Royal Family and the Mesdames of France remain at Caserta.

No one of the Corps Diplomatique except Count Esterhazy the Emperor's Ambassador at this Court has been invited to attend Their Sicilian Majesties at Foggia.

I have the honor to be
My Lord
Your Lordship's
most obedient and
most humble Servant
Wm Hamilton

13) Naples April 29th 1797

My Lord
Altho' it is currently reported that the Preliminaries of a Peace between the Emperor of Germany and the french Republic were signed by the Emperor's Plenipotentiaries and Genl Buonaparte on the 19th instant, the Court being at Foggia I have it not in my power to give Your Lordship any thing authentic on the subject, but from what I heard from the best Authority last Week I can never believe that the Emperor has agreed to a Separate and I may say an ignominious Peace if the Articles of the Treaty which circulate here shou'd be genuine.

May I beg the favor of your Lordship to forward the inclosed (which is left open for your perusal) to the Lords Commissioners of His Majesty's Treasury.

I have the honor to be
My Lord
Your Lordship's
most obedient and
most humble Servant
Wm Hamilton

14) Naples May 16th 1797

My Lord,
It is now reported here, and seemingly with some foundation, that the journey of the Arch Duchess Clementina from Vienna is postpon'd untill next Autumn on account of her Royal Highness being at present indisposed, if this report shou'd prove true it must be a great disappointment to this Court and Government who have been at a very great expence in Sending a Squadron into the Adriatick to bring the Princess to Manfredonia, and Their

Sicilian Majesties with the Hereditary Prince have been waiting for some time passed in Puglia to receive the Princess on her landing at Manfredonia.

By the Letters from Rome of the 12th instant we hear that the Pope's life was despaired of and that His Holyness was now expected to live two days, the disorder is in His bladder[43]. It is imagined that in case of the Pope's decease the Cardinals will proceed to the immediate Election of a new Pope without waiting for the Usual forms. Cardinal Mattei Arch Bishop of Ferrara it is thought will be chosen.

I do not mention any thing of the present desperate Situation of the Venetians, nor of the french refusing to Evacuate Leghorn, and Your Lordship will have earlier and better information on those subjects than I can pretend to give from hence.

We have at last received by the Milan Post a packet of English letters from the 2d. of Febry to the 30th of March.

The Banks here have for some days passed refused to pay in Cash, as was the case some months ago, except a trifling Sum they give in money, which causes much murmur and Confusion. I beleive the want of Cash in the Banks now proceeds from the former stoppage of payment as those who have Money no longer send it as formerly to the Banks but change it for Bank paper to great advantage.

I have the honor to be
My Lord
Your Lordship's
most obedient and
most humble Servant
Wm Hamilton

15) Naples May 30th 1797

My Lord
We are still in a State of uncertainty with respect to the arrival of the Arch Duchess Clementina, but as Their Sicilian Majesties, the Prince Royal and General Acton remain in Puglia, it is to be imagined that the Princess must have left Vienna and is expected soon at Manfredonia.

Monsieur de Canclaux, the french Minister[44], with his Wife and family are arrived here.

By the last letters from Rome We hear that the Pope is declining very fast and that his death is daily expected.

Cardinal Lorenzana and the Spanish Prelates sent from the Court of Spain are arrived at Rome, but as yet have had no intercourse with the Card. Azar.

By the last Post from Tuscany We hear that the french had completely Evacuated Leghorn, but that two french Ships of the Line with two Frigates and two Bomb Ketches had since enterd that Port.

I have the honor to be
My Lord
Your Lordship's
most obedient and
most humble Servant
Wm Hamilton

16) Naples June 6th 1797[45]

My Lord
If we may judge from the Revolution that has lately taken place at Venice, the actual and precarious Situation of Affairs at Genoa, and the probability of a Revolution there, added to the confusion that the death of the Pope (which may be expected daily) must naturally occasion, and that a formidable French Army is now on the March towards the Roman State, I beleive your

Lordship will think with me, that this Kingdom, notwithstanding its Peace, and that a French Minister actually resides at this Court, is by no means secure. It is certain that the aggrandizement of the Duke of Parma was the temptation that induced the Court of Spain to join the French Republick.

The Neapolitan officers are ordered to their Posts, but by death and desertion His Sicilian Majesty's Army is greatly reduced; and I fear that the discontent that prevails in this Kingdom has likewise in some degree infected the Army – perhaps I may see Things in too unfavourable a view; but unless some Stop is put immediately to the rapid progress of the French increasing Army, it appears to me that it may very soon give the Law to all Italy, now that the King's Fleet has left the Mediterranean, and a Squadron is come out of Toulon. In case of any accident here it would be difficult to escape from Naples either by land or by sea; which circumstance is indeed so alarming considering the present residence of His Royal Highness Prince Augustus at Naples – however your Lordship may be assured that we shall keep a good look out, and do the best we can in case of any accident; and we are sure of every assistance that this Government can afford. I have only to assure your Lordship that what I have written is from my own reflection on this Government, it having never intimated to me any apprehension of immediate danger.

I have the honor to be
My Lord
Your Lordship's
most obedient and
most humble Servant
Wm Hamilton

17) Downing Street June 16th 1797

Sir,
Having submitted to His Majesty your Request to be permitted to return
to England for a short time on your private Affairs, I have the satisfaction to
inform you that His Majesty is graciously pleased to grant you leave of
Absence for that purpose. You are therefore at Liberty to set out on your
Return home as soon as you think you can do so without any prejudice to
His Majesty's Service – leaving the Cyphers, Decyphers, and the official Cor-
respondence in the care of some proper Person on whom you can count.

18) Naples June 20th 1797

My Lord
Her Royal Highness The Arch Duchess Clementina, Spouse to the Hereditary Prince of the two Sicilies. arrived at Manfredonia on Sunday last, to
which place Their Sicilian Majesties and the Hereditary Prince went to
receive Her Royal Highness, and yesterday conducted Her to Foggia, where
the Court will probably remain a few days and then proceed to Caserta. Great
preparations are making in this City to celebrate the Nuptials and the Opera
Theatre of St. Carlos has undergone a thorough repair on the occasion[46].
The Pope in addition to His late serious Complaints has had a Paralytick
Stroke, so that His Holyness's dissolution may be daily expected and which,
as it is generally beleived, may cause the greatest confusion at Rome. The
french have already, as we hear, advanced fifteen Thousand Men as far as
Rimini.
Your Lordship will have heard of the rapid progress the french are making in the Democratizing the different States of Italy, and that Genoa has
undergone the same fate as Venice, and there is no saying how much further
they may go, By the inclosed printed paper your Lordship will see the language they hold in Italy, and which can not fail to be pleasing the ears of the
Majority of it's inhabitants, discontented with their Governments, and in

extreme want and misery. Although it is generally reported that it is the firm and avowed intention of General Buonaparte to come on to Naples, this Government does not appear to be in the least alarmed at so general a report. It has punctually hitherto fulfilled every Article of it's late Treaty of Peace with the french Republick, and I am well assured that both Monsr. Canclaux, the french Minister here, and the french Commissaries are loud in their praises of His Sicilian Majesty for the great punctuality of His Payments etc, and that the Neapolitan Minister at Paris has been remarkably well received by the Directory. However it is impossible to be here free from all Alarm whilst the french remain so powerfull in Italy, and when both the french Directory and their General Buonaparte have of late given so many instances of a total want of good faith. The french being in the possession of the Ships in the Arsenal at Venice is also a very unpleasant Circumstance.

His Royal Highness Prince Augustus continues to enjoy perfect health, but is not quite easy in his present Situation when, Shou'd the french realy have any Evil intention against Naples (which I can hardly think possible) it wou'd be very difficult for His Royal Highness to escape, either by Land or by Sea[47].

I have the honor to be
My Lord
Your Lordship's
most obedient and
most humble Servant

19) Caserta July 4th 1797

My Lord
His Sicilian Majesty arrived here on Wednesday last from Foggia and the Queen of Naples with the Hereditary Prince and Princess of the Two Sicilies Yesterday morning. The Court will probably remain at Caserta a f ew days in repose before it removes to Naples for the Ceremonies and Fetes that are preparing to Celebrate the late marriage of the Hereditary Prince.

General Buonaparte seems to be increasing his Army in the Romagna, or near it, probably with a view of seizing on the Pope's death such parts of the Roman Territory as may suit the present views of the french Directory, or the General's particular interest. His Holyness it is said may hold out some lit-tle time longer but there is no hope of His recovery.

We hear from Rome that part of the Castle of St. Angelo was by some accident blown up last week. The Explosion caused the greatest alarm at Rome, it is said that only thirteen lives were lost but that more than half of the Windows of Rome were broken.

The Mesdames of France are removing to the Old Palace of Caserta which has been completely repaired for their reception and constant Residence, and where as I understand they are to defray The Expences of their own House-keeping, Whereas, in the New Palace They have hitherto lived, with their numerous Suite, at the sole expence of His Sicilian Majesty.

A General Peace is much talked of and as much desired but I fear the fate of most part of Italy is already decided and past recovery.

The Count Muschin Puschin the New Minister from Russia to this Court with His Lady is arrived at Naples, They came from Trieste on board one of His Sicilian Majesty's Ships of War.

I have the honor to be
My Lord
Your Lordship's
most obedient and
most humble Servant
Wm Hamilton

P.S. The inclosed Gazette contains the Authentick List of the Promotions on the late marriage of the Hereditary Prince of the two Sicilies.

20) Naples July 18th 1797

My Lord
On Monday last His Sicilian Majesty came to Naples from Caserta and Monsieur de Canclaux presented his Credential Letters as Minister from the french Republick the same day in the Morning, and Count Muschin Puschin, the new Minister from the Court of Russia to that of Naples, presented his Credential Letters to His Sicilian Majesty in the Evening.

On Tuesday Evening The Queen of Naples with the Hereditary Prince and Princess of the two Sicilies arrived at Naples from Caserta. The Concourse of people in the Streets and at the Windows of every house was prodigious, and all testifying the highest Satisfaction on seeing the Royal Bride who appeared indeed to be very amiable, and highly accomplished. There were three days of Grand Gala and Illuminations in this City on this occasion. On Wednesday last there was a general Baccio Manos at Court after which Their Sicilian Majesties and the Hereditary Prince and Princess dined at the same table in Publick; at Night the Court went to the great Theatre of St. Carlos which having been newly decorated and highly illuminated made a most magnificent Appearance.

Monsieur de Canclaux behaved with great politeness to all the Diplomat-ick Corps, not aiming at any kind of Precedence? but placing himself below all the Ministers of Crowned Heads that were standing as Usual on the side on the side of the Table of their Sicilian Majesties whilst They dined in Pub-lick.

General Acton gave a great Dinner on Thursday, and another on Sunday last to all the Diplomatick Corps, and the Principal officers of the Court. Monsieur de Canclaux was dressed in a handsome embroider'd Uniform and a rich Sash round his waist, Madame Canclaux in a simple Chemise that scarcely cover'd her shoulders, the rest of her Arm being quite Naked, and Madamoiselle Canclaux came to this formal dinner with a morning blue silk bonnet in her head; there were also four Secretaries of the french Legation whose appearance was very mean indeed, particularly that of the first Secre-tary, Mons. Trouvet, the person that formerly had the direction of the Moni-teur at Paris. His hair very black was cut short all round and stood up on end in all directions, he wore a pair of large Spectacles through which he con-stantly Stared every one full in the face, a dark blue Coat with brass buttons and button'd up close to his Chin, a pair of black leather buskins with a nar-row gold lace at the top and a huge Scymitar hanging to a black leather broad belt going over his Coat. Your Lordship may imagine the Effect of such a figure in the midst of a great Company dressed in the highest Gala, however as They call it the Uniform of the first Secretary of the french Lega-tion he will, I suppose, be received every where in this Extraordinary dress.

Your Lordship will see by the inclosed Letter which I received Yesterday from the British Vice Consul at Messina that on the 5th instant Six french Ships of the Line and three Frigates from Toulon passed through the Phare of Messina on their way to the Adriatick. The french have actually four or five Ships of the Line and some frigates at Corfu, and as the Venetian Resi-dent here assured me Yesterday, the french have fitted out from the Arsenal of Venice five more Ships of the Line which were nearly ready to Sail, so that the french Maritime power begins to appear formidable in these Seas.

The Pope continues in the same weak State of health and his death is daily expected, whilst a considerable body of french and Cispadan Troops is assembling in the Romagna, an other body of french are already arrived at Ancona and it is said that a third body of french is marching to Urbino which movements give room to think that some great Event is at hand, and which may finally determine the future fate of Italy.

His Royal Highness Prince Augustus Frederick has lately had a Slight attack of His Asthmatic Complaint but is now perfectly recover'd. His Royal highness (tho' Weak) was able to go to the Court Galas and His dress and Equipage were most magnificent on the present occasion[48].

I have the honor to be
My Lord
Your Lordship's
most obedient and
most humble Servant
Wm Hamilton

21) Naples August 1st 1797

My Lord

I have been honor'd with Your Lordship's Letter N. 1 dated the 16th of June, and am truly sensible of Your goodness in having so readily procured for me the King's permission to return to England for a short time on my private Affairs; Your Lordship in returning my most humble thanks to the King will be pleased to assure His Majesty that I shall not think of profiting of that Gracious permission until it shall be clear that I may do so without the smallest prejudice to His Majesty's Service at this Court.

The Bailli de Rohan Grand Master of Malta died lately and the Bailli Humpesh, a German, has been elected the Grand Master in his room.

Two Danish Frigates, one of Forty Guns and the other of Twenty Six, came into this Port about ten days ago from Tripoli, having succeeded in making the Peace with that State. The Commodore's Ship having lost its Main Mast was supplied with a New one from His Sicilian Majesty's Dockyard, and both the Frigates have left this Port with the view of cruizing some time longer in the Mediterranean. The Commodore's name is Billy.

Two British Privateers fitted out from Gibraltar have taken and carried into Palermo a french and a Spanish Polacca both of which by the diligence of His Majesty's Pro Consul at Palermo, after long disputes, have been acknowledged legal Prizes as Your Lordship will see by Mr. Bomeester's Letter N. 1 inclosed.

The Consulship of Sicily of late Years, owing to the great decrease of Trade in that Island has scarcely afforded the Consul his basic Subsistance, I therefore imagine that your Lordship has not had many applications from that Consulship, vacant by the death of Mr. Daniel Bomeester.

From the personal knowledge I have of Mr. John Bomeester, son to the late Consul, I shou'd think him capable of executing the King's Consular business in Sicily exceedingly well, having been bred up by his Father at Palermo, and being a perfect Master of the Italian language, tho' not quite so of the English, as your Lordship will see by his Letter to me inclosed; and the poor man has been left with the Charge of a young Mother in Law without any sort of provisions, notwithstanding his Father's long and meritorious Services as British Consul, both in Spain and in Sicily.

I have the honor of inclosing N. 2 A Copy of a Curious printed paper published by Genl. Buonaparte at Milan and circulated in Italy, and which seems to shew decided marks of dissention between the Army of Italy and the 500.

The french Minister's behaviour in publick continues to be highly proper and decent but I have been well assured that he gave a Fete a few day's ago in his house to all the Democratic and french at Naples, and actually planted the Tree of Liberty in his Garden round which they assembled and Sung their popular songs. Madame de Canclaux has open'd her house, but as yet very few of the Neapolitan Nobility have visited her notwithstanding this Court's having expressed a desire that they shou'd.

I have the honor to be
My Lord
Your Lordship's
most obedient and
most humble Servant
Wm Hamilton

22) Naples August 8th 1797

My Lord

By the last Letters from Rome We hear of many persons having being arrested on Suspicion of their being concerned in a fresh Conspiracy against that Government, and that there are constant patroles of the Civic Guards in the Streets, and Cannon loaded with grape Shot planted in the principal Streets of Rome. The Castle of St. Angelo is put into the best state of defence and a great quantity of provisions has been sent into the Castle. The Pope remains in the same weak state of health as mentioned in my former Letters.

We hear that there is as usual at this time of the Year a very great mortality in the french Army in Italy, however it continues to be active, and Ancona has lately been reinforced by a considerable body of french Troops.

I have reason to believe that the french Minister and his Wife are not satisfied with their residence in this City, as it is Evident that the Neapolitan Nobility avoid them as much as possible altho' every sort of attention has been shewn them by the Court and Ministry.

I have the honor of inclosing a Copy of Monsieur de Canclaux's Speech to His Sicilian Majesty when he presented his Credential Letters, and of His Majesty's Answer, both of which I beleive to be nearly genuine.

The Heat here is at present excessive the Thermometer in the day time being seldom lower than 80 and often above 90 degrees.

I have the honor to be
My Lord
Your Lordship's
most obedient and
most humble Servant
Wm Hamilton

23) Naples August 22^d 1797

My Lord
The Fetes on account of the Marriage of The Hereditary Prince of the two Sicilies still continue. On Saturday last being the Birth Day of the Hereditary Prince, His Sicilian Majesty gave a Superb Fete at St. Leuce near Caserta with a Ball and Supper, Fire Works and Illuminations, which Fete is to be repeated next Friday on the 10th instant. The Nobility of Naples gave a Concert and Ball at their Academy to Their Sicilian Majesties and The Hereditary Prince and Princess. His Royal Highness Prince Augustus having been invited to that Fete under the Title of Prince Augustus, Son to His Britannick Majesty, and finding that there were only four Armed Chairs prepared and destin'd for Their Sicilian Majesties and the Hereditary Prince and Princess, sent Count Munster to Enquire of the Directors of the Academy if it was their intention to leave him in the Crowd without any mark of Distinction, they replied that they must wait for the decision of His Sicilian Majesty. The Prince waited the arrival of Their Sicilian Majesties and the Concert beginning without any place having been alotted to H. R. Highness, He thought proper to retire, in which H. R. Highness was certainly fully justified, and the next day Count Munster wrote me a letter stating the Affairs as above mention'd. I went with the Letter directly to General Acton being well assured that no intentional Slight cou'd have been intended to His Royal Highness by this Court or the Nobility of the Country, and wishing to have the Affair cleared up without my being obliged to move a formal Complaint to this Government of the Nobility of this Country having been wanting in the proper respect to The King's Son.

Your Lordship will see by the inclosed Copy of a Billet which I received from the Prince Castel Cicala that His Sicilian Majesty sent for Prince Augustus in order to place Him near Him at the Academy as soon as He heard of what had passed, but His Royal Highness had already left the Academy. It seems that the Directors had misled the Prince Castel Cicala by having assured him that Prince Augustus had not been invited as His Britannic Majesty's Son, whereas in the Original Billet of invitation now in my possession, at the bottom are these precise Words *A. S. A. Il Principe Augusto, Figlio di S. M. Britannica* which your Lordship will see I have explained in my Answer N. 2) to the Prince Castelcicala's billet and now all that remains is for the Directors of the Academy to make a proper excuse for their having made a false report to the Secretary of State's Office; in every other respect H. R. H. Prince Augustus is perfectly Satisfied and was at the King of Naples' s Fete at St. Leuce on Friday last where He was very particularly distinguished by Their Sicilian Majesties, who placed H. R. H. near Them during the Firework.

As this Affair might perhaps be misrepresented I thought it my duty to write this very Circumstantial account of it to Your Lordship. Certain it is that This Court on all occasions has consistently Shewn a very particular regard and Esteem for every branch of the King's Family that have visited Naples and have been pleased likewise to distinguish His Majesty's Subjects from those of every other Nation during the Course of my long residence at this Court.

I have the honor to be
My Lord
Your Lordship's
most obedient and
most humble Servant
Wm Hamilton

P. S. Since writing the above I have received an other Billet from the Prince Castelcicala desiring me to make His excuses to Count Munster, and assuring me that His Sicilian Majesty Had been much displeased that the Directors of the Academy shou'd have made a false representation of their Invitation of His Royal Highness Prince Augustus, so that this occurrence is now finished to the compleat Satisfaction of His Royal Highness.

24) Palermo 31st August 1797[49]

My Lord
His Majesty has graciously been peased to appoint me Consul of the English Nation in this island of Sicily and Malta; an honor which I acknowledge with gratitude and thankfulness; I beg leave to assure Your Ldp. That no pains will be spared on my part for the promotion of the trade and Navigation of my Country.

It is now twenty three years since I reside in this City, was only twenty four when I first came over, wherefore I am pretty well acquainted with the trade, policy, and customs of this island.

A fertile soil: a healthy and mild climate: a number of good harbours, and ports are the natural advantages of the island of Sicily; but with all these favourable circumstances commerce is far from being in flourishing state, the principal obstacles against its improvement are, the great inequality of riches and conditions; The money which people that live in Celibacy do monopolize, or lay out on objects of little use to the nation: Husbandry and industry are neglected on account of the many possessors of landed property: We have no kind of Manufactures to encourage labour and activity by making use of the produce of ye Land.

Effeminacy and idleness are the favorite inclinations of the inhabitants – The only means to employ the people is the Church, and the Bar, hence the vast number of Priests that foment superstition and Ignorance, and of Lawyers that make a commerce of Justice!

The number of inhabitants in Palermo can not be known with any degree of exactness; the general opinion is for one hundred and forty thousand : Lawyers and Churchmen make at least the fifth part. No wonder then it is so difficult to obtain justice, and that all Laws and principles of honor, and probity are transgressed against with impunity, and Arrogance. The interior part of our island is in the most abject state of misery, ignorance, and rusticity. The Regnicoli/forgive the expression!/[50] all flock to the Capital to find the means of living, and carrying on an existence. What an immensely rich Country this would be if Industry, arts, sciences, navigation, Husbandry, freedom of trade, toleration, natural liberty, and circulation of money were encouraged and protected! And Injustice, the Despotism of the Powerful, and arbitrary laws for ever abolished, and detested!

The trade of this island with Great Britain is not very considerable: Brimstone, Barilla[51], Shumaco[52], oil, and Silk are the principal materials which our manufacturies import from Sicily: Cantharide[53] and Manna by our druggists: raisins, almonds, figs, currents, and green fruit by our Grocers – All kinds of cotton, woollen, and linen cloths, heardware, Lead, tin Earthenware are imported in this island from England. It is true the imports in England exceed the exports, but considering that the freight and primage is paid to British Subjects, that the materials are purchased at the first hand: and that our Manufactures have a recompense for their industry, I think that on the last Analysis, the trade is not unprofitable to our Country.

The wheat of this Island is in general of a very hard kind, and not for the English Markets – The superfluous is exported to Italy, Spain, and Portugal: The most profitable trade of Sicily is with Marseilles.

Our Government has prohibited the exportation of Brimstone to England, notwithstanding that a permission is easily granted for France. The Prohibition does not proceed from bad will, but is repugnant to our Principles.

If Your Ldp. wishes to have any further intelligence about the trade of this Country, your orders shall be punctually obey'd by him that has the honor to subscribe himself with due respect and veneration.
Sir
Your Lordship's
Most obedient & humble Servant
James Tough
Consul in Sicily and Malta

25) Naples September 5th 1797

My Lord
The Reports on the Emperor's Peace are so various and contradictory that I dare not say any thing on that subject, but by the last accounts We are assured that General Buonaparte is at Udine to finish the business.

General Buonaparte's Brother is arrived at Rome, as Minister from the french Republic, in the place of Monsieur Cacault[54].

Three french Commissaries that came here to settle the pecuniary article of the late Peace between the Court of Naples and the french Republic are returning to Paris, they are loud in their complaints of the treatment they have met with from the Neapolitans in general who they say fly from them as if they had the plague; it is certain that every attention has been shewn to the french by this Court and Ministry but it is as true that they are generally detested in this Country.

Monsieur Bouligny the Spanish Charge d'Affaires at this Court gives out (which I hope in God may not prove true) that the Gallant Sir Horatio Nelson was killed by a Shot from a Spanish Gun Boat during the late Bombardment of Cadix.

Lieutenant General Gunning died here On Saturday last of a dropsy in his breast, and Mrs. Duberly who in returning hom immediately through France desired me to apply to Your Lordship's goodness for an Order that She may be permitted to land at Dover with a Man Servant, a Maid Servant and a Child.

Lord Berwick and Mr. Vernon are arrived at Naples and as soon as the Corps of the late Lady Berwick shall have been brought from Manfredonia and interred in the Protestant Burying Ground at Naples they propose to return directly with the two Miss Hills to England.

A Considerable body of Cavalry and Infantry are kept in readiness to march at a moment's warning towards the Confines of this Kingdom bordering on the Roman state. His Sicilian Majesty's Army has been considerably Weaken'd by the late Epidemical Disorder and frequent Desertions.

The Heats are somewhat abated and the Court proposes to remove to Portici in the Course of the Next Week.

I have the honor to be

My Lord

Your Lordship's

most obedient and

most humble Servant

Wm Hamilton

26) Naples September 19ᵗʰ 1797

My Lord

The reports are that the Peace between the Emperor of Germany and the french Republic has been concluded at Udine, but the Articles are not mention'd. The great point for the future safety of Italy wou'd be the Emperor's repossession of Mantua without which even this part of Italy will be in the utmost danger of being overwhelmed, sooner or later, by the present french Contagion.

Their Sicilian Majesties are at present in this City, but the Court will remove to Portici the beginning of the next Month.

His Royal Highness prince Augustus has been slightly indisposed with a Sore Throat but is now perfectly recover'd.

It is not the custom here at the Theatres for the audience to applaud when any of the Royal Family are present but a few days ago Monsieur Canclaux, the french Minister, being in a box at one of the Theatres with some of his Secretaries of Legation who were preparing to applaud, He prevented them with difficulty as His Sicilian Majesty was at the Theatre and I have been confidentially assured that Monsr. Trouvet, one of the Secretaries, has made a Complaint to the Directory of Monsr. Canclaux being too much of the Courtier to represent properly the french Republic and at the same time has requested to be recall'd[55].

I have the honor to be

My Lord

Your Lordship's

most obedient and

most humble Servant

Wm Hamilton

27) Naples September 26th 1797

My Lord

The important Change that has lately taken place in the french National Assembly and of which We have as yet but imperfect accounts, keeps Naples in an Awfull Suspence and has greatly diminished it's hopes of a general Peace being near at hand. If the War shou'd be revived in Italy it is but too obvious that the french Maroders, who can not expect Subsistance or money from home, will turn their Eyes towards Rome and the two Sicilies, the only part of Italy that they have not compleatly robbed and plunder'd.

Mr. John Bomeester acting as His Majesty's Pro Consul at Palermo (Mr. Tough His Majesty's newly appointed Consul not having as yet receiv'd his Exequatur[56]) represented to me in his Letter of the Seventh of Septr. that a french Prize brought into the harbour of Palermo by two British Privateers called The two Brothers and the Fortune, and declared a legal prize had been nevertheless Siezed in that harbour by an armed force of french and Genoese Sailors and that notwithstanding his timely and strong application to the Sicilian Government it had contrary to the Law of Nations suffer'd the Robbers to be supplied with provisions and other Necessaries, and to carry off quietly the Ship and Cargo.

Immediately on the receiving of this Letter I wrote a billet to the Prince Castelcicala inclosing the documents which Mr. Bomeester had sent me to prove the truth of his Complaint and requesting of His Excellency to lay them and the complaint before His Sicilian Majesty, whom I did not doubt wou'd highly disapprove of so unheard of a proceeding, and Order that immediately justice shou'd be done to the Owners of the British Privateers.

Yesterday I receiv'd a Satisfactory Answer to that Billet from the Prince Castelcicala, a Copy of which is inclosed for Your Lordship's perusal.

I have the honor to be
My Lord
Your Lordship's
Most Obedient and
Most humble servant
Wm Hamilton

28) Portici October 10th 1797

My Lord

We remain in the same anxious State of Suspence with respect to the result of the Negociations at Udine, as mentioned in my last.

There has been a great Military promotion here as Your Lordship will see by the inclosed printed List and General Acton appointed Captain General, or Commander in Chief of His Sicilian Majesty's Land and Sea Forces.

The Prince Belmonte Pignatelli, who Negociated the late Peace between this Country and the french Republic has (besides the Order of St. Januarius) been rewarded by His Sicilian Majesty with Crown Lands of the Annual value of Six Thousand Ducats and which will surely produce Twelve thousand to His Excellency.

Their Sicilian Majesties, all the Royal Family and most of the Nobility and Gentry of Naples are now at Portici, and twice a week the Royal Gardens at the Favorita are open'd to the Public. There is a band of Musick and all sorts of rural diversions such as Swings and Wooden Horses that turn round the riders running at the ring or firing pistols at a Turk's Head etc. Last Week there was a Magnificent Ball at the Favorita on account of it's being the Birth Day of the Prince Royal of the Two Sicilies, and on Sunday Next being Santa Teresa the Name day of the Empress of Germany the Ball will be repeated at the Favorita; There is also a temporary Theatre here, where either a Play or an Opera is performed every Night; but Alas! with all this I can not say that there are many gay faces. Every thing is dear, there is here, as in most parts of Europe, great scarcity of Money; the chief currency is in Paper, which you can not exchange for money under, at least, Seven per Cent Loss.

The Mesdames of France are very conveniently lodged at the Old Palace of Caserta and seldom go out, unless to pay their Court in private to Their Sicilian Majesties.

The Pope has had an other narrow escape, but after having remain'd some time with little Signs of Life, is recover'd, and goes to His Devotions at St. Peters, as usual.

I have the honor to be
My Lord
Your Lordship's
most obedient and
most humble Servant
Wm Hamilton

29) Portici October 24th 1797

My Lord
Last Night a Messenger dispatch'd by the Marquis de Gallo from Udine brought to this Court the welcome News of the Peace between the Emperor

of Germany and the french Republic having been Sign'd there on the 18th instant but without any further particulars.

This News, as Your Lordship may well imagine must afford much Satisfaction to this untouched oart of Italy, which wou'd assuredly have been in danger of sharing the fate of it's Neighbours, and been plunder'd by the cruel and Lawless french Banditti, had the War been renew'd and the Emperor's Arms proved as Unsuccessfull as they have hitherto been in Italy.

Lord Berwick, Mr. Vernon and the two Miss Hills set out from Naples yesterday in perfect health on their return to England, the remains of the late Lady Berwick having, by His Sicilian Majesty's particular, and Gracious permission, been deposited in a Vault at Manfredonia purchased by the Family.

I have the honor to be
My Lord
Your Lordship's
most obedient and
most humble servant
Wm Hamilton

30) Portici November 7th 1797

My Lord
Untill the ratifications of the Emperor's Peace with the french Republick are exchanged the Articles of the Peace will not be published, but as soon as that is completed We shall see what intentions the french have with respect to the rest of Italy. Ancona is according to the Eighth Article of the Pope's Peace with the Republick to be evacuated by the french as soon as a general Peace shall take place.

Last Week a sudden Gust of Wind attended with thunder lightening and Rain did infinite damage to the Campagna Felice, in a a moment it either broke, or tore up by the roots, upwards of thirty thousand of the large Poplar trees that support the Vines in the Campagna, many houses were unroofed and Windows broken, the effects of this hurricane are visible from Naples to the Mountains of Caserta, which is Sixteen Miles in length and in breadth about twelve miles.

I have the honour of inclosing a Letter directed to Your Lordship's which I received yesterday

by a boat from Cagliari, and which Count Ghillini His Majesty's Consul there desires me to forward to Your Lordship. I likewise inclose a List of the

Squadron of french and Venetian Ships of War at Corfu, or expected there soon, which I have just received from the British Consul at Messina who tells me he got it from the Master of a Merchant Vessel who came directly from Corfu to Messina, and which he has reason to beleive is Correct.

The Royal Family will not remove from hence to Caserta untill the end of this Month.

I have the honor to be
My Lord
Your Lordship's
most obedient and
most humble Servant
Wm Hamilton

31) Caserta November 21st 1797

My Lord

The Gazette Extraordinary of the 13th of October which your Lordship was pleased to order to be forwarded to me by Mr. Hammond gave me and all His Majesty's Subjects at Naples the most compleat Satisfaction; The total defeat of the Dutch Fleet by His Majesty's Fleet under the Command of Adml. Duncan can not fail of producing the best consequences besides that of humbling the pride of our insolent and treacherous Enemy.

The Articles of the Emperor's Peace with the french Republic do not give any sort of Satisfaction here, particularly as it is Understood that Mantua is to remain with a french Garizon altho' the Mantuan is included in the Cisalpine Republic. The behaviour of the french to the Venetians is a fresh proof that no trust can be placed in french promises and Allurements. It is certain that the Italian States, United, might have prevented the french from ever entering Italy and as certain that there have been, during this War, many precious moments lost, when in all probability they might have driven them out, so that, shou'd this unfortunate business end ill for them, they may take the blame on themselves.

His Sicilian Majesty is come to Caserta to resume His Usual hunting and Shooting Parties, The Queen and the rest of the Royal family are expected here from Portici the end of the Month.

The two Mesdames of France are quietly established in the old Palace of Caserta, live in perfect retirement, and have every attention shewn them by Their Sicilian Majesties. I paid my respects to them lat Night when Their Royal Highnesses expressed their joy on the News of the total defeat of the Dutch Fleet.

I have the honor to be
My Lord
Your Lordship's
most obedient and
most humble Servant
Wm Hamilton

32) Caserta December 5th 1797

My Lord
On Thursday last Mr. Tatter One of His Royal Highness Prince Augustus's Gentlemen came to me here to complain of the extraordinary treatment Mr. Sani a Messenger sent by the King with Letters for His R. Highness the Prince and Count Muster, had met with at Fondi and having left me in writing (which paper your Lordship will find inclosed) a Statement of the facts I wrote the Billet (a Copy of which is inclosed N. 1) to the Prince Castelcicala; and to which billet I received the Prince's Answer (likewise inclosed N. 2) and which, in my opinion, being perfectly Satisfactory I have expressed myself accordingly in my last Billet to His Excellency a Copy of which N. 3) is inclosed, and I flatter myself that when Your Lordship shall have informed the King of every circumstance of the Affair His Majesty will perceive that there was no real intention of shewing disrespect to His Majesty's Messenger either at Fondi or at Naples, and that this Government has given a proper Satisfaction for the indiscreet officiousness of the Director of the Custom House at Fondi.

All the Letters from Rome agree that it is impossible that Government can go on there much longer without a total change of System, and an approaching Revolution is talked of publickly in every Coffee house.

The Municipality of Ancona have declared Ancona a Republic under the protection of the french, and this New Republic has hoisted a flag Striped yellow red and blue, to distinguish it from the Cisalpine Flag, which is red, blue and Green.

I have the honor to be
My Lord
Your Lordship's
most obedient and
most humble Servant
Wm Hamilton

33) Caserta December 12th 1797

My Lord
The Prince Belmonte Pignatelli, who Negociated the late Peace between this Country and the french Republic has been appointed Ambassador extraordinary from this Court to that of Rome, and the Bailli Pignatelli, the Neapolitan Minister now at Rome has been appointed Grand Maitre to the Hereditary Princess of the two Sicilies in the room of the Prince Luzzi who has been Named Grand Maitre to the Queen of Naples in the room of the deceased Duke of Andria.

Letters of good Authority from Rome say that the Cisalpine and french Troops are in force at Rimini, that in Urbino there are signs of a revolt and that five hundred of the Garrison of Ancona had marched to take possession of Senigaglia, which Step leaves little room to doubt of the fate of that part of the Pope's State. We look forward to the Congress of Radstad for the final Settlement of Italy, and General Buonaparte is said to be on his journey to Radstad[57].

The Venetian gazette as Your Lordship will see by one of the latest received here (and which is inclosed) has not undergone any alteration since Venice has been ceded to the Emperor.

The Queen of Naples and the Young Royal Family will not probably remove to Caserta untill after Christmas, but His Sicilian Majesty will continue his residence chiefly here, as there is abundance of Game in this Neighbourhood. On Saturday last His Majesty with His Usual Party (of which I had the honor to be one) killed, in the wood of Matalone, four miles from hence, no less than five Wolves besides a number of Wild Boars Stags and Fallow Deer.

The last Post brought us the melancholy account of the death of Mr. Lambton at Pisa.

I have the honor to be
My Lord
Your Lordship's
most obedient and
most humble Servant
Wm Hamilton

34) Caserta December 19th 1797[58]

My Lord
I can assure Your Lordship that the French have offered to cede all the Venetian Islands except Corfu to His Sicilian Majesty who will not accept any unless He has them all.

The French are desirous of having the Grand Duchy of Tuscany. But this Court does not seem to be inclined to give it to them. The remarkable attention shewn here of late to the French Minister and the Spanish Chargé d'Affaires indicates a preservation of good Understanding between the Court of Madrid the Court of Naples and the French Republic and that this Court will be at length induced to join France and Spain in their great Object of obstructing the Trade of Great Britain on the Seas.

This Country is certainly in a very critical situation, full of discontent and ripe for Revolution, waiting only for the moment of the Certainty of Support which seems to be approaching by the rapid increase of the Italian Republicks.

I have the honor to be
My Lord
Your Lordship
most obedient and
most humble Servant
Wm Hamilton

SICILY

Letters and Papers from sir William Hamilton at Caserta and Naples; Consul Tough at Palermo, and others to the Secretary of State with Drafts.

From January 2ⁿᵈ 1798 to December 28ᵗʰ 1798

1) Caserta January 2ᵈ 1798

My Lord

By an Express from Leghorn this Government has just received the disagreable intelligence of the Plague having broken out in the Island of Corsica, and as the certainty of it is no longer doubted, every precaution will be taken here, and in Tuscany, as usual on such melancholy Occasions.

An Insurrection at Rome has been long expected, and there is no doubt of the french having long wished for an opportunity of Anihilating that Government, and that they Secretly fomented discontents in that City. On the 28ᵗʰ December some of the Roman populace began to be riotous and wearing french Cockades insulted the Pope's Soldiers, who drove them for refuge to the door of the french Minister Buonaparte's House. Monsieur Buonaparte came out with another french General and General Dufort to endeavor (as it is said) to calm the riot, but one of the Pope's Officers imprudently ordering his men to fire the Minister narrowly escaped and Genl. Dufort was killed on the Spot. This General had been appointed second in command under General Buonaparte to the Army insolently termed, The English Army, by the french Directory. I have the honor of inclosing for Your Lordship's perusal the two last letters received from my best Correspondents at Rome, Mr Jenkins and Mr. Denham, confirming the above.

The Queen of Naples has not been well of late and Her Majesty has still some remains of an intermittent fever but without being confined to Her bed.

Allow me to wish Your Lordship a happy New Year. We certainly do not here enter upon the New Year with any agreeable prospect before us.

I have the honor to be

My Lord

Your Lordship's

most obedient and

most humble servant

Wm Hamilton

2) Caserta January 9th 1798

My Lord

By our last letters from Rome dated the 5th instant all was very quiet in that City. The body of the french General Dufort was it seems buried at Rome with great pomp and not carried off as mentioned in my last. The french Minister Buonaparte on leaving Rome order'd his Horses and Household furniture to be Sold and advised all the french Republicans to leave Rome as soon as possible, there is News of his having been insulted at Viterbo, but that he arrived safely with his family at Florence the 31st of December.

Cardinal Braschi and Monsignore Galeppi have been at Naples, as is imagined, to Sollicit the Assistance of this Government at this most critical period but they returned immediatly to Rome, as is said, with the Answer that His Sicilian Majesty cou'd not take any Step without first consulting the Court of Vienna but offer'd to receive the Pope if His Holyness shou'd think fit to retire to Naples. The Pope was so ill at the time of the late attempt towards a Revolution at Rome, that He cou'd not even be made acquainted with it, and it is probable the circumstance of the Pope's illness encouraged General Dufort to try the experiment in which he had succeeded at Genoa, and bring about the revolution quietly before a New Pope cou'd be Elected.

We hear from Rome that the Cisalpine Army is in possession of Perugia, Urbino, Gubbio, Tollentino and Macerata, and that it is expected that they will join and act with the french Army very soon against Rome. The Roman people are encouraged to beleive that a powerfull Assistance is coming to them from Naples, and the Preachers from their Pulpits assure their auditors that they have no thing to fear. The precarious State of the Pope's health and the very unfortunate affair of the 28th of Dec.r certainly leaves Rome in a very hazardous Situation and this Government seems to be taking proper precautions in order to be prepared for all events from the Roman quarter, as well as against the Plague which is now said to be at Cagliari in Sardinia as well as in Corsica.

General Canclaux has to the regret of this Government left Naples; he passed through Rome two days after the disturbances of the 28th of December and went on directly to Florence.

Monsieur Trouvè, who is left Charge des Affaires of the french Republic at Naples, seems not to be a very Conciliating Character.

I have the honor to be
My Lord
Your Lordship's

most obedient and
most humble servant
Wm Hamilton

3) Caserta January 16th 1798

My Lord
On friday last being the Birth Day of His Sicilian Majesty there was a
Grand Gala and Baccio manos at the Palace of Naples, and as usual a New
Opera and triple Illuminations at the Theatre of St. Carlos. It was universally
remarked that Monsieur Trouè, the french Charge d'Affaires did not pay his
Court to Their Sicilian Majesties in Gala at the Palace as all other Foreign
Ministers did on Friday last, but was in his box that Night undressed and
without powder (as were all the Secretaries of the french Legation) at the
Opera opposite to their Sicilian Majesties, and that they were the only persons in the Theatre that kept their Seats when the Royal Family stood up
between the Acts, and what offended the public still more, there were two
of the most common and Noted Women of the Town in the Box with them.
We hear from Rome that most of the foreign Travellers have left that City
and are either gone to Naples or Florence, some of the Roman Nobility are
already arrived at Naples, and the Palace belonging to the Pope's Nuncio at
Naples is preparing, as is said, for His Holyness. It is imagined that General
Berthier is waiting for orders from the french Directory to chastize the
Romans, and revenge the death of General Dufort; in the meantime a large
body of french and Cisalpine Troops are assembled on the Borders of the
Romagna, they write also from Rome that a small body of french Troops
were lately marching from Ancona upon some Expedition, and passing along
the common road without the Walls of Urbino were fired upon from the
Town, that four Soldiers were killed and the Commanding Officer wounded
in the Shoulder, that they return'd to Ancona, and having been reinforced
took possession of the Town of Osimo and immediately raised a Contribu-
tion there of Seventy thousand Crowns.
French[59] Commissaries are said to be arrived at Lucca and one at Pisa but
they have not yet open'd their Commissions which must naturally be to raise
Money for money they must get in Italy to maintain their Army as they do
not receive any from France.
It is now said that the french refuse to give up Venice at this moment to
the Imperialists altho' the last Letters from Venice and Trieste assured us that
General Mack[60] was arrived, and on the point of marching into that City at
the head of the Imperialists.

This Government has now order'd Four Thousand Cavalry to be ready to march at a moment's warning. It is certainly right to be well prepared at this uncommonly critical Moment but with respect to the fate of the Pope's State, the most natural Conjecture is, that its final Partition has been settled and agreed upon in the Congress of Udine, and to take place on the death of the Pope, daily expected but it is also natural to imagine that the french will in the mean time profit of the late accident to plunder Rome and lay that Unfortunate City under further Contributions.

The Marquis Gallo has been appointed Secretary of State for the foreign department and the Marine, and the Prince Castelcicala has been promoted from having the Direction of Foreign Affairs to the Post of Secretary of State per gli Affari di Grazia e Giustizia as Your Lordship will see in the inclosed Copy of a billet which I received from His Excellency[61] on the occasion.

The Letter inclosed and directed to Your Lordship, I have just received from Corfu.

I have the honor to be
My Lord
Your Lordship's
most obedient and
most humble Servant
Wm Hamilton

3) Naples February 6th 1798

My Lord
Since I had the honor of writing to Your Lordship last I have been on a Hunting Party with His Sicilian Majesty at Venafro fifty miles from this Capital, His Majesty returned to Naples on Thursday last, and the whole Court was to have removed to Caserta the 2[d] instant, but the near approach of the french Army to Rome has occasioned the Court's remaining at Naples, where frequent and long Councils are held on the present very critical Situation of Affairs.

By the last accounts We receiv'd from Rome, dated February 2[d]. We hear that General Berthier passed through Bologna the 22[d] of January for the Romagna and was supposed to be then at Ancona and that a great number of Troops are daily pouring into the Romagna so that in the whole it is conjectured that the Army is to consist of Sixty Thousand men, forty thousand of which french comprehending the Thirty one Thousand arrived from the Venetian Territories, and the rest Cisalpines and Poles. They have also an immense Train of Artillery so that it wou'd seem (if this account is not as I suspect greatly exaggerated) as if They had some other object in view, besides Rome and its State. One of my Letters from Rome says that twenty Thousand french are actually at Macerata, and that forty Carts are arrived at Rome with the Plate, Church furniture and other costly things from Perugia, Foligno, Terni, Narni and other places, and all deposited in the Castle of St. Angelo, which Castle has been furnished with plenty of provisions. The general opinion of Rome is that The Pope and all the Cardinals will retire to Benevento, They and their baggage are ready to depart at a moment's warning. The french are expected at Rome in about three Days from the date of this Letter, if that shou'd prove true I know not when I shall be able to write to Your Lordship again by Post, with any degree of Security.

His Royal Highness Prince Augustus has had a very long and severe attack of His former asthmatic complaint so that The Prince's Birth Day, that was to have been celebrated at my House, cou'd not take place untill Saturday last when all the foreign Ministers except those of Spain and France paid their Compliments to His Royal Highness, all the first Officers of the Court and Nobility of this Country were present at this fete in Gala, and the Cabinet Ministers as they wrote me word wou'd have certainly paid their Court to H. R. H. had they not been prevented by a long Council that lasted untill four o' clock on Sunday morning. Her Sicilian Majesty was pleased to honor Lady Hamilton with a Letter on that day full of Expressions of Her attachment to the King, Our Royal Master, and all His Family, and to the British Nation, and with Her kind Compliments to Prince Augustus, whom She declared that She loved as if He was her own Son, adding that, if Circumstances had permitted, Her Majesty wou'd certainly have been present Herself at the Fete.

I have the satisfaction of assuring Your Lordship that Prince Augustus is now perfectly recover'd, but neither His Royal Highness nor any of His Majesty's Subjects here are perfectly at their ease with the idea of a faithless Enemy being so near the Confines of this Kingdom, and particularly as they come (like Hamlet's Ghost) in such a Questionable Shape[62].

It appears that the false report of the Plague having manifested itself in Corsica was purposely raised and spread abroad by the Corsicans in order to prevent a great Body of french Troops from coming there from Genoa to chastize them, all the Letters from Corsica agree in their accounts of those Islanders having massacred some hundreds of the french and being actually in possession of every strong place in the Island except Bastia.

I have the honor to be
My Lord
Your Lordship's

most obedient and
most humble Servant
Wm Hamilton

4) (Private) Naples February 6th 1798

My Lord
Your Lordship is I dare say well acquainted with the Character of the Earl
of Bristol, and the warmth with which his Lordship follows up any object he
may have in View.

He is at present at Trieste confined with a fit of the Gout and writes to
me continually on his present favorite object. I take the liberty of transmitting to Your Lordship by a private channel Lord Bristol's last 3 Letters to me
as they contain some curious information relative to Corfu, but I have
answer'd His Lordp. that I knew that our Government was well informed of
the present State of Corfu and coud best judge whether it was an object or
not for detaching a Strong Naval force but that I wou'd not fail to inform
your Lordship of the Zeal His Lordship had manifested on this occasion.

I have the honor to be
My Lord
Your Lordship's
most obedient and
most humble Servant
Wm Hamilton

5) Naples February 19th 1978

My Lord
I profit of the opportunity of the return of the Messenger sent to this
Court from London by the Marquis Circello to inform Your Lordship of the
Revolution that is taking place at Rome and nearly compleated, without a
drop of blood having been as yet shed. In my Dispatch of last Year of the 6th
of June (N. 19) I ventured to mention to Your Lordship my conjectures with
respect to the critical Situation in which this Country wou'd probably soon
find itself, by the approach of the french Army, and which Conjectures are
now compleatly verified.

On the 10th instant the french Army, under the command of General
Berthier consisting of about twelve Thousand men including a body of Cavalry, which is the best part of their Army, enter'd Rome and took possession

of all the Castles Gates and high grounds, about the City Three Trees of Liberty were erected but after twenty four hours were taken down by order of Berthier. The Pope was obliged to sign Nineteen heavy Articles, but there was no mention in any of them of Religion or cession of Territory, but all the Pope's force and Government Authority to be annulled, Hostages having been given chosen from the rich and well affected and some immediately imprisoned, as Your Lordship will see by the inclosed Note N. 1) The Roman people to be disarmed and all monuments of Antiquity, and works of Art, to remain entirely at the french disposal; All sorts of British Manufactures prohibited, six Million of Roman Scudi to be paid within the Month, four in money, the rest in Effects. They likewise demand immediatly three Thousand Horses to recruit their Cavalry. The Six Thousand of the Pope's Troops disarmed and disbanded have two Months pay, and liberty to retire where they please, but it will probably end in most of them inlisting in the french Army. The Pope's Civic guard do duty at Rome in conjunction with the french. Notwithstanding the Pope's having agreed to these hard terms, by a Messenger from Rome Yesterday We hear that the french Army and the Roman people were now in perfect harmony and in full revolution burning and destroying all the Arms and inscriptions of the Pope to whom nothing is left but His Ecclesiastical power. Your Lordship may judge of the effect of such tidings upon this Court and Government, who now seem to be truly allarmed, particularly as they know that Berthier has order'd Ten thousand more french and a large Train of Artillery to join him immediatly at Rome. This must be evidently with a view to encourage a rising and to bring on if possible a Revolution in this Country, and Whilst so powerfull and faithless, call it either Friend or Enemy[63], is so near us We can not count upon a Moment's Security and indeed the Circumstance of His Royal Highness's Prince Augustus residence here at so very critical a moment is truly alarming, altho' We are sure of every assistance from this Court and Government in case of Necessity, but shou'd the french and Venetian Ships that are at Corfu come to Naples, as they probably wou'd in case of a rising in this Country, all means of escape wou'd be entirely cut off.

A french Gentleman Emigré called upon me lately and proposed that I shou'd pay his expences to England where he cou'd give such lights and intelligence to our Government as wou'd probably defeat the present plan of the french Directory to anihilate the British Superiority at Sea. I desired him to send me in writing some idea of his Plan and that I wou'd forward it to Your Lordship, without whose directions I cou'd not take upon me to send him to England. I have now the honor of inclosing N. 2 the paper he gave me. I see by several papers he shew'd me sign'd by all the french Emigrant Princes that he has realy been employ'd by them Confidentially in many very important Commissions at Naples Spain and in Germany. I can not add more at present as I was not informed of the Messenger's immediate departure untill about an hour ago[64].

I have the honor to be
My Lord
Your Lordship's
most obedient and
most humble Servant
Wm Hamilton

6) Naples March 6th 1798

My Lord
The french being in possession of the Roman Post I take the opportunity of writing to Your Lordship by a friend who sails this day for Leghorn in one of His Sicilian Majesty's Frigates. Your Lordship will certainly have received constant and fresh advices relative to the Unfortunate State of Rome from the Paris papers as special Messengers are frequently going between Rome and Paris. I have the honor of inclosing the three last Bulletins received from my old correspondent at Rome who is obliged to make use of different forms to send me the News of the day from Rome. What he says in N. 1) of the french being thirty Thousand strong there is absolutely false, they never were more than twelve thousand and having sent detachments to Ancona are not now more than Eight Thousand according to the best accounts received by this Government. The Differences between the Officers, the Commissaries and Generals of the french Army at Rome as mentioned in the Bulletin N. 2) may be attended with good consequences, if the whole is not a plan concerted amongst Them to furnish a pretext for calling more Troops to Rome. Whilst the french remain in force there this Country can never be Secure, but I am glad to see that this Government is seriously occupied in putting their Confines in the very best State of defence His Sicilian Majesty and His General Officers are inspecting the Troops Themselves in company with the Austrian General Colli who is universally esteem'd and allowed to be an Excellent Officer and who fortunately chances to be at Naples at this moment on account of his health.

I mean to profit of the very first opportunity to get to England according to the King's Gracious permission, either by land or Sea but as I think there is but little chance of a secure voyage home by Sea, I think in the Spring I may get a passage from Manfredonia to Trieste in one of His Sicilian

Majesty's Armed Vessels, and go on to Vienna. As I am totally ignorant of the present State of our Court with respect to that of St. Petersburgh, but see the importance of there being at this moment a perfect Understanding between them, shou'd our Government have a wish to try any new ground with the Emperor, perhaps it cou'd not employ a person that wou'd be more agreable to His Imperial Majesty than myself. I had the honor of attending the Great Duke of Russia and the Duchess during their whole stay at Naples some years ago, and lived with them in the utmost confidence and since which His Majesty has several times honor'd me with his correspondence and invited me to His Court. I throw this out to Your Lordship, not with any wish or view of Serving myself, but out of pure Zeal and earnest desire of serving My Good King and Country to the utmost of my Ability, and it wou'd be of little consequence to my private concerns whether I shou'd return home a few Months sooner or later or travel some Leagues more or less. If your Lordship wou'd be so kind as to send the Answer to this hint directed to me under Cover to Sir Morton Eden[65] I shou'd either receive it at Vienna or it might be forwarded to me here[66].

May I beg the favor of Your Lordship to order the inclosed Letter (which is left open for Your perusal) to be forwarded to the Lords Commissioners of His Majesty's Treasury.

I have the honor to be
My Lord
Your Lordship's
most obedient and
humble Servant
Wm Halmilton

P. S. Mr Livingston arrived here from Trieste the day before Yesterday.

7) Naples March 13th 1798

My Lord
By an Estafette that arrived here from Corfu three days ago We hear that the french and Venetian Ships of War, Eleven of which of the Line, loaded heavily with the Spoils of Venice and other parts of Italy Sail'd from that Port the 24th of February, Supposed for Toulon, altho' the french gave out that they were going upon the Expedition against Great Britain. The inclosed, which I received by the Estafette directed to your Lord.p, will inform You of the particulars of the Sailing of this Fleet. Having had the honor of inform-ing Your Lordship very particularly of the State of Rome and Naples at this

critical juncture by a safe and Speedy conveyance in my Letters of the 19th and 7th of March I have nothing to add at present.

I have the honor to be
My Lord
Your Lordship's
most obedient and
most humble Servant
Wm Hamilton

8) Naples March 27th 1798

My Lord
Whilst the Post at Rome remains in the hands of it's present rulers, it is in vain to write with any degree of Security, but Your Lordship may be assured of my taking the advantage of Writing to You as often as a safe opportunity shall offer.

The report of an additional Army of Thirty Thousand french being on it's march to reinforce that already in Italy, gives great alarm both here and in Tuscany, but as this Government is realy exerting itself to the utmost to put the Country in the best State of defence, and that the Neapolitans are by no means well disposed towards the french, They will not be able to penetrate into this Kingdom so easily as they did into the Pope's State.

I have the honor of inclosing a List of the Spanish Fleet that Sail'd from Cadix the 7th of Feb.y which I have reason to beleive to be correct, that Fleet is now said to be returned to Cadix. We have reports that a portion of the french Fleet from Corfu endeavor'd to get into the Port of Malta, but that the Grand Master being well prepared would only suffer a limited number of Ships to enter, and that they sail'd away as supposed for Toulon with marks of great discontent.

There are several small french Privateers always hovering about this Bay and they have made many prizes but having attacked a Jersey Merchant Vessel well armed, he beat off three of the Privateers and sunk one of their boats with twenty five men all of whom were drowned.

I have the honor to be
My Lord
Your Lordship's
most obedient and
most humble Servant
Wm Hamilton

9) Naples April 3ᵈ 1798

My Lord

your Lordship will have heard of the french having laid an Embargo on the Shipping at Genoa. By the last Letters from Leghorn of the 27ᵗʰ of March We are told that the french Secret Expedition fitting out at Genoa will carry Cavalry with them, and are to take from Corsica Troops and a General Officer. Most of the Squadron from Corfu are in the Gulph of Specia, but some Ships of the Line are supposed to be gone to Toulon with the rich Spoils from Venice and Ancona. The destination of the Expedition is given out to be for Sardinia or Malta, others think differently.

As the french have certainly occasion for a reinforcement both in Corsica and at Corfu if they mean to keep their ground in those Islands I shou'd think that must be the present object of the Expedition. That when they can, they will take all they can, in this, and every other part of the World (according to the present System of the french Republic) is as clear as day light.

Inclosed is a Packet directed to Your Lordship which I received last Week from Corfu.

I have the honor to be
My Lord
Your Lordship's
most obedient and
most humble Servant
Wm Hamilton

10) Caserta April 17ᵗʰ 1798⁶⁷

My Lord

A Strong Squadron of Neapolitan Ships of War will be ready in the Adriatic to carry his Royal Highness Prince Augustus in safety to Trieste. I have reason to suspect that the Queen of Naples and a part of the Young Royal Family mean to profit of this Opportunity of getting to Vienna to avoid the danger with which these Kingdoms are threatened at this very critical moment.

I have the honor to be
My Lord
Your Lordship's
most obedient and
most humble Servant
Wm Hamilton

11) *Secret* Naples April 20th 1798

My Lord

I have the honor of inclosing my Letter to The Lords Commissioners of His Majesty's Treasury, acquainting Their Lordships that I had drawn on Them for the Sum of Two Thousand Pounds, which was the full extent of the Credit Your Lordship directed to me in Your Letter of the 22.d of Dec.r last in favor of Edm.d Livingston Esq.r, and may I beg the favor of Your Lordship to forward my Letter to Their Lordships.

M.r Livingston has found it necessary to call upon me for the whole Sum of Two Thousand Pounds, in order to arrange the confidential Business on which he is employ'd by His Majesty and Your Lordship will receive from me, or M.r Livingston, by the first safe opportunity a full account of what We have thought incumbent upon us to do at this uncommonly Critical Moment.

I have the honor to be
My Lord
Your Lordship's
most obedient and
most humble Servant
Wm Hamilton

12) Downing Street, April 20th 1798
By the Messenger Bassett

Sir,

Your dispatches to N. 7 inclusive have been received and laid before the King.

In the uncertainty whether this dispatch may find you still at Naples, I inclose it to Sir Morton Eden, with directions either to forward it to you, or to deliver it to you, if you shall actually have reached Vienna. In the latter case, you will not fail to take such measures for transmitting the substance of it to the Neapolitan Ministry as may ensure their receiving it in so short a time as possible, and accompanying it with such expressions as may convince them in the strongest manner of the loyalty and sincerity with which His Majesty enters into the interests, and feels for the present situation of Their Sicilian Majesties.

It would have been impossible for His Majesty to witness the plain and undisguised declarations of the French government of their intention to overwhelm the dominions of His Sicilian Majesty without feeling the most lively desire to interpose, so far as he might have the means and opportunity, to rescue from destruction a Power with whom He has always been anxious to maintain the most friendly intercourse. The discussions which have lately taken place between His Majesty and the Court of Vienna respecting the common interests of the two Governments and of Europe lead His Majesty to hope that he may find occasion to interfere with effect, provided the period at which his assistance can be afforded be not too remote to prevent the difficulties which appear to be impending over Naples. And he has only to lament that the other Powers of Europe have so tardily awaked to the true sense of their general danger as to leave any doubt upon this point, and to have made it impractical for Him to be either more early in His offers of assistance or more certain of their success.

His Majesty has come to the determination of sending a Fleet into the Mediterranean for the protection of Naples so soon as it is possible for it to be brought forward – without detriment to the indispensable objects of His Naval Service, or imminent hazard to the safety of His dominions.

I have endeavoured to explain fully to Mr. Circello – and I shall shortly recapitulate here the circumstances in the present situation of this Country, which make it impossible that this measure however much His Majesty has it at heart should take place, as immediately as His own wishes, and perhaps the necessity of the case, require.

No reasonable man can look at the present situation of this Country without being convinced that the providing and maintaining for the defence of His Majesty's European dominions such system of naval defence as may be sufficient to meet all attempt on the part of the Enemy to invade these Kingdoms, is the first and most indispensable duty of the Naval Administration.

The next service in point of importance is the blockade of the harbour of Cadiz. And it will perhaps be no difficult matter to convince the Neapolitan Ministry of the impossibility of abandoning altogether, or diminishing in any material degree the system which has so long locked up in that port the greatest part of the maritime force of Spain when you have to prove to them (as you may easily do) that even the abandonment, or the partial suspension of it would not enable His Majesty to afford effective or permanent assistance to the Court of Naples. For if Lord St. Vincent were to sail into the Mediterranean with his whole Fleet, the Spanish Fleet would be left at liberty to join the French Fleet at Brest, and would constitute such a superiority on these Seas as must necessitate the recall of the Mediterranean Squadron almost as soon as it had arrived at it's destination. If he were to detach a portion of it as might be thought sufficient for the immediate defence of Naples, there could be no security that the remainder might not be found insufficient to prevent the Spanish Fleet from making its way into the Mediterranean also, when joined with the Toulon Fleet, it would so far outnumber the British Squadron as if not to render a Contest doubtful at least to make the service which it could render to the particular object of its destination precarious both in duration and extent.

It is therefore evident that an augmentation of the naval establishment of Great Britain is necessary for enabling her to furnish to Naples the succour which it required, that this augmentation will take some time, and be attended with considerable expence and some difficulty.

I am enabled, however, to transmit assurances to Naples that this augmentation will be made, and that a fleet sufficient for all the purposes of protection and assistance will sail for the Mediterranean from this Country with the first fair wind after the beginning of June.

I need hardly explain to you the natural consequences of such an exertion on the part of His Majesty is a demand for the free and immediate admission of His Fleet or of any part thereof as the service may require into the Neapolitan ports, with the fullest liberty to the commander of the Fleet to supply himself there with every species of provisions, store, etc. without restriction, and also that these ports shall be shut to all Enemy's Ships, and all commerce between them and the Enemy effectually prohibited. But I am under the necessity of stating distinctly that if, at least the first part of this demand, that which relates to the admission and supply of the Fleet in the Neapolitan Ports, be not complied with, His Majesty's Admiral commanding that fleet will have orders forthwith to quit the Mediterranean, and to return to these Seas.

And as the principal difficulty in this Country in making the proposed augmentation will arise from the deficiency of Men, His Majesty further demands that a number of Seamen not less than 3000 or even more if they can be spared shall be furnished from the ports of Naples (the like number being also to be supplied from those of Austria in the Adriatic to strengthen the Crews of those Ships which His Majesty shall send there) and that the Sailors being furnished shall be bound to serve (on board the King's Mediterranean Fleet only) during the whole War, subject to the same discipline and entitled to the same pay and victualling allowances as the British Seamen.

It remains to speak of the degree of assurance that can be given for the continuance, in the Mediterranean, of the Fleet which His Majesty destines to this service. And this must plainly be affected by the same considerations which render it impossible to deduct from the present existing force a squadron sufficient for the purpose. The two points of home defence, and of the Blockade of Cadiz must retain the same importance in the scale of our naval preparation so long as the state of Europe and of the War continues the same as at present, as between Great Britain and France and Spain.

It is possible, tho' I trust not probable, that the Naval force of the Enemy may by the efforts we understand they are making, be augmented to a considerable degree, and be brought to bear with an increased pressure upon these two points. This would necessarily require a proportionate augmentation of force on our part to meet it, and it might happen therefore that the Fleet prepared with a view to the Mediterranean Service might be necessarily recalled to the reinforcement of one or other of these Stations. Under these circumstances it would be impossible to engage in the first instance continuance of the Fleet in the Mediterranean to an indefinite period. There are but two Events which could make it possible that a positive and unqualified engagement should be taken in this respect: the first is the total discomfiture and destruction of the Maritime force of France employed (if she should so employ it) in an attempt to invade these Kingdoms. The other, one which it seems not improbable that Naples and Austria might take a considerable share, as they will have a considerable interest, in accomplishing, the inducing the Court of Spain to come to a separate accommodation with Great Britain, and thenceforth either to maintain a perfect neutrality during the remainder of the War or to accede to the General defensive Alliance now in Agitation.

You will mention this to the Neapolitan Ministry, not as a matter loosely thrown out with a view merely to the single object which is here in question[68], but as one which is well worth the serious consideration of the Courts of Naples and Vienna, and in which the Ministers of those Courts at Madrid might be instructed to exert themselves in a manner by no means unlikely to lead to a conclusion highly beneficial to the Common Cause.

You will inform the Neapolitan Minister (in the strictest confidence) that, from the reception which certain overtures, which His Majesty directed be made, no long time ago, met with at Madrid, there is every reason to believe that the Court of Vienna is not (or was not at least previous to the late change in the Administration there) averse to entertaining proposals for a separate peace with His Majesty provided it had been possible to do so without incurring the immediate and active hostility of France, and that His Majesty for a purpose so advantageous to the general interests of Europe, was, and is ready to sacrifice without scruple and without compensation the Conquests which He has made on Spain in the course of the War, and to make Peace on the footing of the strict Status ante Bellum.

It is impossible not to add that the danger which Spain apprehends from a French Army already hovering over her frontiers is one which may fairly be supposed to counteract her strongest inclinations for separate Peace especially as it is one from which the power of Great Britain could in no way defend her[69]. But it is conceivable that this apprehension once removed there would be no true motive remaining which would be sufficient to outdo the sense of the serious difficulties under which she labours, the alarm which she must naturally feel for her Commerce and her Colonies from the Continuance of hostility with this Country, and the obvious, imminent, and growing danger to her internal Peace and Tranquillity, and to the Monarchy itself from the uncontrouled admission and encouragement of French Principles throughout her Provinces, to say nothing of the possible introduction of a French Army, into the heart of the Country. This state of Things would of course be materially varied, and the dread of impending destruction from French Arms in a great degree removed by the circumstance of the French Government finding sufficient employment for her whole military force elsewhere as would necessarily be the case if Austria renews the War.

It can hardly be doubted therefore that if a confidential communication were to be made at Madrid of the intention of the Court of Naples (so soon as they were finally matured) the overture of His Majesty might be renewed with Spain thro' the Neapolitan and Austrian Ministers, and that the fear of France being removed, Spain might then be persuaded by the state of the plainest and most urgent considerations of her own interest to exchange a state of unprofitable and perilous War, for a safe neutrality if not for an Alliance with the remaining powers of Europe, cemented by the principles of common interest and common security.

In this case one of the most pressing exigencies of our Naval Service would be effectually removed, and His Majesty could then safely engage to keep a force in the Mediterranean superior to that of the Enemy during the remainder of the War. Even if this should not take place every Consideration of interest would certainly make Him desirous of doing so and in the common course of the events of War, there is little doubt that this might be done, but an absolute engagement to that effect can be taken only in the case above-mentioned.

I trust that these assumptions will be sufficient to inspire into the Neapolitan Government the Courage which is required to meet the present trials and difficulties. And you may add the strongest expressions of the sincere and lively Interest which His Majesty takes in a thing that concerns Their Sicilian Majesties and of His desire and determination rather to execute than fall short of all that he has engaged to do for the defence and preservation of their Honour and Interests.

13) Downing Street April 27th 1798

Sir,

The Messenger whom Mr. Circello sends tonight to Naples, & by whom I now write to You, is charged with the account of Mr. Circello's conferences with me on the subject of the applications which he was directed to make here, and of my answers to them.

As I have written to You very fully on this subject through Vienna, I think it only necessary to repeat to You on this occasion that the conditions which have been proposed from hence are considered as absolutely essential, and that as the ready & liberal compliance of His Majesty has been formed on His confidence that these will be punctually fulfilled, so any hesitation in the execution of them must of necessity annul all the measures taken from hence, & replace the whole subject on its present footing[70].

14) Caserta May the 8th 1798

My Lord

Yesterday I was honor'd with Your Lordship's Letter of the 27th of March N. 1.) The instructions your Lord.p was pleased to give me with respect to the French and Corsican Emigrants under His Majesty's Protection in this Kingdom, has releived me from a great Embarassment. Your Lordship's conjecture with respect to the probability of their approaching expulsion from His Sicilian Majesty's Dominions has been partly verified, having about Ten days ago received a Billet from the Marquis Gallo, desiring of me in the Name of His Sicilian Majesty to acquaint the Corsican Emigrants that they must quit this Kingdom as soon as they cou'd so with any degree of safety. These unfortunate Men having represented to me the impossibility of their going out of the Kingdom any other way than by Sea, and that the expences of their moving wou'd be more than their present finances wou'd admit of, requested some extraordinary allowances from The King's Bounty. As the Instructions left me by Sir Gilbert Elliot did not authorize me to comply with their request I promised to represent their case to your Lordship, and that I wou'd sollicit this Government that they might be allowed to stay until I cou'd receive Your Lordship's Answer. The Marquis Gallo insisted upon their quitting the Capital in ten days, and going, at their choice, either to Manfredonia or Gaeta, in order to embark on the first favourable opportunity; and that in the mean time they shou'd not be molested. As to the french Emigrants (from what reason I can not well comprehend) there has been no mention except the requiring of those who wear the Croix de St. Louis, to lay them aside.

In the present moment there is no saying where a place of perfect safety can be found for these unfortunate Emigrants, but as soon as that can be ascertain'd I will make a discreet use of the power Your Lordship entrusted me with by His Majesty's command of supplying them with the money necessary for transporting them to the nearest Port in His Imperial Majesty's Dominions, drawing upon the Lords of the Treasury, at as long a date as possible, for the amount of such advances, and I shall not fail of giving their Lordship's (through the channel of Your Lordship) notice of my Drafts.

Yesterday Monsieur Garrat presented at Naples His Credential Letters, as Ambassador Extraordinary from the french republic to the King of the two Sicilies.

This Morning early His Royal Highness, Prince Augustus Frederick, M.r Livingston and His Royal Highnesses Physician, set off Post for Manfredonia in order to embark directly for Trieste, His Sicilian Majesty having been Graciously pleased to send round from Naples one of the Ships of the Line and a Frigate to Manfredonia for the purpose of conveying His Royal Highness and His Suite safely to Trieste. Count Muster and M.r Tatter sat out for Hanover through Rome about ten days ago, and as they had a french and Roman Passport we have heard already of their safe arrival at Florence.

I shall now begin to think of profiting of the King's Gracious permission for me to return home for a short time to look into my own Affairs and which permission Your Lordship was so kind as to procure for me as long ago as the Month of June last, but I cou'd not think of quitting my Post whilst the King's Son remain'd at Naples, and an inveterate Enemy so very near us.

The two Spanish Ships of the Line loaded with Quick Silver and blocked up so long at Trieste, are now at Palermo in very bad Condition.

His Sicilian Majesty has taken quiet possession of Benevento and other temporary arrangements seem to be in Agitation between this Court and the french Directory. The prospect here however, I must own, appears to me but gloomy, and the fate of this fine Country to depend but too much on the Chapter of Accidents[71].

I have the honor to be
My Lord
Your Lordship's
most obedient and
most humble Servant
Wm Hamilton

P.S. The inclosed for His Majesty was left by H. R. H. Prince Augustus desiring me to forward it
to Your Lordship.

15) Caserta May 15th 1798

My Lord

We hear by a Messenger that arrived here three days ago from Paris that the extraordinary conduct of the late Ambassador of the french Republic at Vienna did not meet with the entire approbation of the Directory, and was not likely to produce the expected rupture between the Court of Vienna and the Republic.

The Ambassador of the Republic at this Court, Mons.r Garrat, at his first Audience read a Speech of Six pages to His Sicilian Majesty, in which, as I am informed, He bragged of the generosity of the Great Nation[72] in having given so good a Peace to the Emperor of Germany, and of it's Magnanimity in having granted a Peace to an other power which was by no means in a Situation of defending itself[73]; and then He utter'd much abusive language against Great Britain. Your Lordship will probably soon read this Extraordinary Speech at full length in the Paris Papers.

It certainly was not civil in the Directory to send as Ambassador Extraordinary from the french Republic to a Court of the House of Bourbon the very man who carried the Sentence of death to the Unfortunate Louis XVI and who attended His Execution.

We hear from Rome that the french are carrying on their depredations there without mercy, and that they are now come to the point of taking One pair of Sheets from a house that has only two pair, and leaving a man with only One Shirt to his body. We hear also that they have now plunder'd the Houses of the English Artists whom they had permitted to remain at Rome, and have order'd them to leave the Town immediatly.

The report still prevails of a British Fleet's being on the point of coming into the Mediterranean, of which I much doubt, when I consider the Necessary Occupation of the King's Fleets, at this moment, for the defence of Great Britain. I think it however my Duty not to leave my Post untill this point shall have been cleared up, and which I flatter myself will be in a very few days.

The Enormous preparation for a Grand Secret Expedition is said to be carried on at Toulon with great vigour, but its immediate Object is now thought to be the Two Sicilies as it was in the beginning.

Their Sicilian Majesties and most of the Young Royal family are at this Palace, and the Mesdames of France (by whose desire I take the liberty of troubling Your Lordship with the inclosed) continue to reside in the Old Palace of Caserta.

The Hereditary Princess of the two Sicilies is three Months gone with Child.

I have the honor to be
My Lord
Your Lordship's
most obedient and
most humble Servant
Wm Hamilton

16) Naples May 22^d 1798

My Lord
Very fortunately, as your Lordship will have seen by my Dispatch of the
15th of May N. 12.) I had determined not to leave Naples untill all hopes of
a British Fleet's coming speedily into the Mediterranean were at an end, so
that I had the honor of receiving here Your Lordship's very important Dispatch N. 2) from Sir Morton Eden, the day before Yesterday and have already
communicated it's contents to this Government, the result of which Your
Lordship will receive by a Messenger Extraordinary that I propose to send off
as soon as I get the Answer which I flatter myself can not fail of being Satisfactory.

The Prince Belmonte Pignatelli has been appointed Minister to the Court
of Great Britain in the room of the Marquis Circello, and as I hear, proposes
setting out soon for London. I can take it upon me to assure Your Lordship
that the King of Naples cou'd not have made a better choice, I have known
the Prince from his early Infancy. He has been perfectly Educated (which is
a rare circumstance in the Nobility of this Country), is a good Classical
Scholar and speaks most of the modern Languages, particularly the English,
fluently, but what I esteem above all He is an honest worthy young man, and
will I am convinced give perfect Satisfaction to the King and His Majesty's
Ministers.

The Prince has desired me to trouble Your Lordship with the inclosed for
Lord Malmesbury[74] whom He had the honor of knowing during the late
Negociations at Paris.
I have the honor to be
My Lord
Your Lordship's
most obedient and
most humble Servant
Wm Hamilton

17) Naples May 29th 1798

My Lord

We know little more about the Earl of Bristol's Arrest and present con-
finement at Milan than was (as I see by the last Newspapers) known in England the 24th of April, but We all know that His Lordship's freedom in conversation, particularly after dinner, is such as to make him liable to accidents
of this nature. The latest and most authentic account I have of Lord Bristol
is in a letter to me from Mr. Alex.r Day a Printer employ'd by His Lord.p,
it is dated from Rome May 26th. He says, "I am just returned from Milan, I
have been in hopes of having the pleasure of seeing Lord Bristol, but not suc-
ceeding after waiting ten days, I thought it most prudent to return home. I
understood from His Servant Giunti that His Lordship was in good health,
indeed I had the honor to receive several billets from his Lord.p which as
usual were replete with Spirit and brilliancy; the artists here all feel his Loss
most sensibly."

The Court proposes to come to Naples from Caserta this day, Tomorrow
being the Name day of His Sicilian Majesty and consequently a Grand Gala,
There will be neither Baccio Manos nor Tavola Publica as formerly at the
Palace, but the Royal Family will be at the Royal Theatre of St. Carlos,
which is to be decorated as usual with a triple Illumination.

His Sicilian Majesty gave a Fete Champetre at St. Leuce near Caserta on
Sunday last, to which the Forreign Ministers and all the Nobility of this
Country were invited. Monsieur Garrat, Ambassador Extraordinary from the
french Republic and two of his Secretaries of Legation, were there dressed, or
rather undressed in their new exaggerated Stile, that is with rough cropt
black hair, their frock closely buttond up, boots and a huge Sabre hanging to
a black leather belt over the Coat. The Ambassador and one of his Secretary's
wore large Spectacles constantly, as did the late Minister of the french
Republic, Monsieur Trouet and his attendants, perhaps it may be a Diplomatic Etiquette of the New Republic. Their terrific appearance actually
frightend the Ladies, they must have perceived that they were universally
avoided and they did not stay for the Supper altho' they had been honor'd
with marked attentions by Their Sicilian Majesties, the Royal Family, and
principal Officers of the Court.

General Acton told me yesterday that Mons.r Garrat had assured him seriously that the Grand Expedition from Toulon, which was commanded by
General Buonaparte, was realy destin'd for Egypt, that they were to establish
a Colony and rebuild a City on the Spot on which stood Ancient Berenice,
and that he did not doubt of their being able soon to put in Execution the

ancient plan of cutting a Canal across the Isthmus of Suex, for that the french Republic had never been in so flourishing a Situation as this Moment.

I have the honor to be
My Lord
Your Lordship's
most obedient and
most humble Servant
Wm Hamilton

18) Naples June 5th 1798

My Lord

Your Lordship will have seen by my late dispatches that however desirous I was to profit of the King's gracious permission to return home for a short time to look into my private concerns (and which permission I have had ever since the month of June 1797) I did not think of leaving Naples untill I cou'd do so without the smallest prejudice to His Majesty's Service. The Formation of the Cisalpine and Roman Republics and the french having taken possession of Rome put this Country immediatly in such a perilous situation that I began to be apprehensive for the safety of His Royal Highness Prince Augustus but when General Acton informed me that the french Directory had actually declared to the Neapolitan Minister at Paris (who had required a explanation as to the object of the great Armament at Toulon) that if the King of Naples did not satisfy the Republic in several points, particularly in that of Money in exchange for Benevento, that Armament wou'd be employ'd in republicanizing the rest of Italy, I thought it high time that Prince Augustus shou'd be removed to a place of more security, and accordingly applied to this Government for their Assistance to convey H. R. H. from Manfredonia to Trieste, the only door now open for His retreat. His Sicilian Majesty was pleased to order immediatly that a Ship of the Line shou'd be prepared with every conveniency and sent round to Manfredonia to convey His Royal Highness and His Suite to Trieste and no doubt before this time The King will have received Letters from Prince Augustus dated from Vienna. As soon as my mind was at ease with respect to the safety of the Prince, I began to prepare for my departure when I had the honor of receiving from Sir Morton Eden Your Lordship's important Dispatch of the 20th of April last N. 2) and which determined me to defer my departure as certainly shou'd a British Fleet come to Naples and the Commander of it not find either The King's Minister or Consul here might be under the greatest difficulties and what made it still more necessary fro me to stay was the death of M.r Andrew Davenport, who is universally regretted, He had been appointed Pro Consul by M.r Goddard, and had been constantly employ'd in the British Consular business upwards of forty Years, with much honor to himself and benefit to His Majesty's Service.

Your Lordship will now see the Necessity of His Majesty's appointing as soon as possible a Consul for Naples; in the mean time I will assist M.r Market, the present Vice Consul, as far as I am able, but We already feel the loss of M.r Davenport, french and Spanish prizes being brought frequently into the Ports of Naples and Sicily by our Privateers, and the french and Spanish Consuls making every possible objection, founded or not as to the legality of those Prizes[75], which objections will naturally be attended to by this Government whilst the Mediterranean is in the power of Spain and the french Republic.

I had the honor of informing Your Lordship by my Secret Letters dated April 17th 1797 N. 12), and forwarded to Your Lordship by M.r Ragland, of the exact state of this Court and Government to the best of my judgment, at that Period, and as no alteration of consequence has taken place since I have not any reason to alter my opinion and I beg leave to refer Your Lordship now to that Secret Dispatch. The Marquis de Gallo indeed has since been appointed Secretary of State for the foreign Department, and is extremely jealous of any interference in His department, particularly from the quarter of General Acton, but as the General is now as much supported by the King of Naples as He was formerly by the Queen, I look upon His Excy still as the Prime Minister of this Country. The person who has been particularly distinguished for some time past by Her Sicilian Majesty and certainly in great favor at this moment is the Prince Belmonte Pignatelli, lately appointed to succeed the Marquis Circello at our Court, but I have reason to beleive that He is not consulted in affairs of a public nature. The Marquis de Gallo does not appear to me to be greatly in the Esteem of either the King or Queen of Naples. He seems like the Marquis de Sambuca (who had also been His Sicilian Majesty's Minister at the Court of Vienna before his being appointed Secretary of State) to have an ambition to be thought like that great man, the late Prince Kaunitz[76], and indeed as to all the outward appearance of magnificence and foppery, the Marquis Sambuca did, and the Marquis Gallo does, represent Prince Kaunitz very exactly. The Marquis Sambuca's Understanding was very weak indeed, and as far as I can judge as yet, the Marquis de Gallo has not any great depth of Understanding.

As soon as I receiv'd Your Lordship's dispatch N. 2) of the 20th of April, I wrote a billet to request an Audience of the Marquis de Gallo as soon as possible, that I might communicate to His Excy the Substance of a most important dispatch which I had just receiv'd from Your Lordship, but the Marquis at that time being confined to his bed at Naples with a severe cold I did not see him until three days after at Caserta. However as I have constantly kept alive that very friendly intercourse that has existed with little or no interruption for so many years between General Acton and me I went immediately to His Excy[77] and in confidence read to him Your Lordship's Dispatch. He wished to have a Copy of it, but I told him that cou'd not be granted as I must now carry on the King's business through it's proper and regular channel, that of the Marquis de Gallo, and that I even begged of His Excy to keep it secret even from their Sicilian Majesties that I had made him this confidence, as it was highly proper that the Marquis de Gallo shou'd be the first to communicate the substance of Your Lordship's dispatch to Their Majesties.

I waited upon the Marquis de Gallo the moment he came to Caserta and communicated to his Excy according to Your Lordship's directions the Substance of Your Dispatch N. 2) which seemed to give him great satisfaction, I then observed to His Excy that after the King's having so readily complied with the earnest desire of Their Sicilian Majesties and Their Government and order'd at a great expence a fresh Fleet to be fitted out immediatly for the sole purpose of protecting Their Sicilian Majesties and Their Dominions from imminent destruction, that His Excy wou'd authorize me, by a Messenger that I intended to dispatch without delay, to assure your Lordship in the Name of Their Sicilian Majesties that when The King's Fleet shou'd come into the Mediterranean, His Majesty's Ships without controul or limitation might freely enter any of the Ports of the two Sicilies, and from which those of the Enemy were to be excluded; and also that they shou'd allow of the Commander of the British Fleet, being Supplied with the necessary Provisions and stores for the Fleet in those Ports. I likewise dwelt on the necessity of Their Sicilian Majesties complience with the Article of the three thousand, or more, Neapolitan Seamen being permitted to serve on board the British Fleet during the War. I found the Marq.s very unwilling to give a decided Answer to these points and His Excy begged that I wou'd not send off a Messenger to England until the Marquis Circello's Courrier, who was expected daily from London, shou'd arrive. That Courrier is arrived and I still find the same indecision, saying that it is necessary for this Government to see more clearly into the intentions of the Emperor before it decides a question, which in Effect, wou'd be a declaration of War against the french Republic. I told His Excy that I cou'd do no otherwise than to send off my Messenger immediatly and endeavour if possible to prevent the sailing of the Fleet for the Mediterranean, when after putting Great Britain to such an enormous Expence it cou'd be of no Use unless the principal Articles in Your Lordship's Dispatch were fully complied with by this Government, for that His Excy knew, that the Commander of the Fleet wou'd have positive Orders to return home immediatly unless they were complied with. Not hearing more from the Marquis de Gallo I wrote a Confidential Billet to General Acton to tell him my reasons and determination of sending off my Messenger and I have the honor of inclosing His Excy's Answer N. 1). The want of decision and half-Measures will I fear be the ruin of this Country. I have spoken my mind freely and often to Gen.l Acton on this Subject and I take the liberty of inclosing a Copy of a billet N. 2) which I wrote to His Excy in the year 1796 soon after which His Sicilian Majesty made his Peace with the french Republic, after the British Fleets having been detain'd in the Mediterranean at a great Expence and at the sole earnest request of Their Sicilian Majesties and their Ministry.

The present moment seems to be very similar to the one above mention'd, in the Copy of my Letter to Lord St. Vincent N. 3) inclosed your Lordship will find a Copy of Gen.l Acton's billet of Confidence to me dated the 3d of April last – in that Letter with expressions so anxious for the implored assistance of Lord St. Vincent's Fleet, threaten'd as they were by the french Directory unless such a Sum as wou'd content the Directory was paid to them in exchange for Benevento – it is natural to imagine, seeing soon after Benevento in the possession of His Sicilian Majesty, that the Directory has been contented, and the immediate danger from the french Toulon Fleet being thus removed this Government is returning again to it's Half-Measures[78].

Genl. Acton was so good as to communicate to me on Sunday last the dispatches of the Marquis Circello dated to the 11th of May, in which I saw, with great pleasure, that by a new Arrangement the British Fleet may be most probably in the Mediterranean by this time, and as the great Armament from Toulon Sail'd and was seen off Piombino on the Coast of Tuscany the 25th of last Month Steering southwardly, The King's Fleet may be in time to counteract the Operations of that Fleet whether it is against Sicily, Malta, or for the wild project of the Settlement of a french Colony in Upper Egypt.

Not to detain Your Lordship longer – I have told the Marquis de Gallo and Gen.l Acton fairly my opinion that as Your Lordship had repeated in your last Dispatch to me of the 27th of April N. 3) that the Sine qua non of His Majesty's Fleet's remaining in the Mediterranean wou'd be His Sicilian Majesty's compliance with the above mentioned Articles – that I shou'd also take the opportunity of that Fleet's returning home (which it is to do if not admitted freely into the Ports of the two Sicilies) to profit of His Majesty's gracious permission and return to England with it.

The Marquis Gallo promised me however that I shou'd have a possitive Answer in a few days, and that I might profit of a Courrier they meant to send to London to forward my Dispatches to Your Lordship. Never the less I flatter myself that Your Lord.p will not disapprove of my having dispatched M.r

Small the bearer with this packet particularly as he is directed to go to Vienna on his way home to take any Packets that His R. Highness Prince Augustus or Sir Morton Eden may wish to forward by him, and as M.r Small is to remain in England nothing more will be required than the indemnification of the Expence of his Posting from Naples to London.

I have the honor to be
My Lord
Your Lordship's
most obedient and most
humble Servant
Wm Hamilton

19) Copy of my Letter to Sir John Acton in Answer to His Excy's Confidential Letter of the 28th October 1796
Naples October 29th 1796

Dear Sir

Returning Your Excy. my warmest thanks for Your Confidential Letter of Yesterday's date You may be assured that I shall not fail in my Dispatches to Sir Gilbert Elliot and Sir John Jervis to express the great Satisfaction of Their Sicilian Majesties and Their Government on the friendly reslution they have taken of not abandoning the Mediterranean; your Excy., by adding *as yet*, seems to doubt of the King's Fleet remaining here for any considerable time. Now, with the same frankness that your Excy. has permitted me to write to You on all occasions, I must say that I understand by Sir John Jervis's Letter of the 19th October no more than that the stay of the King's Fleet in the Mediterranean must depend upon Succours and Provisions sent from hence. Allow me, Dear Sir, to speak out freely, and I do not do so as the Minister of Great Britain, but as an impartial Englishman, who from very particular Circumstances during a Residence of 32 years in this Country, is nearly as much attached to it as to his Native one, and feels equally for the Prosperity, Honor and Glory of Both.

After the Compliance of Sir John Jervis and Sir Gilbert Elliot to the Wishes of Their Sicilian Majesties and of their Government, by which I verily beleive They have saved the Two Sicilies and all Italy from the most imminent danger of absolute Ruin and Subversion, it must be expected that this Government will as soon as possible (with propriety) Exert itself to the utmost and join Great Britain with all it's power to distress the Enemy. It is plain that Naples will never have reasonable offers of Peace from the french Directory by following half Measures; the french will continue to delay, and give hopes, but will not Conclude. In my humble Opinion then the Armistice shou'd be broken as soon as possible (and indeed I have reason to think that Your Excellency is of the same opinion) and as many of His Sicilian Majesty's Ships, Frigates, Galleons, Zebecks, Gun Boats etc. etc. as can be spared, consistently with the immediate safety of These Kingdoms, shou'd be directly prepared and sent to Sir John Jervis, in short, knowing as We do how very ill – not to say wickedly inclined the Court of Spain is at this Moment towards that of Naples, the latter shou'd not I think hesitate on the first favourable opportunity to put itself entirely under the protection of Great Britain, and join issue with it against every Enemy. At present indeed this Government has only to think of it's breaking the Armistice without delay, of marching forward its Land Forces and of assisting The King's Fleet to the utmost of its power in annoying the Enemy and protecting its own Dominions and the rest of Italy against the french: Violent disorders require violent Remedies, half Measures seldom or ever turn to good account as the Celebrated Pontano how well observed in the following Inscription, which he has left to Posterity in a Chappel dedicated by him to the Virgin Mary in Naples at a place called La Pietra Santa, and which Inscription appears to me to be very applicable to the present circumstances of Italy

AUDENDO AGENDOQUE
RES PUBLICA CRESCIT
NON IIS CONSILIIS
QUAE TIMIDI
CAUTA APPELLANT

I have the honor to be
Dear Sir
Your Excellency's
most obedient and most
attached humble Servant
Wm Hamilton

20) Copy of Sir Wm Hamilton's Letter to Lord St. Vincent dated April 15th 1798 and sent to his Lordship by the Terrible Privateer of Gibraltar Express.

My Lord
When Your Lordship shall have perused the inclosed Coppies of two Letters which I received lately from General Acton, Prime Minister here, You

will see the miserable Situation to which this Country is reduced by having, as Your Lordship well knows, follow'd *mezzi termini* or half measures,
which seldom or ever succeed. Notwithstanding it's apparent Peace with
the french Republic, this Monarchy is threaten'd with immediate destruction. The last message from the french Directory at Paris is exactly the language of our Highway men – Deliver your money or I will blow your
brains out.

As it is natural for a Person in danger of drowning to catch at every twig
Your Lordship will see that the greatest hopes this Government entertains
of being saved from the impending danger is on the protection of the
King's Fleet under Your Lordship's command; my answer to General
Acton's first Letter of the 3.d of April was that I was ready to dispatch the
Gibraltar Privateer to acquaint Your Lordship of the present very dis-
tressed Situation of these Kingdoms but that I was persuaded, however
willing Your Lordship might be to give them every assistance in Your
power, that in the critical Situation of Great Britain at this moment You
cou'd not take it upon You to move without absolute Orders from home.
Your Lord.p will see by the General's Second Letter of the 9ᵗʰ that Their
Sicilian Majesties even at the exorbitant price asked by the Captain of the
Privateer to carry this packet to You still desire it to be sent and wish me
to say all in my power to induce Your Lordship to take Their Situation into
Consideration. I meant to have inclosed the Original Letters of the General
to me but reflected afterwards that it might be necessary one day for me to
produce them; the inclosed Copies are exact and of my own hand writing,
altho' Gen.l Acton does not write our language correctly, it is intelligible,
and highly expressive, and therefore I did not alter or correct one Word,
but after all I can see this Affair in no other light than I did at first; if in
consequence of the application of this Government to the Cabinet of St.
James's by a Messenger sent from hence to London Six Weeks ago, a British
Fleet shou'd have been order'd into the Mediterranean it will come and the
Country will be saved, if not the only chance of a respite from Republicanism is in the Austrian Army already in Italy and which as Your Lordship will see is to be immediatly Augmented.

As every intelligence relating to the actual french Maritime force in
these Seas will be found in the Copies of Genl. Acton's Letters inclosed, I
have nothing further to add but to assure your Lordship that no circumstance cou'd make Lady Hamilton and me so happy as that of having the
honor of receiving Earl St. Vincent at the King's Court at Naples, and then
if possible to get a passage to Gibraltar and so home in one of the King's
Ships as I have had the King's Leave to return home for a short time ever
since the Month of June last without having been able to profit of it.

I have the honor to be
My Lord
etc.
Wm Hamilton

21) *Separate* Naples June 5th 1798

My Lord
One of my reasons, and indeed the principal one, for sending off the bearer
M.r Small from hence with my Dispatches to Your Lordship of this day's date
is the knowing well how very delicate the King is on the subject of His
Majesty's private and Family concerns and that it might hurt His Majesty's
feelings if the papers inclosed shou'd from any accident have been made public, and whilst the Roman Post remains in the hands of the french no sort of
confidence can be placed in it.

I suppose that His Majesty will have been already informed by Mr. Livingston of the pressing Necessity there was for coming to some speedy resolution to Satisfy Prince Augustus's Roman and Neapolitan Creditors, without which His Royal Highness wou'd have actually been detain'd here at the
moment the french Armament at Toulon was openly threatening an Invasion
of these Kingdoms.

No remedy cou'd before but that I shou'd (as His Majesty's Minister at
this Court) give my Word, the only Word they wou'd take, that such debts
of His Royal Highness Prince Augustus as appeared to be just (and shou'd
be thought so in England) Wou'd be discharged by the House of Gibbs and
falcon at Naples, as soon as an Answer cou'd come from England.

I did not hesitate in agreeing in opinion with Count Munster M.r Tatter
and M.r Livingston (whose Letters to me on that Subject are here inclosed)
with a Short Statement of such debts of H. R. H. Prince Augustus for the
payment of which I have taken upon me to Answer, and may I beg the favor
of Your Lordship to lay these papers before His Majesty and at the same time
most humbly entreating for me His Majesty's forgiveness if it shou'd be
thought that I have taken upon me more than I ought to have done. I fdid
it for the best, at a most critical moment, when The King's Son was not only
in danger of being arrested, but taken Prisoner by our inveterate Enemy, and
this became a National Concern.

As my stay at Naples is so very uncertain, Whatever resolution the King,
or His Ministers, may be pleased to take with respect to the satisfying Prince
Augustus's Creditors at Rome and Naples by being communicated to Abraham Gibbs Esqr.with proper instructions to him from Your Lordship, they

will be attended to with that fidelity and punctuality for which this British Mercantile Gentleman has ever been distinguished at Naples[79].

I have the honor to be
My Lord
Your Lordship's
most obedient and
most humble Servant
Wm Hamilton

22) Downing Street, June 5th 1798

Sir,

I take the opportunity of a Messenger whom the Marquis de Circello sends to his Court this day, to acknowledge the receipt of your dispatches up to N. 11. inclusive and to apprize you in addition to the information which I conveyed to you in my dispatch N. 2. with respect to the resolution taken by His Majesty to send a Fleet into the Mediterranean to the succour of the Court of Naples that the re-inforcement, by which Lord St. Vincent was to be enabled to make the detachment necessary for that purpose, will in all probability have joined that Officer off Cadiz on the 20th of last month – and that the detachment in question must therefore, by this time, be actually in the Mediterranean.

It is hardly necessary for me to enlarge here upon the considerations which have engaged His Majesty at a time when so much is required for the security of His own Dominions, to make an exertion of such a nature for the preservation and protection of those of His Sicilian Majesty. You will not fail to express to the Neapolitan Minister the degree of interest which His Majesty has invariably taken in all that concerns the safety and honour of Their Sicilian Majesties, and to put in its proper light the strong proof which he gives of His disposition by his ready Compliance with their wish in the present instance.

You will at the same time represent the confident expectation which His Majesty justly entertains that in an effort made so immediately on account of Naples, His Fleet will receive every assistance that the Ports and Means of that Country can supply; that Lord St. Vincent, therefore, or the Officer commanding the detachment will be given to understand that he will find the Port of Naples open to him; and that any attempt on the part of the Enemy, to restrict the admission of His Majesty's Ships, will be steadily rejected as wholly incompatible with the effectual execution of the Service.

23) Naples June 18th 1798

   My Lord

General Acton having been so good as to inform me that a Neapolitan
Messenger wou'd be dispatched this Evening for London I profit of it to
inform Your Lordship that Capt. Bowen in His Majesty's armed Sloop Transfer arrived here on the 10th instant with Dispatches to me from Lord St. Vincent with the joyfull account of His Lordship's having detached a powerfull
Squadron under the Command of Sir Horatio Nelson into the Mediterranean
for the Protection of His Sicilian Majesty and His Dominions, and that the
Squadron was actually on it's way to the Sicilian Coasts. This News which I
communicated instantly to Their Sicilian Majesties and Their Ministry,
gave, as Your Lord.p may well imagine, the utmost Satisfaction, and all
expressed in the strongest terms their heartfelt gratitude to The King and
His Majesty's Ministers for this fresh and strong proof of their Friendship
towards them and without which the present situation of Their Sicilian
Majesties and Their Kingdoms wou'd be, indeed, desperate.

Not having received a satisfactory Answer upon my verbal demands of the
Marquis de Gallo for the free and unlimited ingress of His Majesty's Ships of
War to the Ports of the Two Sicilies & that they might also be permitted to
provide themselves with Provisions and Stores of all kinds in those Ports, I
wrote a regular official Billet to the Marquis de Gallo demanding of His
Excy. a categorical Answer to those two essential points, and that if they were
not granted His Majesty's Fleet cou'd be of no use in these Seas. A Copy of
the Marquis's Answer is inclosed and I flatter myself that Your Lordship will
agree in opinion with me that, considering that the Defensive Alliance
between the Courts of Vienna and Naples has not been ratified, The Court of
Naples objecting to many Articles that were agreed upon by the Prince
Campo-Chiaro the Neapolitan Minister at Vienna & contrary to his instructions, that this is a fair and satisfactory Answer, particularly when I am
assured by Their Sicilian Majesties that every assistance will be given to His
Majesty's Ships that can be consistently with their present critical Situation,
that they only wait for an Answer from London and Vienna, to take a more
open and decided part.

The Toulon Armament under the Command of General Buonaparte consisting (according to a List I received from Gen.l Acton) of 16 Ships of the
Line, 10 Frigates, 20 Gun Boats, some armed Brigs and Cutters with 280
Transports containing as they say forty thousand Troops was for Several days
on the Coast of Sicily between Trapani and Marsala. Gen.l Buonaparte sent
a boat on shore on the Island of Favignana to inform the Governor that His

Sicilian Majesty had nothing to fear from the Armament He commanded, the french Republic being in perfect peace with the King of Naples, and that Armament having another object – not Sicily – in View.

On the 8th instant The french Fleet left the Sicilian Coast and reached Malta the same day, they captured a Maltese Polacca, and this Government has received an Account from Malta last night that the french had landed on the 10th instant and taken possession of the Island of Gozzo, and that an other body of Troops had landed at the Cala of St. Paolo, North of the Harbour, but that the Maltese were making every where the most vigourous defense.

Yesterday morning The Squadron of His Majesty's Fleet Commanded by Rear Admiral Sir Horatio Nelson appeared at a distance in this Bay, Capt. Troubridge[80] and Capt. Hardy came ashore from the Fleet in the Lutine Sloop of War, with Dispatches to me from Sir Horatio Nelson. The Admiral was desirous of information respecting the position of the Enemy's Fleet and to know particularly from me if the Ports of the two Sicilies were perfectly open for His Majesty's Ships of War, and whether they cou'd depend upon Supplies of fresh Provisions, Stores etc. in those Ports. As Sir Horatio in his Letter to me said that His Friend Capt. Troubridge knew his mind and wou'd explain it to me, I thought the shortest way wou'd be to carry him to General Acton and We did more business in half an hour than we shou'd have done in a Week in the Usual official way here. Capt. Troubridge went straight to his point and put strong Questions o the General who answered them fairly and to the satisfaction of the Captain. As no time was to be lost the Admiral being now informed of the position and strength of the Enemy and desirous of attacking them as soon as possible. I prevail'd upon General Acton to write himself an Order in the name of His Sicilian Majesty directed to the Governors of every Port in Sicily to Supply the King's Ships with all sorts of Provisions and in Case of an Action to permit the British Seamen sick or Wounded to be landed and taken proper care of in those Ports. When Capt. Troubridge had received this Order from the General and put it into his pocket his face brightend up and he seem'd perfectly happy. I gave him likewise a Copy of the Marquis Gallo's Dispatch, the same as the inclosed to carry on board to Sir Horatio Nelson and which fully explains the delicate Situation of His Sicilian Majesty at this moment. Capt. Troubridge did not stay two hours on Shore, and went off perfectly contented with General Acton who he said was a true man of business rarely to be met with.

This attack of the french upon Malta is certainly an indirect one on His Sicilian Majesty to whom the Island belongs supposing the Knights to be driven from it. However we look upon it as a very fortunate circumstance as it will give time for Admiral Nelson to get up with the french Armament and which, as he goes through the straights of Messina, he may very easily do in three days from the time We lost sight of the Squadron Yesterday at four o' clock in the Afternoon.

By all accounts the french Ships of war are visibly crowded with all sorts of lumber and the Sans Culotte on board of which Ship is General Buonaparte and all the Peasants, Astronomers, Mathematicians, Naturalists etc. etc. is said contain more than 2000 men.

We have certainly every reason to expect that such fine Ships with such a chosen band of brave and experienced Officers as Lord St. Vincent has sent out will soon give a good account of this boasted french Armament. Capt. Troubridge expressed only his Wish to get in sight of them.

That God may continue to prosper his Majesty's Arms in so good a Cause an against so perfidious and profligate an Enemy is the Earnest Prayer of My Lord.

Your Lordship's
most obedient and
most humble Servant
Wm Hamilton

24) Naples June 20th 1798

My Lord
Fortunately the Neapolitan messenger was not dispatched last Night so that I have now a moment to inform Your Lordship that Yesterday a french Officer on board a Maltese Speronara with french Colours brought from General Buonaparte advice to the french Ambassador at this Court, that Malta has surrender'd the 12th instant and was now in the possession of the french Republic. Little or no resistance was made and Treachery was every where Evident. Some accounts say that all the french Ships of the line are in the harbour of Malta and it is certain that Gen.l Buonaparte remains there. As they have landed from 10 to 12 thousand men at Malta, other accounts say that a part of the Fleet and Transports went off directly upon another Expedition but as they must have had notice of the King's Fleet approaching, it is most probable that the greatest part of the Armament has taken refuge in the Harbour of Malta and where by this time they must be compleatly blocked up by Admiral Nelson's Squadron.

I think now the Courts of Vienna and Naples must see the Necessity of joining offensively with Great Britain against the Robbers and Violators of Treaties for certainly Malta itself belongs to the Crown of the two Sicilies.

I have the honor to be
My Lord
Your Lordship's
most obedient and
most humble Servant
Wm Hamilton

25) Naples July 3ᵈ 1798

Since I had the honor of forwarding to Your Lordship my two last Dispatches by a Neapolitan Messenger on the 20ᵗʰ of June, and which I flatter
myself will have been safely deliver'd to Your Lordship, this Government has
received the certain account of the french Armament having left Malta the
19ᵗʰ of June, that they had let there a Garizon of between Six and Eight
Thousand men french, Cisalpines and Polonese with three of their Frigates
and that there was also in the harbour of Malta a small Maltese Ship of the
Line and a frigate and that an other large Maltese Ship of the Line quite new
was just ready to come out of the Dock.

Monsieur Garrat the Ambassador of the french Republic at this Court gives
out that General Buonaparte wrote him word that he is gone to the Levant. I
am hoping however that we have reason to beleive that Genl. Buonaparte left
Malta without having received advice of the King's Squadron being so near
him, for it was only the 17ᵗʰ of June at Night that Mons.r Garrat dispatched
the french Vice Consul in a boat from Naples to inform Gen.l Buonaparte that
He had that morning seen Sir Horatio Nelson's Squadron off the Bay of
Naples, and it requires four days for a boat to go from Naples to Malta and this
Government has received accounts from Sicily of Admiral Nelson's Squadron
having been seen off Siracusa on it's way to Malta on the 21ˢᵗ of June in the
morning. I had sent a Maltese Speronara with a dispatch to Sir Hor. Nelson the
18ᵗʰ. The boat returned on Saturday after not having been able to get up with
the Admiral, The boatmen who I have reason to beleive speak the truth assured
that on the 21ˢᵗ of June in the Afternoon they had nearly reached one of the
Ships of the British Squadron, then between Siracusa and Cape Passaro, but
that an English Brig coming from the Levant, made Signals, upon seeing
which the Squadron instantly alter'd its Course and with a crowded sail stood
to what they called Scirocco Levante which is I beleive South East but that particularly said towards Cotrone which leads to the Adriatick. If this be true it
is most certain that the King's Squadron must have been up with the
Unweildy Armament before it cou'd take Shelter in Corfu or any other Port
and probably a day or two may bring us great News.

On Wednesday last the 27th of June Captain Hope in His Majesty's Frigate Alcmene in Company with the Terpsichore, Emerald and Bon Citoyen came into this Port. They were all except the Terpsichore Captain Gage who had refreshed at Leghorn in want of Bread and Water. Capt. Hope sent off the Terpsichore directly to join Admiral Nelson and I got for the other three Frigates their Water and Necessary Provisions compleated by Saturday at Noon when They saild also to join the Admiral.

Monsieur Garrat receiv'd on Friday last a dispatch Boat from Toulon with Letters from the french Directory and wanting to send back the boat the same Night with his Answer had the impudence to apply to this Government, requiring, has he said according to the Laws of Neutral Ports, that His Majesty's Frigates might be detain'd twenty four hours from the time of his french boat's sailing; and Capt. Hope received this Notice from the Neapolitan Captain of this Port, as I did in a confidential letter from the Marquis Gallo. Our Answers were that the King's Ships did not trouble themselves with little french boats and wou'd certainly Sail as soon as they thought proper.

Monsieur Garrat had taken leave of this Court some days ago and went to Rome on his way to Paris on Sunday last having left as Chargé d'Affaires Monsieur de la Chaise.

I have the honor of inclosing a Copy of the Infamous Convention between the french Republic and the Knights of Malta under the Mediation of His Catholic Majesty. Trusting in God that we may very soon have joyfull News from the brave Admiral Sir Horatio Nelson I have the honor to be

My Lord
Your Lordship's
most obedient and
most humble Servant
Wm Hamilton

26) Downing Street 6th July 1798

Sir,

M. de Circello delivered to me yesterday your dispatch N. 13 announcing his recall and the Appointment of the Prince de Belmonte to succeed him.

As you refer me to your Dispatches by the Messenger, whom you were on the point of dispatching for information on the important points, which you have recently been instructed to bring forward at the Court where you reside, I shall wait the Arrival of that Messenger before I say any thing further on the subject of the Measures, which I have just learnt from you, than simply to acknowledge the Communication of it.

It seems not improbable that the Information which you were enabled to communicate to the Ministry of His Sicilian Majesty may have made some Change in the determination as to the Arrangement which you announce to me.

At all Events you will use every proper endeavour to prevent any farther step being taken towards it's completion until you shall hear distinctly from me upon the subject.

His Majesty perfectly approves of your resolution not to avail yourself of your leave of Absence during the present very critical Situation of Affairs in the Mediterranean.

27) Naples August 4th 1798

My Lord
Your Lordship will see by Rear Admiral Sir Horatio Nelson's Letters to me, dated from Siracusa the 20th and 22.d of July, and which Your Lordship will find in my Letter directed to the Earl Spencer N1.) left with a flying Seal for your perusal, that this Squadron of the King's Fleet after having gone as far as Alexandria and Caramania, a run of 600 Leagues[81] in 27 days, is returned to Siracusa in Sicily without having been able to gain the smallest intelligence of the french Armament under the command of General Buonaparte, and that He is still unfortunately without a single Frigate. I can not do better than to inclose a Copy of my Answer to Sir Hor.o Nelson's Letter N. 2.) in which, and in the Copy likewise inclosed of Lord St. Vincent's Letter to me of the 15th of July N. 3.), Your Lordship will find every circumstance respecting the King's Fleet that has come to my knowledge since We saw the Squadron off the Bay of Naples on the 17th of June last, and it is as extraordinary as it is provoking, to know for certain that no less than Seven of His Majesty's Frigates and a Cutters have been for more than a fortnight passed in the Levant looking out for, and earnestly desirous of joining Admiral Nelson's Squadron.

Your Lordship will observe that Sir Horatio Nelson, in his Letter to me of the 22.d of July, appears to be very angry that the smallest difficulties shou'd have been made by the Governor of Syracusa in admitting the Whole of His Majesty's Squadron into that Port. Inclosed N. 4) is a Copy of the report made by the Governor, Brigadier Don Giuseppe della Torre, to General Acton of what passed on that occasion.

After what The King, our Royal Master, has done for Their Majesties, and of which Their Majesties and Their Ministry appear to be perfectly Sensible,

I shou'd be the first, as His Majesty's Minister at this Court, to take up the matter very highly indeed, if I perceived any Unfair dealings, or the smallest Neglect of this Government in Affording every Assistance in it's power to the King's Ships, sent here at the express and earnest request of the Court of Naples, to save these fine Kingdoms from impending ruin. I flatter myself that my Answer to Sir Hor°. Nelson's Letters will explain the behaviour of the Governor of Syracusa, to the entire Satisfaction o the Admiral, for as Your Lordship will see by Gen.l Acton's Billet to me of the 1st of August a copy of which is inclosed N. 5) the whole Mystery was, that the Court cou'd not without great risk throw off the Mask until it had received the ratified Treaty with the Emperor of Germany and with the two Supplementary Articles, by which the Emperor was bound to Defend His Sicilian Majesty in case of an Attack from any Enemy, in Consequence of His having Open'd His Ports to the King's Ships without any limitation; and that Treaty arrived here from Vienna in the Night of the 30th of July and was Officially Communicated to me the next day by the Marquis de Gallo, the Treaty having been finally Concluded at Vienna the 16th of July.

As soon as I had received Admiral Nelson's last Letters I shew'd them, Abuse and all, to General Acton as His Excy mentions in his Answer to that Communication, but I flatter myself, having sent to Sir Hor.° Nelson the Original Letter of General Acton to me of the 1st of August, that He will be perfectly Satisfied, as I am, with this Ministry on this head, and indeed I have no other fault to find, but the fatality which attends this Government, in common with many others in Europe, of adopting half Measures, which have brought some of them to the brink of Destruction and must end in the ruin of all, shou'd they persevere in them.

I am happy in having a safe and expeditious Opportunity of Conveying this Dispatch and Inclosures to Your Lordship by a Neapolitan Messenger, Sent, as I understand, with His Sicilian Majesty's Full Powers to the Marquis Circello to Conclude immediatly a New Treaty of Alliance with Great Britain. We already here look upon us as United, and there can be no doubt but that the french will resent the King's Fleet having been admitted in to the Port of Syracusa. Why then shou'd The King of Naples hesitate one moment to take advantage of the present discontent and rising of the Roman Peasantry (as mentioned in my Letter to Sir Horatio Nelson) and march on to Rome, where there are not now more than three Thousand Poles and french? And Why does not the Emperor come forward and assist the King of Naples in driving, whilst they can, the french Maroders compleatly out of Italy and before they can be reinforced? Why? Because They are infatuated and will not attend to the learned Pontano's Salutary Advice *Audendo, Agendoque, Res Publica crescit, Non iis consiliis quae Timidi, Cauta Apellant* (sic).

Altho' I feel myself with all my Personal property[82] in danger of being involved in the general ruin of this Country which threatens it from the land Side (for We can have nothing to fear on the Sea Side whilst The King's Fleet remains in the Mediterranean) I am still happy that I did not profit of The King's Gracious leave of Absence as my presence here at this Moment has been, and appears stittl to be, essential to His Majesty's Service, Nor will I quit Naples untill I can do so with a good Conscience, let what may, be the Consequence.

M.r England His Majesty's late Consul at Malta having lost all and taken refuge at Messina but having no pay or Subsistance from the British Government, I have taken upon me to give him a Credit of One Hundred Pounds on my Banker at Naples untill he can get an Answer from Your Lordship to his Letter inclosed, and I flatter myself Your Lordship will not disapprove of what I have done and allow me to charge the same in my Bill of Extra — Extraordinaries.

I have the honor to be
My Lord
Your Lordship's
most obedient and most
humble Servant
Wm Hamilton

P. S. Since I wrote the above this Morning the Marquis de Nize with the Portughese Squadron, as detail'd in Lord St. Vincent's List inclosed, enter'd this Port, except The Falcon Brig of 22 Guns, who was unfortunately lost at Sea by being run down by the Principe Reale, the Commodore's Ship, but the whole of the Crew were Saved.

The inclosed N. 6) is a Proclamation just published by His Sicilian Majesty's Command at Naples & which I hope will have a good Effect[83].

28) Naples August 8th 1798

My Lord
To my great sorrow The Neapolitan Messenger has not yet been dispatched, as I can well Conceive the Anxiety at Home to obtain Authentic News from Rear Admiral Nelson, such as contain'd in my Dispatch N. 18) but I flatter myself the Messenger will go off for Vienna and London this Night or Tomorrow Morning, and this delay affords me the opportunity of transmitting to Your Lordship some further Intelligence of Consequence.

Altho' a report prevail'd at Naples that the french Armament was at Tunis the 30th of June, We have private Letters here from Major Magra, His Majesty's Consul at Tunis dated July the 7th and which prove that report to be without any foundation.

Yesterday Sig.r Caracciolo, the Agent of Ragusa at Naples, came to me by order of that Government to inform me of their Unhappy Situation – That a french Ship of the Line, and a Brig had been at Ragusa with a Commissary on board who had demanded of the Republic of Ragusa, in the Name of the french Directory, a Loan of One million of Livres tournois, for two Years; threatening that if that demand was not complied with in twenty four Hours they wou'd take possession of the Port and Overturn their Government as Your Lordship will see in the inclosed Copy N. 1) of the Memorandum left with me by Sig.r Caracciolo, and who desired me in the Name of the Ragusan Republic to communicate the same to Your Lordship and to the Commanding officer of His Majesty's Squadron in the Mediterranean.

The present object of the french Directory being so evidently to get Money wherever it is to be got and even by the most infamous Robberies and Plunderings, How can this Government be so blind as not to see that the Kingdom of the Two Sicilies must Necessarily be one of their immediate objects, and when alone money can be found in Italy and yet no active measures are taken and the poor Roman Peasants on the Confines of this Kingdom, mention'd in my last dispatch, for want of support have been obliged to take refuge in the Mountains and the french and Patriots maintain their ground at Rome. They say here that they wait to be sure of the Support of the Emperor of Germany and as I understand the Emperor is waiting to be sure of that of the King of Prussia, and in the mean time the french are pouring a fresh and formidable Army into Italy, and in my humble Opinion, Unless some Unforeseen and fortunate Event shou'd prevent it, the french will pass their Christmas merilly at Naples.

Monsieur de la Chaise the Charge d'Affaires of the french Republic at this Court say's that the french have taken possession of Leghorn which seems highly probable.

I have the honor of inclosing N. 2) a Copy of a Curious paper that has fortunately fallen into my hands and from a quarter that leaves no room to doubt of its being genuine.

May I beg the favor of Your Lordship to forward the inclosed to the Lords Commissioners of His Majesty's Treasure, Your Lordship will observe that according to Your directions I draw my Bills with as long a Date as possible.

No news of Sir Horatio Nelson since he left Syracusa the 26th of July.

We have many Cardinals residing now at Naples and of the Number are the Cardinals Stuart and Busca.

I have the honor to be
My Lord
Your Lordship's
most obedient and
most humble Servant
Wm Hamilton

P.S. I beg leave to remind Your Lordship that We are in extreme Want of
a Consul here, whose business I am obliged to transact without having had
any former experience in it, but am much obliged to M.r Gibbs, an intelligent and respectable British Merchant here, for his kind and voluntary Assistance.

The Portughese Squadron and His Majesty's Ship Lion, and fire Ship[84]
Incendiary, will probably Sail from hence Tomorrow in search of Admiral
Nelson.

29) Naples August 21st 1798

My Lord

The Portughese Squadron is gone round by Palermo to Syracusa, in order
to join Rear Admiral Sir Horatio Nelson as soon as possible, The Admiral
having left in that Port instructions for His Majesty's Ships to meet with
him[85]. The Lion Captain Dixon is gone for the same purpose to Syracusa, but
through the Straits of Messina, and His Spanish Prize Frigate, The Dorothea,
is gone to join Lord St. Vincent off Cadix.

Captain Bowen in the Transfer Brig charged with Dispatches from Lord
St. Vincent and Letters from me for Sir Hor: Nelson, in going to Syracusa,
fell in with, and captured, a french Polacca from Malta the 5th instant, She
was going to Civita Vecchia for Charcoal and other Necessary Articles for the
Garizon of Malta, and Captain Bowen has sent to me a packet of Letters
which had been concealed in the ballast of his Prize, and which I shall have
the honor of forwarding to Your Lordship by the first safe opportunity; in the
mean time I shall not fail to make a proper Use of the intelligence they contain for the immediate Service of His Majesty. They are chiefly Duplicates of
the Dispatches sent to the french Directory from Malta in the french Frigate
la Sensible, Captured by His Majesty's Frigate the Sea Horse.

It appears by these Letters that at Malta they have no more certain intelligence of General Buonaparte than We have here, but have received Sea
reports of his having landed his Army at Alexandria the 10th of July. They
are in want of every thing at Malta, and complain heavily, and in the most

insulting terms, of the King of Naples for His having laid a Quarantine on all Vessels coming from Malta to Sicily, at the same time that Admiral Nelson's whole Squadron had been admitted into the Port of Syracusa, and Supplied with all sorts of provisions and in abundance, and they vow Vengeance on His Majesty for having shewn such an evident partiality to the English.

They are in total want of Wine, and wou'd have been without fresh Meat if the Bey of Tunis[86] had not sent them a few Oxen and Sheep; but Money seems to be the principal Want at Malta, and the Directory upon their representations on that Subject, has answer'd them, Patience.

In one of the Official Letters from Malta I was very sorry to find that His Majesty's Frigate L'Aigle was cast away & lost on the Barbary Coast, near Tunis; Six men of that Ship's Company having been brought to Malta in a Speronara; however I have the satisfaction of adding that by the report of those Sailors, the Whole of the Ship's Company was Saved.

It is incomprehensible that We shou'd still be without any positive News of General Buonaparte and his Fleet, consisting of near four hundred Sail, of one sort or other, and that left Malta th 19th of June, they must undoubtedly have obliged every Vessel they met with to join them.

As I write by the Common Post, and probably may have soon an opportunity of a much safer conveyance I shall add no more at present. We are most Anxiously expecting every Moment a Cutter or Brig from Admiral Sir Hor: Nelson's Squadron that left Syracusa the 26th of last month having got, as is beleived in Sicily, intelligence of the position of the Enemy.

God send that the Admiral's Activity and unwearied perseverance may at last be attended with the Success it deserves.

I have the honor to be
My Lord
Your Lordship's
most obedient and
most humble Servant
Wm Hamilton

30) Naples August 27th 1798

My Lord
By a Letter of the 9th instant from the British Vice Consul at Syracusa I am informed that Capt. Foot of His Majesty's Frigate the Sea Horse, was arrived there in search of Sir Horatio Nelson, having himself seen General Buonaparte's Fleet, and Convoy, at one of the Mouths of the Nile, near

Alexandria, on the 21st of July. The Sea Horse sail'd immediatly for the Ren-
devouz which Admiral Nelson has left for the British Ships at Syracusa.

By a letter of the 18th instant from the British Vice Consul at Messina I
am informed that Capt. Gage, in His Majesty's Frigate the Terpischore,
arrived there from Alexandria, having likewise seen the Enemy's Fleet near
that port, and was looking out for Sir Hor: Nelson to give him that Information. An Unfortunate accident happend on board the Terpsichore a few
days before that of her arrival at Messina. One of the Marines cleaning his
firelock, that was loaded, it went off and blew up a Chest of Cartridges and
fireworks, by which Explosion more than twenty men were wounded. Captain Gage's hands were violently scorched, and his Surgeon was wounded,
but they are both in a fair way of recovery – two of the Seamen died on board
Ship, and three more are left in a dangerous way in the hospital at Messina.
Capt. Gage sailed from Messina in Company with his Majesty's Ship the Lion
Capt. Dixon to join the Rear Admiral on the 17th instant.

General Acton has been so good as to inform me that an Ottoman Vessel
from Alexandria (which he left the 25th of July) bound to Leghorn had put in
to the Port of the Island of Procita the 2$^{.d}$ instant. By the deposition by the
Captain of that Vessel it appears that General Buonaparte had demanded to
enter with his Whole Fleet the Port of Alexandria, but, it being denied, He
had Answer'd that as He was closely pursued by an Enemy, he wou'd go in,
and that if any resistance was made he wou'd put the Garrizons of the Forts
to death; that a resistance had been made in Consequence of which Gen.l
Buonaparte had landed a part of his Army, stormed the Forts and putting
every Man to the Sword Secured His Fleet in the Old Port of Alexandria. The
Captain adds that on his way hither, he had met with the British Fleet, off
Candia, but does not give any date, and that he had informed Admiral Sir
Hor: Nelson of what he had seen at Alexandria. If this important information is true the King's Fleet must have blocked up the french in Alexandria
and the Turks become their declared Enemies, We may expect good News
from that Quarter. The Portughese Squadron, with the Incendiary Capt.
Barker, passed through the Fare of Messina the 13th instant and may probably by this time have joind Admiral Nelson.

By a Letter which I have received from M.r Spencer Smith, His Majesty's
Minister at Constantinople, dated the 7th of July, I find that the Ottoman
Government had open'd its Eyes with respect to the french Arts and Arms,
and were eagerly expecting to hear of a British Fleet's being in those Seas that
they might Cooperate with it against such a perfidious Enemy. However Letters, which I have seen of the 21st of July from Constantinople to this Government, say that the Porte[87] was still hesitating whether it shou'd declare

War, or not, against the french, who on their side, were using every endeavour to pacify them.

Every thing wears an hostile Appearance here, but I do not know that this Government has yet come to any decision.

I have the honor to be
My Lord
Your Lordship's
most obedient and
most humble Servant
Wm Hamilton

31) Naples September 4ᵗʰ 1798

My Lord
I profit of the Opportunity of a Neapolitan Messenger's going to Vienna to send Your Lordship through the Channel of Sir Morton Eden the Original Dispatches of the french Ministry at Malta that were found under the ballast of a french Brig captured by Captain Bowen of His Majesty's Sloop of War the Transfer, as mention'd in my Dispatch to Your Lordship of the 21ˢᵗ of August N. 22).

Since my last We have not any certain intelligence or Either the french Fleet or of His Majesty's Squadron, commanded by Rear Admiral Sir Horatio Nelson, who is supposed to be blocking up the french Fleet in the Port of Alexandria.

This Government is making every effort to augment the Army, and eight men out of every thousand, capable of carrying Arms without destination have been required, at the same time the want of current coin in this capital is extreme the Exchange of the Bank Policies being this day at Thirty per cent, and which falls so hard upon the lower class of people that they begin to lose patience and unless some remedy is speedily found against the Monopolies that are supposed to have occasion'd this scarcity of Money, the worst consequences may be expected, and indeed I perceive that this Government is much alarmed but appears to be quite ignorant of Affairs relative to finance, so that I fear the Evil will increase.

I have the honor to be
My Lord
Your Lordship's
most obedient and
most humble Servant
Wm Hamilton

P.S. This moment Captain Capel arriv'd here in His Majesty's Brig the Mutine with the glorious News which he carries to England of the total defeat of the french Fleet at the mouth of the Nile on the 1st of August by the Brave Admiral Nelson. I most sincerely congratulate Your Lordship on this happy Event which can not fail of producing the best Consequences. Cap.t Capel will have the honor of delivering this Packet to Your Lordship.

WH.

32) Naples September 11th 1798

My Lord

Since I had the honor of writing to Your Lordship by Captain Capel We have not had any News directly from the Brave Admiral, Sir Horatio Nelson, but We know from Malta that The Guillaume Tell, and the two french Frigates, the Diane and La Justice, that escaped from the Glorious Battle of the Nile on the first of August, have got into Malta, the Genereux having founder'd at Sea.

The Maltese provoked by new and repeated french Robberies and having received the joyfull Tidings of the total defeat of the french Fleet in Egypt and the great probability of Buonaparte and his Army being destroyed likewise, immediatly rose and murder'd many of the french Maroders. It was reported last Night that they had taken all the Forts but One, and Sunk the Guillaume Tell, and the two Frigates in the Harbour; but this wants Confirmation. What is certain, and that I know from the Authority of this Government, the Maltese Insurgents are in possession of the Bormola Fort, which Commands the Arsenal on the right side of the Port, and of all the Islands and Casali. The City of Valletta, The Forts of St. Elmo and St. Angelo are still in the possession of the french but their force at present does not amount to more than Two Thousand men, unless, as is supposed, the Crews of the Guillaume Tell, that saved from the Genereux and of the two Frigates have joined them, but if they have not, and the Maltese of the Valletta shou'd join those of the Islands, the french will certainly be Exterminated.

I have the honor of inclosing Copies of the two last accounts that have been received by this Government from Malta.

His Majesty's Frigate the Terpsichore Capt. Gage came in here four days Ago for a Supply of provision, from a cruise off Candia, and will Sail this Night to cruize off Malta, and the Mutine Brig, Captain Host, will sail at the same time with my Dispatches for Sir Horatio Nelson informing the Admiral of the present State of Malta.

Captain Gage having been informed by me of the Unfortunate loss of His Majesty's Frigate the Aigle near Tunis and that by a Letter lately received at Naples from Major Magra, dated from Tunis the 3^d of August, Captain Tyler was there with the whole of his Ship's Company, that were fortunately saved, proposes after his Cruize off Malta, to go for them and bring them to the Admiral.

The Illuminations of His Majesty's Subjects residing at Naples, on account of the signal Success of the King's Ships under the Command of the immense Sir Horatio Nelson, were most brilliant for three Nights. The french and Cisalpines were bursting with Envy and rage, whilst the Neapolitans expressed the highest joy and Satisfaction.

I have the honor to be
My Lord
Your Lordship's
most obedient and
most humble Servant
Wm Hamilton

33) *Private* Naples September 14th 1798

My Lord
M.r Scott a British Merchant going from hence to England has promised to deliver safely this Letter to Your Lordship's Office.

Your Lordship may be assured that The Prince Belmonte who is gone to Vienna will not go further untill I shall hear from Your Lord.p that his arrival in England wou'd be Agreable to Our Government.

I have known the Prince from his Infancy, and have never had the smallest reason to doubt of his Principles & Loyalty.

The inclosed Letter from the Queen of Naples to Lady Hamilton was written I believe on purpose for me to Explain to Your Lordship the Intrigues which His Majesty imagines to have thrown a difficulty in the way of Prince Belmonte's arriving at his favorite object of being Employ'd at the Court of S.t James's.

I have the honor to be
My Lord
Your Lordship's
most obedient and
most humble Servant

34) Naples September 17th 1798

My Lord

I profit of the Opportunity going to Vienna to send this Dispatch and inclosures to Sir Morton Eden under a flying Seal to be forwarded to Your Lordship by the first opportunity.

General Acton's Letter to me a Copy of which is inclosed N. 1) will give Your Lordship full information of what is known here of the Insurrection at Malta. Your Lordship will perceive that the principal Motive of the General's Letter to me was that Capt. Gage shou'd be informed of the State of Malta and attack the french Frigate La Diane at the entrance of the Port of Malta. The Terpsichore had Sailed two hours before I received the General's Letter and a boat I sent after him with this Intelligence and not get up with him, but He knew of the Insurrection and also that the Guillaume Tell and two Frigates that escaped from the Glorious Battle of the Nile were in Malta, and that the Genereux had founderd at Sea and he went purposely to assist the Maltese as Effectually and as Speedily as possible.

Capt. Host that Sailed from hence the day before in the Mutine to join Sir Horatio Nelson was also acquainted with the same Circumstances. It Seems that both Vienna and Naples are well pleased that We shou'd do the business for them but I must own and declare that I do not Comprehend Their not profiting of the present most precious Moment, when the french might be driven out of Italy with the greatest Ease, and as it is very probable that Sir Horatio Nelson will soon be before Malta, the retaking of that Island may be Effected by His Majesty's Squadron, that has already evidently Saved the Two Sicilies from utter destruction.

The inclosed Copies of the Queen of Naples's Letters N. 2) will show Your Lordship how sensible Her Majesty is of the abovementioned Truth, and how Gratefull at the same time.

I have the honor to be
My Lord
Your Lordship's
most obedient and
most humble Servant
Wm Hamilton

35) September 18th 1798

My Lord

Very fortunately the Neapolitan Messenger was not dispatched last Night for Vienna but is now going. In the Night time Captain Nisbet in His

Majesty's Frigate the Bonne Citoyenne came into this Port and brought me two Letters from the Brave and Indefatigable Admiral, Sir Horatio Nelson, Copies of which I have the honor of inclosing, knowing Well how Anxious our Government must be to get any Authentic News from that, His Majesty's, most Valuable Squadron.

The Bonne Citoyenne is still in Quarantine and two large Ships are in Sight in the Bay, which We think may be The Vanguard and Culloden.

General Acton assures me that He has order'd every accommodation to be prepared at Castel a Mare for the Culloden and that a fore Mast and Bow Sprit etc. are already prepared for the Vanguard. I flatter myself that the Admiral's arrival at Naples may induce this wavering Government to come to some determination.

I have the honor to be
My Lord
Your Lordship's
most obedient and
most humble Servant
Wm Hamilton

P.S. I have just heard from Capt. Nisbet that the Alexander & Thalia are with the Vanguard and Culloden coming in.

36) Naples September 25th 1798

My Lord
His Majesty's Ships The Culloden, Captain Troubridge, and The Alexander, Captain Ball, and the Frigate Bonne Citoyenne came into this Port on the 18th instant in the Evening. His Sicilian Majesty went out in His boat into the Bay to meet them, as did Numerous boats of English and Neapolitans. The Ships gave the Royal Salute to His Majesty. The Brave Admiral Sir Horatio Nelson in the Vanguard, accompanied by the Thalia Frigate, did not make his appearance in this Bay untill Saturday last, the 22.d instant, (the Day of Our Good King's Coronation) having been becalmed off Sicily.

The King of Naples not only went off to meet The Admiral but instantly went on board the Vanguard, and taking Sir Horatio by the hand made Use of the strongest Expressions of Gratitude to him for the infinite Services that his Intrepidity and good Conduct and that of the Brave British Squadron under His Command had render'd Him, His Family, and His Kingdom.

His Majesty stay'd on board untill the Vanguard was at Anchor in the Port. The Royal Salute was given by all the King's Ships, both on His

Sicilian Majesty's arrival on board The Vanguard, and on His leaving the Ship. The day being remarkably fine, (the Numerous boats with Colours and Musick attending the Vanguard, all the Shores and Wharfs of Naples crowded with a Multitude of rejoicing People, was, I can assure Your Lordship, a Sight that can not easily be described, and When The Admiral came on Shore the reception the Neapolitans gave him, was so expressive of kindness and Gratitude, that I saw affected him greatly.

Not a french Cockade is now to be seen in the Streets of Naples, neither do the french or Cisalpine Ministers make their appearance abroad, and since Sir Horatio Nelson's Prisoner, Admiral Blanquet, has been put on Shore, on his Parole, the french can no longer deny (which they did to that moment) the truth of Sir Horatio Nelson's most Glorious and compleat Victory over the french Fleet at the Mouth of the Nile on the first of August.

The Account of the Battle of the Nile published at Rome by the french Government is perfectly ridiculous, and will certainly amuse Your Lordship. A Copy of it is inclosed for that purpose.

Every Assistance has been immediatly given to His Majesty's Ships, and the Culloden is hove down at Castel a Mare. All these Ships, that had many and great wants, will be repaired and fit for Service in three or four days more, as The Admiral has been assured by this Government.

The State of health of Sir Horatio Nelson when He arrived here, was but indifferent, but He is visibly mending daily, and he is now without fever. The deep Wound on his Forehead (which wou'd have surely proved fatal if He had been without His hat that was torn to pieces) is now quite heal'd.

Your Lordship may well imagine the hurry that the Arrival at this Critical Moment of so distinguished a Character as that of Sir Horatio Nelson must have occasion'd here so that I hope Your Lordship will Excuse my not saying more at present, particularly as I write by the Common Post.

I have the honor to be
My Lord
Your Lordship's
most obedient and
most humble Servant
Wm Hamilton

37) Naples September 28th 1798

My Lord
General Acton having just informed me that a Neapolitan Messenger was to be dispatched to Vienna in a few hours I hasten to acquaint Your Lordship

that The Brave Admiral Sir Horatio Nelson, who does me the honor of Lodging in my House, is gaining health and Strength daily – That every mark of Honor, Distinction and Gratitude is daily Shewn to Him by Their Sicilian Majesties, Their Government and all the Neapolitans and Sicilians, from the highest to the lowest Class; but what gives most pleasure to Sir Horatio Nelson is that Every Assistance has been given to the Vanguard, The Culloden and Alexander from His Sicilian Majesty's Dock Yards so that these His Majesty's Ships will be fit to go to Sea again in three or four days more – and it appears to me that the Admiral's first object is to go off Malta and assist the Maltese Insurgents in recovering that Island and Fortress and to restore it to it's ancient Sovereign, The King of the Two Sicilies. It appears to me likewise that Sir Horatio Nelson's arrival at Naples, and the Confirmation of the most glorious and complete Victory of the first of August has induced this Government to take a decided part and march on immediatly a part of it's Army without waiting for the decision of the Court of Vienna and take possession of Rome. Probably the object of the dispatching this Messenger to Vienna is to acquaint The Emperor of such a Salutary Determination.

Yesterday His Majesty's Ship Colossus[88] Capt. Murray with four Victuallers from Gibraltar came to an Anchor in this Port; the arrival of this Convoy seems to make The Admiral completely happy as nothing now can retard His going to Sea again, in order to compleat what has been so gloriously began.

This Gallant Admiral by no means Elated with his late most Signal Victory, is continually occupied in the desire of following it up by every Effort in his power for the honor and good of the King's Service and the Security and repose of Europe.

This morning Sir Horatio Nelson has received a Letter from Sir James Saumerez dated from the Port of Augusta in Sicily the 17th instant reporting all Well in the Squadron under his command, and that he hoped having got Water and fresh Provisions to sail from thence for Gibraltar the Wednesday following.

Monsieur La Combe S.t Michel[89] the Newly appointed Ambassador from the french Republic to this Court in the room of Monsieur Garrat, is expected here this Evening. It is a curious moment for the arrival of an Ambassador from the french Republic.

Most humbly and most Sincerely, Congratulating His Majesty, through the kind Channel of Your Lordship, on the important Victory of His Majesty's Squadron so generously sent into the Mediterranean to rescue These Kingdoms from the Jaws of Destruction,

I have the honor to be

My Lord

Your Lordship's
most obedient and
most humble servant
Wm Hamilton

P.S. September 29th 1798

The Neapolitan Messenger that was going to Vienna last Night being
now order'd to proceed directly to London without touching Vienna I have
only time to add that Capt. Gage in the Terpsichore arrived here this Night.
He left Malta the 26th instant When Sir James Saumerez with his Squadron,
in Conjunction with the Portugheze Squadron under the Command of Marquis Nizza, had Summon'd the french to Surrender and Evacuate Malta
which was refused by Mons.r Vaubois, the Commander in Chief of the
Valette, and that Sir James Saumerez was proceeding with his Squadron and
french Prizes to Gibraltar, having left the Portugheze to Block Malta and
having at the request of the Maltese Insurgents Supplied them with plenty
of Ammunition and twelve hundred Stand of Arms from his french prizes.
The Maltese say that the french are in the greatest want at Valetta. This Government as yet has not (at least openly) given any assistance to the Maltese
Insurgents to recover an Island which they Claim as their Own, and the
Insurgents are fighting under Neapolitan Colours – *Most extraordinary*

38) Downing Street 3[d] October 1798

Sir

By the last Messenger M. Circello received, as he informed me, Full Powers
to conclude a Defensive Alliance with His Majesty in the name of the King of
Naples. I expressed to him by the King's command His Majesty's readiness to
enter into engagements of this nature (founded on the Basis of the Convention
of 1793) whenever the situation of Affairs shall be such as to induce His Sicilian Majesty to place Himself again in a situation of open War with France, I
apprized him however that H. M. was not insensible of the danger which must
attend such a resolution taken without the fullest assurances of support from
the Court of Vienna; tho' on the other hand it could not be denied that the
other alternative, that of remaining a patient spectator of the intrigues, insults,
& aggressions of France, was also full of danger to H. S. M's interests and security. In this situation it appeared that the decision both in point of substance
and time must be left to H. S. M's own determination, and that the most
friendly conduct which His Majesty could pursue on this subject was to refer
the Negotiation to Naples, and thus to leave it to H. S. M. to act in this respect

as circumstances may require, & particularly as may be found most expedient
from a view of the final resolutions (whatever they may be) of the Court of
Vienna. In pursuance of this idea I herewith transmit to you by the King's
command His Majesty's Full Powers for negotiating and signing a treaty of
Defensive Alliance with the Court of Naples; such treaty to be either in the
form of a general Defensive Treaty, or in that of a special Convention applicable to the particular case of the present War against France. Which of these
forms shall be preferred by the Court of Naples may be adopted by you, and
in either case you will take the Convention of 1793 for the basis of the Negotiations modifying the stipulations there contained according to the nature of
the case, and the tenure[90] of the following Instructions.

In the case of a General Defensive Alliance the usual stipulations may be
inserted for mutual good understanding & friendship and for guaranteeing
to each Party their Dominions *as they now stand* or, (if the Court of Naples
should prefer that alternative,) *as they stood at the commencement of the War*. It
may be stipulated that in the case of an attack from any European Power,
made in whatever quarter of the world against the Dominions of either Party,
the other will furnish such assistance as the nature and circumstances of the
case will allow, which shall be regulated at the time by a sincere & friendly
concert. This stipulation appearing on the whole better suited to the circumstances of this Alliance than any distinct specification of mutual succour
other than that which the subsequent Articles of the Treaty may contain
agreably to the remainder of these Instructions.

With a view to providing for any case in which the two Parties may find
themselves engaged in a Common War, it should be stipulated that in that
event all the Articles of the Convention of 1793 should be held to apply. But
from this general rule you must except the 8th which had reference to that
particular & temporary circumstance. Some alterations must also take place
respecting the specification of Neapolitan force in the third & the engagement in the fourth for maintaining a decisive superiority in the Mediterranean, which of course cannot be engaged for before hand under all the
unforeseen contingencies of future Wars. Nor indeed would the succour of
6,000 land Troops and 4 Ships of the line together with 4 Frigates and a like
number of smaller Vessels appear sufficient on a general principle of reci-
procity to compensate for the engagement of maintaining a Naval force in
the Mediterranean superior to that of the Enemy, & sufficient to provide for
the safety of Naples against all attacks by Sea. It may therefore be better to
consolidate the stipulations of these two Articles and to provide that H. M.
will in the case of a common War send a respectable force of Ships of War
into the Mediterranean to act in concert with that which the King of Naples
would also engage to furnish in such case to the extent of his ability, the

whole to be jointly employed for the defence of the two Sicilies and for the general annoyance of the Enemy. The remarks which I have here stated respecting the Convention of 1793 are to be considered by you as equally applicable to the course of any Negotiation which should relate not to a general & prospective Alliance but to the renewal of that Convention with a view not only to the case of the present War. But if it should be much preferred you might consent in the framing such a Convention for the limited purpose last mentioned to insert the whole of the fourth Article as it now stands. The return which the King would desire for this would however be different from that which now stands in the third Article. The Neapolitan Ships of the line and Frigates should be engaged for in the same manner as it is there done. But in lieu of 6,000 land troops the King would require a much larger number of small armed Vessels such as it is easily within the power of H. S. M. to furnish & as would, in the manner I shall explain in a separate Dispatch, be of the utmost advantage to the common cause.

M. Circello has orders to make application here on the subject either of a Subsidy or the guarantee of a Loan. For both these applications I am under the necessity of saying in the most decided tho' friendly manner that it was wholly out of H. M's power to listen to them. The demands of the Naval service here, & the engagements already taken being such as not to leave no ground for encouraging any even the smallest expectation on this head. Having now completed the Instructions which I had it in charge from H. M. to convey to you on the subject of the treaty I have only to add that in every event of the Negotiation you will not fail to express H. M's confident reliance on the justice & friendship of H. S. M. for the continuance of the liberal reception which according to your late Dispatches His Majesty's Fleet has experienced in the Neapolitan Ports and in which the King sees with pleasure a new proof of the attachment and friendship of a Sovereign whose interests H. M. considers a His own. The grounds on which this request is to be urged are too well known to you to make it necessary for me to dwell upon here, especially as the recent conduct of the Court of Naples in this respect has shewn the Satisfaction which H. S. M. feels in rendering this important and necessary service to that Navy by which alone His Coasts enjoy a moment's security from the designs of the Enemy.

P.S. Since the above was written the intelligence has been received here of the glorious result of the attack on the French fleet at Aboukir. This happy event makes no change in His Majesty's disposition to consider the views and interests of H. S. M. respecting the conclusion of an Alliance in the manner stated in the above dispatch, and it evidently affords still greater facility for fulfilling the stipulations of it at present to both sides[91].

39) Downing Street 3$^\text{d}$ October 1798

Sir,

Among the first Objects to which His Majesty's Attention would be directed in case of the renewal of the War between Naples and France would be that of establishing an effectual Blockade of Malta. The importance of this Point to the Interests of the Court of Naples is sufficiently obvious, as well as the means by which that Court may promote its accomplishment by supplying to His Majesty's Fleet a number of light armed Vessels of different descriptions, such as are best calculated effectually to cut off all Intercourse between that Island and the neighbouring Shores. This is therefore to be stated by you as a principal and sine qua non Condition of future Concert. You will of course communicate on the subject with the Commanding Officer of His Majesty's Fleet stationed at or near Naples and you will shape your requisition by his Advice. And I have no doubt that in the event abovementioned this demand will meet with a ready Acquiescence from the Court of Naples. It may also be for your Consideration whether further Assistance might not be afforded to His Majesty's Fleet by the supply of Neapolitan Sailors in the manner suggested in my Dispatch Nr of this Year: – the stipulated Aid of Land Forces under the Convention of 1793 being wholly useless to His Majesty and inapplicable to the present Circumstances and State of the War.

In order to render the Blockade of Malta more effectual it will be necessary that a strong Declaration should be published in the name of the Allies, in all the Ports of Italy, and notified to all the Neutral Powers, that all Vessels attempting to enter the Ports of Malta, or found hovering within a certain distance of the Coast of that Island will invariably be sunk.

If by these Measures the Island of Malta should be wrested from the French it will remain to be considered what future System shall be adopted for it's defence and Government. The Communications made to His Majesty on this subject from the Court of Naples are in the highest degree liberal and friendly. But His Majesty does not entertain any idea of acquiring the Sovereignty to Himself, or any of the Venetian Islands. He is ignorant how far any such wish is entertained by the Emperor of Russia or by His Sicilian Majesty though it does not appear to His Majesty that such an Acquisition would be advantageous to either of those Sovereigns. He has however directed the Court of St Petersburgh to be sounded on the Subject, and in the mean time I have His Majesty's Orders to transmit to you the Copy of a Suggestion which has been made here on the subject of the Restoration of the Order as the best means of placing the Island in the most beneficial Situation for the Interests of all the Allies. You will converse with the Neapolitan Ministry on this Point but without expressing any decided preference for an Arrangement to which His Majesty attaches no other value than as it shall appear to His Allies to provide for their Interests.

40) Naples October 9ᵗʰ 1798

My Lord

On Thursday last His Majesty's Minister at this Court, His Lady, Admiral Sir Horatio Nelson and the Captains of the Ten British Ships of War Lying at Anchor in this Port were invited to dine on Board of His Sicilian Majesty's Ship the Samnite, commanded by Captain Caracciolo, lying also at Anchor in the Port of Naples.

His Sicilian Majesty, the Hereditary Prince, and the Young Prince Leopold, received the Company and did the honors on board the Samnite, with such attention, kindness, and affability as never to be forgotten His Sicilian Majesty and the Hereditary Prince taking every opportunity of expressing their Eternal Gratitude to the King and Sir Horatio Nelson for the Signal Service render'd to Them and these Kingdoms.

After a most Sumptuous Dinner His Sicilian Majesty proposed the Healths of the King, of His Majesty's Rear Admiral Nelson, and of the Brave Squadron under his Command, which was acompanied with a Royal Salute of twenty One Guns. The Company returned the Compliment drinking the Healths of Their Sicilian Majesties and all Their Royal Family with Three Cheers according to the British Marine Custom.

Your Lordship may imagine the effect this Scene must have had on Monsieur La Combe S.t Michel who had only the day before presented his Credentials Letters as Ambassador from the french Republic, and lodges in a House, the Windows of which are in full View of the Harbour, however he has not yet made any Official remonstrance against the British Squadron having been admitted and repaired in this Port, contrary to an article of Their Treaty.

General Mack, who is to Command the Neapolitan Army is arrived at Manfredonia and expected to be at Caserta this day Their Sicilian Majesties and Royal Family having removed to that Royal Residence on Saturday last.

As there can be no doubt of the intention of the french Army to plunder the rest of Italy as soon as they shall be in sufficient force, it is a Mystery to Us all, why The Emperor and King of Naples who have a sufficient Force, do not profit of this most precious moment to drive these Cruel Robbers out of Italy – We hope the Arrival of General Mack may clear up this Mystery, and that I may soon have the Satisfaction of informing Your Lordship of the Neapolitan Army's being in possession of Rome – if not it is the Opinion of the Rear Admiral and myself that the sooner We leave Naples the better, and indeed We have expressed as much to this Government. It is however only justice to declare that the assistance that has been given by this Government in repairing the King's Ships, that were in great need of such Assistance, has been most generous and unlimited; and never before was such Activity displayed at Naples. The Colossus and Alexander with the Frigate Terpsichore and bonne Citoyen sailed for Malta (which remains in the same situation as mention'd in my last letters) three days ago, and the rest of His Majesty's Ships will be perfectly fit for Service in the course of this Week.

We fear that the report of His Majesty's Ship The Leander giving been taken by the french Ship Le Genereux and carried into Corfù is but too true, The report is that the Genereux after four hours Engagement had struck her Colours to the Leander, whom She took afterwards by Treachery.

Sir Horatio Nelson's health is perfectly re-establish'd.

I have the honor to be

My Lord

Your Lordship's

most obedient and

most humble Servant

Wm Hamilton

P.S. I have the honor of inclosing a Copy of Mons. La Combe St. Michel's speech to the King of Naples on presenting his Credential Letters and which I have reason to beleive genuine

WH.

41) Naples October 16th 1798[92]

My Lord

Admiral Nelson sailed yesterday with four Ships of the Line and a Frigate for Malta. He proposed to return by half the first week in November. General Mack is arrived to take the Command of the Neapolitan Army, Thirty Thousand of which, as I am assured, will march forward before the last of this Month, The Emperor having consented, and even promised, his powerful Support. The glorious Victory of the first of August seems to have inspired this Court with Courage and Confidence, and We hope that this fine Country may be saved.

It is certain that the French Minister has ordered an Army of Sixty Thousand Men to act against this Country. Their Sicilian Majesties have the utmost Confidence in the brave Admiral; and the Conferences we have had with General Acton, have certainly decided this Government to the salutary Dtermination of attacking, rather than waiting to be attacked.

The French Ambassador is still here, and saw the King of Naples go on board the Admiral's Ship Yesterday to take Leave of Him, and was Witness to the Royal Salute from the whole British Squadron. Their Sicilian Majesties, and the Ministry, never ceased expressing their Gratitude to The King, and His Majesty's heroick Rear Admiral; Affording every Assistance in Their Power to His Majesty's Ships. The Culloden's Damages are not quite repaired, and will have to remain here with a Frigate, a Cutter, and the Four transports with Stores from Gibraltar, until the Admiral returns to Naples. The Ships left at Alexandria are expected here every Day to be repaired and victualled.

His Majesty's Sloop Mutine is returned here with Letters off Cadiz, having met with the British Squadron with the French Prizes from the Mouth of the Nile, about Eight Leagues from Gibraltar.

I have the honor to be
My Lord
Your Lordship's
Most obedient and
Most humble Servant
Wm Hamilton

42) Caserta October 23^d 1798

My Lord
On Sunday last the Neapolitan Messenger arrived from London and brought me Your Lordship's Dispatch of the 21st of Sept.r N. 12) and the same day I received from Sir Morton Eden Copies of the two translated papers from Portugal which Your Lordship directed to be sent to me. I have communicated the Substance of those papers to the Marquis Gallo and General Acton, who desire me to return Your Lordship many thanks for so important a Communication. I have strictly obey'd Your Lordship's orders in not having allow'd of any kind of Copy to be taken of these Papers.

His Majesty's Frigate the Emerald Capt. Waller and the Flora Cutter arrived at Naples on Friday last from off Alexandria, the latter left Commodore Hood there the 29th of Sept.r to bring here Dispatches and some from the Sultan to Admiral Sir Hor: Nelson at Naples. Capt. Hood told

Capt. Yawkins of the Flora Cutter, just as he sailed, that he expected every moment a Fleet of twenty two Ships of the Line, Russian and Turkish, besides many smaller Vessels and Transports having had advice of their being arrived at Candia and of their having fall'n in with, and Captured a french Frigate. Commodore Hood had lately received from the Governor of Rhodes an abundant Supply of Bullocks, fresh Provisions of fruits and Vegetables, as a present from the Sultan. The Ships before Alexandria were the Zealous and the Lion with the Sea Horse and another Frigate, I beleive Alcmene. The Swiftsure was gone for Water for the Squadron either to Rhodes or Candia. Captain Hood lays an Embargo on all the Craft he meets with, with the view of facilitating a descent to Alexandria, in case the Troops with the United Fleet shou'd attempt it, but has no communication with Egypt, for fear of disseminating amongst our people some banefull distemper, as there certainly is a great Sickness with the french in Egypt and at Alexandria, but whether Plague or not has not yet been ascertain'd. Buonaparte is said to have fall'n back from Cairo and acts merely upon the Defensive, having thrown up Entrenchments some miles distance on the banks of the Nile. His Situation is deplorable in the extreme, and all his talents are barely sufficient to quell the very serious Mutinies, to which he has been exposed, of his own Troops, whose Eyes are open'd to a sense of their own danger, and as is beleived, inevitable Fate. His main army is said now to consist of no more than Thirteen Thousand men. Captain Waller of the Emerald who left Alexandria only ten days before the Flora Cutter assures me that Buonaparte had before he left Egypt taken most of the Crews out of the Ships and Transports at Alexandria to strengthen his Army. Monsieur Tallien was at Alexandria.

I have the honor of inclosing General Berthier's original Letter to the Cisalpine Republic which Sir Horatio Nelson left with me and which will shew Your Lordship how severely Buonaparte's Army was harrassed in marching over the Desarts just after his landing at Alexandria, and with the greatest Body of Arabs and Mamelucks, did not exceed Six Thousand men, and Now it is said that the french weaken'd Army is surrounded and watched by two Armies of Twenty thousand Men each.

The inclosed are the Copies of the Dispatches and papers brought from Captain Hood by the Flora Cutter and which Captain Troubridge of His Majesty's Ship Culloden, has been so good as to send to me.

The Culloden is now perfectly repair'd and is Expected from Castel a mare this day to Anchor in the Bay of Naples where She will wait with the Alliance Frigate Captain Wilmot and the four Transport Victuallers for the Return of The Rear Admiral Sir Hor:° Nelson.

I have the honor to be

My Lord
Your Lordship's
most obedient and
most humble Servant
Wm Hamilton

43) Caserta November 6th 1798

My Lord
General Mack after having made the Tour of all the Confines, and out
Posts, returned here last Week for a few hours to make his report and to set-
tle with His Sicilian Majesty the Plan of Operations that the Neapolitan
Army might immediatly go on and Secure the most advantageous Posts in
the Roman State. The General told me that he had been much pleased with
the appearance of His Sicilian Majesty's Troops and which he found greatly
beyond what he had Expected. His Sicilian Majesty is determin'd to put
Himself at the head of His own Army, and proposes going from hence with
General Acton, to join the Army on Thursday Next, so that I flatter myself
that No time will be lost in putting into Execution the Salutary Plan this
Government seems at length to have realy adopted. A very few days must
make this Matter clear.

According to the Accounts received here of the Enemy's Force in Italy at
this Moment counting, french, Poles, Romans, Cisalpines etc. it amounts to
no more than twenty six Thousand Men. The King of Naples's Army ready
to march is said to Consist of Sixty eight Battallions of Infantry and thirty
two Squadrons of Cavalry, in all upwards of Thirty thousand men, and
according to the late Treaty between the Courts of Vienna and Naples When
Naples furnishes Thirty the Emperor is to furnish Sixty Thousand men.

Every, and most necessary precaution, is taking here that the Neapolitan
Army going into an exhausted Country may be well supplied with Provisions from hence. We hear from Rome that the french force is there diminishing daily, and it appears that Ancona will be their Fortress, as they have
already errected strong Batteries to Command that Port.

Yesterday I received a Letter from Sir Horatio Nelson dated off Malta the
27th of Oct.r. The Gallant Admiral was then assisting the Maltese in taking
the entire possession of the Island of Gozza, and He does not doubt but that
if His Sicilian Majesty wou'd assist the Maltese properly by affording them
the Necessary Supplies of Provisions Arms and Ammunition Those brave
Islanders who are fighting for The King of Naples and under His Majesty's
Standard, wou'd soon oblige the french (who have been greatly reduced by

several late and unsuccessfull Sorties, and are much distressed for Provisions)
to Capitulate. The Admiral adds that if it had not been for the Supplies of
Arms, Ammunition and Provisions afforded them by the King's Fleet, those
brave Islanders must have long ago bent their necks again to the french Yoke.
At the desire of this Government We expect Sir Horatio Nelson here daily,
and the Admiral say's in his Letter to me that Captain Ball of His Majesty's
Ship, Alexander, will be left with the Command of the Blockade of Malta.
Sir Horatio Nelson mentions his having taken three Vessels loaded with
Oxen from Tripoli, destin'd for the french in the Valette, and that ten more
Vessels were expected from the same Quarter, which wou'd certainly be
intercepted also.

Captain Troubridge in His Majesty's Ship Culloden, now in perfect repair,
with the Alliance Frigate, two Cutters, The Flora and Lord St. Vincent, with
three Transport Victuallers are lying at an Anchor in the Bay of Naples, as is
the Portugheze Squadron under the Command of the Marquis Nizza, which
on Sir Horatio Nelson's arrival before Malta received His Orders to return to
Naples to repair, take in three Months provisions, and prepare for Service
with all Expedition.

Captain Troubridge has sent One of the Transport Victuallers with a flag
of Truce to Corfu with several french Officers Prisoners on board from
Alexandria, and to bring off the Crew of the Unfortunate Leander. The Officers of the Leander have been permitted to go away on their parole.

Captains Thompson and Berry were on their way to Trieste, intending to
go to England, and the first Lieutenant and fourteen Officers are arrived at
Barletta and expected at Naples in a few days.

By a Letter from Captain Thompson to the Rear Admiral, and which he
sent to me under a flying Seal I find that the Leander made a most noble
defence, having engaged the Genereux off Candia six hours and a quarter and
as the Captain says to the Admiral, as close, as he himself cou'd have wished;
but that his powder being nearly expended and his Ship render'd ungovern-
able he was obliged at last to Submit. On board the Genereux there were 100
men killed, and 188 wounded. The Leander's List, if I recollect right, was 32
killed and 60 wounded.

Letters from Corfu say that both Ships are perfect Wrecks, and that the
Genereux had been on the point of Striking her Colours to the Leander, when
She perceived that the Leander's Powder was exhausted.

I beg leave to remind Your Lordship again that we are in the utmost want
of a Consul at Naples as the Consular business increases daily – I do what I
can with the Assistance of Mr. Gibbs a very intelligent Merchant of the
British Factory at Naples, but still His Majesty's Service suffers for want of
a regular and Active Consul[93].

I have the honor to be
My Lord
Your Lordship's
most obedient and
most humble Servant
Wm Hamilton

44) Caserta November 6th 1798

My Lord
My Dispatch of this days date N. 33.) was wrote Yesterday to be ready for
the Neapolitan Messenger that goes to day to Vienna and I have now just
time to add that Rear Admiral Sir Horatio Nelson returned to Naples Yesterday from Malta in the Vanguard in company with the Minatour. The
Admiral came directly to Caserta and informed me that He had written a
Letter to the french Commander of the Town of Valetta to induce him to Surrender the Fortress of Malta and that he wou'd send the Garrizon in safety to
a Port in France, which Mons.r Vaubois having civilly declined The Adm.l
had proceeded to the Island of Gozo, landed a party of his Marines and Summon'd the french Garrizon in the Castle there to Surrender to His Majesty's
Arms that Garrizon consisting of two hundred and Seventy Men immediately Surrender'd and the Admiral after having kept the British Flag flying
on the Castle twenty four hours, Substituted and left in its place the Flag of
His Sicilian Majesty, having brought here The Flag of the french Republic
which he is to have the honor of presenting to His Sicilian Majesty this
Morning. The Island of Gozzo contains Sixteen Thousand Inhabitants.
    Sir Horatio Nelson is also to present to His Sicilian Majesty a Memorial
from the Chiefs of the Insurgents of the Island of Malta, calling themselves the
lawfull Subjects of His Sicilian Majesty, and praying for Aid in Arms, Provisions and Ammunition, that they may be Enabled to reduce the french Garrizon and Town of Valette that the King of Naples might have the entire Possession of Malta and it's Dependancies. The Admiral has given in a List of what
He thought necessary for this purpose from the Neapolitan Arsenal, and there
is no doubt but that this government will immediately grant whatever The
Admiral desires and if so, with the Active Blockade of the British Squadron
and the bravery of the Maltese Insurgents there is every reason to expect that
it will be not long before the french will be obliged to Capitulate.
    Last Night the Hereditary Princess of the Two Sicilies was safely deliver'd
of a Princess, Her Royal Highness and Young Princess are as well as can be
expected.

I have the honor to be
My Lord
Your Lordship's
most obedient and
most humble Servant
Wm Hamilton

45) *Most Secret*
Downing Street November 6th 1798

Sir

I avail myself of the opportunity of the Departure of M. de Circello's Messenger to apprize you that he is charged with the communication of a plan has been suggested here for effecting the Pope's escape out of the Tuscan States. His Sicilian Majesty having as it appears the means of a secret communication with the Pope it will be practicable to fix with His Holiness the day and the hour on which he might be met at some convenient place between Leghorn and Pisa, calculating the distance to that place from the Convent where His Holiness now is, and the necessary time his Journey would take, allowing for his advanced age and infirmities. Those measures once agreed upon it will be necessary that an English Frigate should be sent on a Cruize off that Coast with a small Vessel that could come closer into shore. At a given Signal (previously agreed upon) a Boat should be ready to embark the Person with his Attendants who should have a Letter from the English Admiral.

I have His Majesty's Commands to desire that you will concert with the Neapolitan Government upon this important subject; and also that you will apply to Lord Nelson or other commanding Officer of His Majesty's Navy for such assistance as may be necessary, for the execution of this design observing always the infinite importance of secrecy.

M. de Circello will write more in detail on this subject on which I have conversed with him very fully.

46) Naples November 19th 1798

My Lord

On the 12th instant Sir Horatio Nelson and I went by the invitation of Their Sicilian Majesties to the Camp of St. Germano on the confines of Abruzzo, and were present at a Military Manoeuvre of Thirty two Thousand

men, Cavalry & Infantry, under the Command of Gen.l Mack: a finer Army
was never seen and the General told Lord Nelson (for by the late Gazette We
are informed that the King has been graciously pleased to distinguish that
Brave Admiral by the high Dignity of a Peer of Great Britain) that He had
never in all his Experience seen so fine a Body of Men. They went through their
different Evolutions incomparably well. In the Evening We had a Consultation
with Gen.l Mack & Acton, in which We all Agreed that the boldest Measures
were the Safest. The Uncertainty of the Emperor's Support seem'd to be the
only draw-back, however when We came away it seem'd to be finally determin'd that the Army shou'd march on in a few day's and by a Letter receiv'd
Yesterday from General Acton His Excy assures me it will march, in Seven
Columns, on Thursday next the 23^d inst. Lord Nelson in our Conversations
always expressed a desire of aiding Gen.l Mack in his land Operations with a
Cooperation by Sea of the powerfull Squadron under his Command, now in the
Bay of Naples, consisting of the Vanguard, Culloden, Minotaur, the four Por-
tugheze Ships of the Line, The Terpsichore and Alliance Frigates and Flora
Cutter besides the Benjamin a Portugheze Brig. Gen.l Mack expressing his
fears for Tuscany and the Great Duke having written confidentially to Their
Sicilian Majesties to assist him in His present Distress, Lord Nelson proposed
the sending a body of Neapolitan Troops to take immediate possession of
Leghorn and to put an end to all difficulties offer'd to transport on board His
Squadron five Thousand Infantry to Leghorn, provided that the King of
Naples wou'd write to the G. Duke of Tuscany to allow of their entering
Leghorn. The Admiral's proposal was eagerly accepted and Cap.t Gage was dis-
patched Yesterday in the Terpsichore to carry the King of Naples's letter to the
Duke of Tuscany. The five thousand Neapolitan Troops are now embarking on
board Lord Nelson's Squadron, and His Lordship proposes to Sail Tomorrow if
possible for Leghorn, and We flatter Ourselves all will Succeed if the Great
Duke shou'd but be firm. It seems to be the glorious Lot of Great Britain to
save them all in spite of what they have hitherto been doing to ruin their own
Affairs, and lose Their Dominions.

An Other fine Neapolitan Army of Thirty Thousand men will remain in
this Kingdom after the Army above mention'd has marched forward into the
Roman State.

Whilst Lord Nelson and I went with Their Sicilian Majesties at S.t Germano, The Neapolitan Messenger from London arrived there and brought
me Your Lordship's Dispatches of the 3^d of Oct.r. N. 6 & 7) with the full
Power The King has been most graciously pleased to honor me with. All I
can do at present is to return Your Lordship my gratefull thanks for the confidence reposed in me, and to assure You that I shall strictly adhere to the
Letter of Instructions Your Lordship has been pleased to give me.

All that Lord Nelson requested from this Government on his return from Malta for the more close blockade of that Port, and for the enabling the Maltese Insurgents to reduce the Fortress of the Valette has been granted. Two Neapolitan frigates and a Corvette, have been put Under the Command of Lord Nelson, and His Lordship sends them Tomorrow to Malta, where they are to remain under the command of Captain Ball of His Majesty's Ship Alexander who has been appointed by L.d Nelson to command the blockade of Malta. These Frigates have on board Mortars, Great Guns, two thousand stand of Arms and Ammunition of all Sorts according to the Wish of the Maltese insurgents, and I hope to inform Your Lordship soon of the important Fortress's being reduced. Your Lord.p will probly have heard of the combined Fleet of Turks & Russians being at Corfu, having taken Zante, Cefalonia &c and placed the Russian and Ottoman Flags in those Islands. The Garrizon of Corfu, consisting of One Thousand men, had been driven into the Citadel by the Inhabitants, and the french Ship Genereux with the Unfortunate Leander were under the Guns of the Citadel and Summon'd to Surrender to Seven Russian Ships of the Line that had enter'd the Harbour of Corfu.

We have just heard the report of the Brest Squadron having been mostly captured or destroy'd in the Bay of Killala[94]. God send that it may be true. The fate of this Country seem's now to be near its Crisis, and When I can with certainty assure Your Lordship that the Army has realy advanced, I shall entertain the greatest hope that the Evident wicked Intentions of the french Republic against this Kingdom may be entirely disappointed.

Every day proves more and more the great Importance of the glorious Success that attended His Majesty's Arms in Egypt on the first of August.

I have the honor to be
My Lord
Your Lordship's
most obedient and
most humble Servant
Wm Hamilton

47) Downing Street November 23^{d} 1798

Sir,
Your Dispatches to N. 32, inclusive, have been received and laid before the King.

His Majesty has seen with the utmost satisfaction the honourable and friendly Reception which Their Sicilian Majesties have afforded to Admiral

Lord Nelson, and his Officers and Fleet; and the distinguished proofs which They have given of the Interest which They take in an Event not more glorious to His Majesty's Arms than important to the general Salvation of Europe.

As among all the Consequences which are derived from the signal Victory of the 1st of August there is none which His Majesty contemplates with more pleasure than the Opportunity offered by It to the King of Naples to rescue Himself and His Kingdom, by a vigorous Exertion, from the State of Terror and Subjection in which They have been held by the French, and the Ruin which has long been meditated against them. You will omit no Occasion of expressing His Majesty's fervent hope that the Opportunity thus offered will not be suffered to be lost. Europe may now be recovered; if in proportion as a due sense of It's danger has been felt, there is a proper Spirit to make Exertions by which alone that danger can be effectually repelled.

48) *Private*
Naples November 20th 1798

My Lord
Mr. Livingston in a Letter addressed to me from Vienna dated the 15th of Sept.r say's that in a letter which He had the honor of receiving from The King dated the 24th of July His Majesty had been graciously pleased to approve of his and my proceedings in regard to the advancements made towards Satisfying H. R. H. Prince Augustus's debts and that His Majesty had given M.r Pitt orders to have that matter arranged directly. Therefore as the period demanded for Satisfying H. R. H's Creditors is elapsed and that they become very troublesome I consider myself as fully Authorized by M.r Livingston Letter to satisfy them without further delay, and have in Consequence drawn a bill in date of this day for £ 2500 upon the Lords of the Treasury at 30 days Sight in favor of Messr.s Falconet Gibbs an Co. of this place which I expect will discharge all the demands upon H. R. H. at Naples, Rome, and Florence, independant however of the £ 495.3.7 due to the Executors of the late Lord Hervey and M.r Daveaux's demand of £ 1945 forming together about £ 4940.3.7 the extent of H.R.H.'s debts conformable to the List I had the honor to transmit to Your Lordship by the Messenger M.r Small, and by the first Courier this Court sends to England I shall transmit to Your Lordship the particulars of the Payments to lay before His Majesty.
I have the honor to be
Wm

49) Naples Novemberr 28th 1798

My Lord

On Thursday last the 22^d Lord Nelson with Three of His Majesty's Ships of the Line, Three of the Portugheze Ships of the Line, His Majesty's Frigates Alliance and Bonne Citoyenne and the Flora Cutter, besides two Portugheze Armed Brigs Sail'd from this Port having on board about five Thousand Neapolitan Troops under the Command of General Naselli. The two Neapolitan Frigates under the Command of Lord Nelson as mention'd in my last sailed at the same time with Military Stores for the Maltese Insurgents. The Weather has been very boisterous and one of the Portugheze ships the two Brigs and Neapolitan Frigates were forced back to this Port, but sailed again the day before Yesterday, and I have no doubt but that Lord Nelson in the Vanguard with the Culloden and Minotaur, having each Eight hundred Neapolitan Troops on board are already at Leghorn. The Neapolitan General is on board the Vanguard.

The Neapolitan Army march'd in Seven Columns the 23^d instant into the Roman State, and the 26th His Sicilian Majesty had joined His Army at different points in the Neighbourhood of Rome. The french Troops from Rome, whose number all together is said not to have exceeded Three Thousand men including those driven from Veletri, Veroli, Anagni, Frosinone, Terracina and Valmorone under the Command of General Championet[95] collected together on the Hills near Frascati with an appearance of making a Stand, but having been threaten'd to be attacked by General Mack if he did not retire with his Army immediatly He marched off and abandon'd Rome to his Sicilian Majesty's Army who took quiet possession of that City the 26th instant. It appear'd as if Gen.l Championets next intention was to throw himself into Tuscany, but happily He will, it is hoped, find the Neapolitans in possession of Leghorn and General Mack had already dispatched a Column of his Army to get into Tuscany between him and the Neapolitan Troops gone by Sea.

His Sicilian Majesty's Letter to His Subjects on His Marching forward into the Roman State, and which was actually written by His Majesty Himself has had a wonderfull effect, as realy the Neapolitans are most sincerely attached to His Majesty. I inclose a printed Copy of the King's Letter N.1) as also a Copy of the Royal Manifesto that has been just Published N. 2). As The Queen of Naples told me that the last Letters from Vienna were more consoling than any yet received, it is to be hoped that the Courts of Vienna and Naples having at length resolved upon vigorous Measures, the only Ones that cou'd promise future Security, the french may soon be obliged to retreat from the greatest part of Italy.

Lieutenant Gregory of His Majesty's Ship Leviathan arrived here the 26th in. in a small Boat with Six men from Port Mahon which Port he left in possession of His Majesty's Forces on the 20th of Nov.r and brought a Letter for Lord Nelson and One for me from Commodore Duckworth[96] a Copy of which N. 3) is inclosed. I most sincerely congratulate Your Lordship on this fresh and most important Success of His Majesty's Arms.

Monsieur La Combe S.t Michel Ambassador from the french Republic and the Cisalpine Minister are still at Naples, and the Arms of the Republics over their Street doors, but not a french or Cisalpine Cockade appears in the Streets of Naples.

I have the honor to be
My Lord
Your Lordship's
most obedient and
most humble Servant
Wm Hamilton

50) Naples December 2^d 1798

My Lord
The Marquis de Gallo having given me Notice that a Neapolitan Messenger was to be dispatched in a few hours for Vienna and London, I have only time to acquaint Your Lordship that His Sicilian Majesty enter'd Rome the 29th of Nov.r and was received with acclamations of the greatest joy by every Class of the Inhabitants of that City. The french General Championet and Macdonald[97], who had given Their Words to Gen.l Mack that they wou'd Evacuate Rome and the Pope's States and not enter Tuscany if permitted to retire have according to their custom already broken their words by having left a french Garrizon in the Castle of S.t Angelo at Rome and taken a strong position at Civita Castellana in the Pope's Territory where it is said they have collected a force of between Nine and Ten thousand men. When the last Courier left Rome A Column of the Neapolitan Army had march'd to attack the french at Civita Castellana, and the Neapolitans at Rome were preparing to besiege the Castle of S.t Angelo. An other Column of the Neapolitan Army is marched towards Terni on the road to Loretto, and the vanguard of that Column is said to have suffer'd a little from a french Ambuscade. We have not yet any news of Lord Nelson's arrival with the five Thousand Neapolitan Troops at Leghorn. I find this Government in great agitation on the doubt whether the Emperor's Army will advance in time, and at a moment so very critical for the Safety of this Kingdom.

Your Lordship will receive by the Neapolitan Messenger the new Treaty of Alliance between His Majesty and The King of the Two Sicilies which was Signed this day by The Marquis de Gallo and me. This Court chose rather a Treaty of Alliance than a Convention, and I have endeavor'd to keep as close as possible to the Convention of 1793 which Your Lordship pointed out as the proper Basis for any New Treaty. The Marquis de Gallo and I had many conferences before We cou'd come to this Agreement. A Secret article for a Subsidy or Guarantee for a Loan was his sinequaNon of a New Treaty and Your Lordship will see by the two Letters from The Queen of Naples to L.y Hamilton inclosed how very anxious her Majesty was on that point.: I shew'd the Marquis fairly by my Instructions that I was positively prohibited from giving even the smallest hope of such aid from Great Britain, and therefore coud not treat on that Subject and the Secret Article was at last withdrawn, The Queen of Naples and The Marquis de Gallo desiring me only to represent to Your Lordship in the strongest terms, that it was not possible for the Neapolitan Army to exist without aid, more than five Months in Active Service, as the Monthly expence of it was no less than Nine hundred Thousand Ducats, and that all the Money they had Collected for the War wou'd be exhausted in that time. However I ventured to give, as my opinion only, that the best chance, if there was any chance for such aid from Great Britain, it wou'd be by His Sicilian Majesty's continuing to pursue the vigorous Measures He had at length adopted in the good Cause and against the treacherous Enemy. The Alteration I made in the Article respecting His Sicilian Majesty's obligation to furnish Four Ships of the Line &c was Necessary as most of the Neapolitan Ships of the Line have been Stripped of their Masts and Yards to Supply the King's damaged Ships from Alexandria, and wou'd therefore have appear'd only upon paper, when an Equivalent in Small Armed Vessels, which His Sicilian Majesty is ready and able to furnish, seems better adapted to the present Mediterranean Service. Your Lordship will observe also, that from the hint You was pleas'd to give me in your Dispatch N. 7) I have obtain'd, if required that Three Thousand Neapolitan Sailors shoud be furnished to the King's Ships in the Mediterranean during the War, in lieu of the Six Thousand Neapolitan Land forces given by the Convention of 1793.

It was very unwillingly that I Signed the Secret Article annext to The Treaty[98] but as Your Lordship in Your Dispatch N. 6) of the 3$^\mathrm{d}$ of Oct.r says that His Majesty was not insensible of the danger which must attend His Sicilian Majesty in case of an Open War with France without the fullest assurance of Support from the Court of Vienna and that the Marquis Gallo shew'd me a dispatch from the Marquis Circello giving an Account of his Conference with Your Lordship on the very subject of this Secret

Article, and allowed me to make an extract from that Letter which is inclosed N. 1) I hope Your Lordship will not disapprove of my having at length acquiesced particularly as it can only have its Effect in the sole Case of the Emperor's abandoning the King of Naples. The other two Secret Articles proposed by the Marquis Gallo, Copies of which are inclosed N. 2.) I did not think my self authorized to enter upon not being mentiond in my Instructions.

I have the honor to be
My Lord
Your Lordship's
most obedient and
most humble Servant
Wm Hamilton

P.S. The inclosed paper N. 3) I a Copy of a Letter from the Brother of General Buonaparte to the french Directory. He is now in quarantine at Taranto. This Letter with several in Cypher was sent by a Messenger from Taranto to the french Ambassador here, but intercepted by this Government. Those in Cypher I take for granted represent Buonaparte and His Army in a Situation the very reverse of this Letter, meant only to deceive; I shall do all in my power to prevail upon this Government to detain Louis Buonaparte & his papers, altho they seem much inclined to give the papers to Mo.r La Combe St. Michel and let him go.

His Sicilian Majesty is in possession of Civita Vecchia, The Maremma & the whole Coast to Leghorn, and a Merchant here has just received advice of Lord Nelson's being arrived with the Neapolitan Troops at Leghorn.

N.4 inclosed is a Copy of the Marquis de Gallos full Power[99].

51) Naples December 11th 1798

My Lord
Lord Nelson in the Vanguard with the Culloden and Minotaur, each having from eight to nine hundred men on board from the Neapolitan Army notwithstanding the tempestuous weather arrived at Leghorn the 27th of last Month and the Neapolitan Troops were landed and took possession of Leghorn the 28th. Above Twenty french Privateers and Seventy Two Ligurian, or Genoese Vessels, loaded with Corn for the french were in that Port, and we hear that the Privateers are still detain'd there by his Majesty's Squadron and now under the Command of Captain Troubridge, and that the Corn Vessels, after having been obliged to deposit their Cargoes at Leghorn,

have been permitted to depart, taking away with them all the french and Genoese then at Leghorn, amounting to about fifteen hundred and who were beginning to be troublesome. Lord Nelson at the particular request of Their Sicilian Majesties returned to Naples as soon as he had landed the Troops and came with the Vanguard only to an Anchor in this Port the 3^d instant. Your Lordship will receive the particulars of the Capitulation of Leghorn from M.r Wyndham. The Portugheze Ships with their portion of Neapolitan Troops on board not having been able to keep up with the British Ships were met with by Lord Nelson on his return about Sixteen leagues from Leghorn. This Expedition plann'd and executed so ably and speedily by Lord Nelson it is to be hoped will totally disappoint the intentions of the french, and save the Duchy of Tuscany.

The Operations of His Sicilian Majesty's Army since my last, have been cautiously kept Secret, but from what has transpired, One Column under the Command of Gen.l Micheroux fell into a french Ambuscade near Fermo on the Adriatick, lost all it's baggage and Cannons and was dispersed over the Country, some having fled back as far as Pescara and Chieti. They have however been rallied again and were the 7th instant advanced as far as Ascoli, with an other General, The Prince of Cuttò, as their head. The Main body of the french Army, said to be about Seven thousand, was by the last Accounts at Civita Castellana, three or four Posts from Rome, and Nearly Surrounded by the Neapolitan Army far Superior, under the Command of General Mack. At Civita Castellana also, on some small Attacks, the behaviour of the Neapolitans, particularly of the Officers, is said to have been very pusillanimous, and that the General had degraded some of the Officers and placed Serjeants in their stead. Count Saxe, Son of the Prince Xavier of Saxony, has been severely wounded in one of these Skirmishes, endeavouring to rally and encourage these New Troops.

His Sicilian Majesty and General Acton were still at Rome the 8th inst.t and the Tricolor flag was still display'd on the Castle of St. Angelo, having in it a Garrizon of about five hundred men, it was however expected to Surrender soon, and the Romans are said to be arming against the french and much pleased with His Sicilian Majesty whom they call their Deliverer. As yet the Neapolitans have sufferd no great losses except in honor baggage and Field pieces, having taken and killed as many of the Enemy as the french have killed or taken from them. We hope that the reason of keeping these disasters Secret may be the great probability of General Mack's being able to repair them soon by giving a good account of the french Army surrounded by so superior a Neapolitan force at Civita Castellana.

We do not know the Number of french Troops at Ancona, but hear that they have strongly fortified themselves there, and have by force mannd, but chiefly with landsmen, the three large Venetian Ships of War that were lying and supposed to be richly laden with Spoil in that Port.

We hear of Numerous french Troops being on their march into Italy from Piedmont and Switzerland, but it is to be hoped the Emperors Army will move before they can join the few Troops the french Republic has at this moment in Italy, and which is calculated at Twenty Seven Thousand men. The Neapolitan Army seems to want such encouragement and there can be no doubt but that the Austrians and Neapolitans wou'd have it in their power to drive the french completely out of Italy if theywou'd without loss of time Act with vigor and Loyalty. If the Emperor Shou'd not move this Kingdom will certainly soon be in the greatest danger.

The Arms of the french Republic were on Saturday last taken from over the door of the house of Monsieur La Combe S.t Michel and He was order'd by this Government to be ready to embark the Monday following, which was Yesterday, with all the french, unprovided with the proper Certificates for their Continuing to reside in this City. Vessels were prepared by this Government to transport The Ambassador and his Suite, and the french amounting to about four score persons, to Genoa and they embarked Yesterday. The Marquis de Gallo having applied to Lord Nelson and me for our Passports that Mons.r La Combe S.t Michel and his Suite might not be molested on their passage to Genoa We gave them accordingly. All the papers of the french Emigrants at Naples under my protection and pension'd by His Majesty have been Yesterday Sealed up by order of this Government for examination.

Yesterday Lord Nelson received Letters from the Russian and Turkish Admirals at Corfu, dated the 30th of Nov.r acquainting His Lordship, that they flatter'd themselves that they shou'd soon have the entire possession of that Island as they were then preparing to Storm the Citadel.

I hope that I shall be able in my next to give Your Lordship a better account of the behaviour of His Sicilian Majesty's Troops, and of the Emperor's Army being on it's march into Italy, without which our Situation here must remain very critical.

I have the honor to be
My Lord
Your Lordship's
most obedient and
most humble Servant
Wm Hamilton

52) Naples December 19th 1798

My Lord

It is impossible in the hurry that we are in at the moment to enter into any particulars. The fine Army of His Sicilian Majesty from Treachery and Cowardice is dwindling away without resistance, by the last Accounts Gen.l Mack was at Veletri and the Enemy had advanced into Abruzzo & taken possession of Aquila. It needs no great penetration to foresee that in a very short time unless the Emperor's Troops shoud advance with hasty strides this Kingdom is lost, however fortunately our Brave Lord Nelson is here with the Alcmene and the Portugheze Squadron under His Lordship's Command, which will I hope secure us a retreat, a temporary one at least, in the Island of Sicily, and this is so provoking considering, that a fine Army of more than Forty Thousand men shou'd yield to a handful of rascally french Maroders, almost without striking a Stroke, and I have never yet heard of more than Seven Thousand french having been collected together and when His Sicilian Majesty's Army marched to Rome it was certain there were not in all Italy more than Twenty Seven Thousand french. Reports say the Emperor's Army was to march forward to attack the Cisalpines the 8th instant, but no certain account has been received of Any motion of the Imperial Army.

I have the honor to be
My Lord
Your Lordship's
most obedient and
most humble Servant
Wm Hamilton

53) Palermo December 28th 1798

My Lord

My last Letter will have prepared Your Lordship and prevent Your being greatly surprised at seeing this Letter dated from Palermo. Letters from Gen.l Mack to the Court of Naples were every day more pressing to put Their Sicilian Majesties in safety, and without loss of time, as the Enemy was advancing and the Troops He commanded continued in their treacherous and cowardly Conduct, making little or no resistance, so that on them there cou'd be no kind of dependance. The Populace at Naples began to collect on the 19th instant and went under the Windows of the Royal Palace and intreated of Their Sicilian Majesties not to abandon Naples but to point out to them the Traitors and Jacobins, and they wou'd immediatly do justice by dispatching them, and that Their Majesties wou'd be perfectly safe under their protection, in spite of the ill behaviour of the Army. The Mob was calm'd for that Night, but the next morning a french Emigrant (not under British protection) was taken out of a boat just as he was going to embark and inhumanly butcher'd by the Mob, and having tied a rope round his leg they dragged him through the dirt under the Windows of the Palace and shew'd him to the King of Naples, who expressed to them the greatest indignation on the occasion, and severe orders were immediatly given to disperse the Mob and prevent such unjust cruelties. The Court had already concerted with Lord Nelson and me as to their Escape into Sicily, and it was plain that They cou'd not trust to Their own Ships, on board of which there were many Officers and Sailors supposed to be disaffected, and indeed Seamen cou'd not be found to man even One of His Sicilian Majesty's Ships without Lord Nelson's help. It was impossible to prevent a suspicion getting abroad of the intention of the Royal Family to make their Escape and it was evident that Lord Nelson's Ship alone cou'd effectuate that Escape; however the Secret was so well kept, that We contrived to get Their Sicilian Majesties Treasure, in Jewells and Money, to a very considerable amount, on board of His Majesty's Ship The Vanguard the 20th of Dec.r and Lord Nelson went the next night The 21st at 9 o' clock by a Secret passage into the Palace and brought off in his Boats Their Sicilian Majesties and all Their Royal family with Gen.l Acton, The Prince Belmonte, The Prince and Princess Castelcicala, and some other principal Officers of the Court and lodged them safely in the Vanguard, altho' the Wind was high and the Sea rough. It was not discoverd at Naples untill very late at night that The Royal Family had escaped. Lord Nelson had already concerted that the Portugheze Ships under His Lordship's command, shou'd accommodate any of the Cardinals, foreign Ministers or Officers belonging to the Court of Naples, when it shou'd become necessary to leave Naples to prevent their falling into the hands of the approaching Enemy, and Your Lordship may well immagine that they lost no time in getting on board those Ships as soon it was known that Their Sicilian Majesties were actually on the board the Vanguard. Lord Nelson had likewise given timely notice through my channel, that the Three Transport Victuallers were order'd to receive the Gentlemen of the British Factory, or any of His Majesty's Subjects with their most valuable Effects, in case of Necessity. I had also taken the precaution to freight two Greek Polaccas for the french and Corsican Emigrants under The King's protection, all of which got safe on board those Ships one or two of them having been slightly wounded by the Neapolitan Mob on the 20th of December.

The Imperial Ambassador Lady Hamilton and myself were most kindly and hospitably received by Lord Nelson on board the Vanguard and the Russian Minister and his family are on board of One of the Portugheze Ships.

On the 22ᵈ numerous boats with Neapolian Nobility and others with a lower Class, came along side of the Vanguard to entreat of His Sicilian Majesty to return to Naples, but His My. did not speak himself to any One but to The Cardinal Zurlo ArchBishop of Naples, whom he assured that He by no means meant to abandon Naples, but that Circumstances of the times obliged His Majesty to remove with His Royal family to an other part of His Dominions, that if the Nepolitans behaved as loyal Subjects, They had force enough in hand to repell the Enemy and that when He saw that they did their duty His Majesty and Royal Family wou'd return with pleasure to the Capital.

All His Sicilian Majesy's Ships of War had been for some days before drawn out of the Mole of Naples, and orderd to be fitted out directly for Sea, but the Samnite alone of 74 Guns was in any readiness to accompany the Royal Family, nor cou'd She have saild without a Supply of British Seamen from the Vanguard. Lord Nelson ever Anxious in Executing his instructions to the utmost, told the King of Naples fairly that he was most happy in having fulfill'd that essential part of the instructions which he had receiv'd from The King His Royal Master, and given every assistance in his power to Their Sicilian Majesties & Royal family yet that He cou'd not consistently with the good of the Common Cause allow of such a considerate Naval Force being left to the chance of falling into the hands of the Enemy, and consequently that it wou'd be absolutely necessary to burn such of the Ships as cou'd not immediatly Sail with His Majesty. Lord Nelson perceiving that this resolution, however necessary, gave pain to His Sicilian Majesty proposed delaying it to the last moment, but on the other hand the Royal Family expressing great impatience to get off, it was agreed on all Sides that the Portugheze Ships and His Majesty's Frigate Alcmene Cap.t Hope shou'd remain in the Bay of Naples to assist in the fitting out as many of His Sicilian Majesty's Ships as possible before the Enemy shou'd arrive, and to burn them in the last Extremity. One of His Sic.n Majesy's Ships of the Line in the Port of Castel a mare was sunk by His Majesty's order before we left the Bay of Naples.

On Sunday the 23ᵈ of December in the Evening The Vanguard (with a richer Cargoe on board than was ever risked before in one bottom) saild from the Bay of Naples accompanied by the Samnite and Archimedes Neapolitan 74.s the three British Transport Victuallers and other hired Vessels with the Emigrants and effects of the Neapolitan Nobility attending upon the Royal Family. On the 24th we met with so violent a Gale of Wind accompanied with hail that Lord Nelson himself says he had never met with one of the like violence in his thirty Years Service, it fortunately did not last long, but Your Lordship may imagine that it was a serious moment, as all of the top Sails of the Vanguard were split into rags, and even the precaution was taken to get up the Axes to cut away the Masts[100]. Thank God all ended well and in three hours time new sails were bent and every thing in the best order and on the 25th at Night the Vanguard was safely moor'd in the Mole of Palermo, close along side of the two Spanish Ships with quick Silver that were so long block'd up at Trieste. In the morning of Christmas day and some hours before we got into Palermo Prince Albert, one of Their Sicilian Majesties' Sons, six years of Age, was either from fright or fatigue taken with violent and repeated Convulsion fits and unfortunately died in one of them in the Arms of Lady Hamilton, The Queen, the Princesses and Women attendants being in such confusion as to be incapable of affording any Assistance to the poor Prince. Your Lordship may well conceive the Situation of the Unfortunate Royal Family at this Moment. The Queen is inconsolable but Her Majesty and all the Royal Family appear to be truly sensible of Lord Nelson's and our Exertions to assist them to our utmost under their Severe and accumulated Misfortunes. The Vanguard and Samnite were the only two Ships that got into Palermo the 25th. On the 27th One of the English Trasports and one of the Greek Polaccas with the french Emigrants on board got into this Port, the rest of our dispersed Convoy are supposed to have got into Messina.

The Sicilians are so enraged against the french, that this Government does not think it safe for the Emigrants to come on Shore here and I am now preparing to send them with a Neapolitan Convoy to Trieste. Since Lord Minto[101] left these Unfortunate Emigrants under my care I have constantly endeavor'd to afford them every protection and assistance in my power according to the Gracious intention of The King Our Royal Master, and I shall certainly not neglect them in their present distress I hope they may all soon be convey'd to Trieste or some other safe port of the Emperor's Dominions. The Sicilians appear to be very happy in having Their King and Royal Family in their Capital and vow vengeance on the french. We have not as yet any News from Naples. All seems to depend upon the Emperor's Army having, or not having, marched into Italy, but as the french invading army was Supposed to be at Fondi when Their Sicilian Majesties left Naples, and Gen.l Macks Army made little or no resistance it is most probable that by this time They may have joined the Neapolitan Mob and plunderd the rich City of Naples. I flatter myself that Your Lord.p will excuse my having only set down the heads of so many Extarordinary Events that have taken place rapidly in the short space of a few days. That a fine Army of near fifty Thousand effective Men shou'd be reduced to little more than twenty thousand men in twenty two days, without coming into what cou'd be call'd an Action, is beyond Example. Genl. Mack came from Capua the 23^d of December on board the Vanguard in a most desperate situation of mind assuring their Sicilian Majesties that the only consolation he felt was that of seeing Their Majesties and Their August Family in safety on board of Lord Nelson's Ship; that He wou'd return to the remnant of His Army at Capua consisting of little more than twelve thousand men, and on which he had little dependance, as every day he had discoverd fresh Treachery among the Officers, and the behaviour of the men continuing to be cowardly in the extreme. The Six Thousand Neapolitan Troops transported by Lord Nelson to Leghorn were still there the 21st of Dec.r but Genl. Mack said that he had received accounts of the french having enterd Tuscany. By the last accounts from Malta of the 12th instant there is every reason to hope that the french Garrizon of the Valette is so reduced as to be on the point of Surrendering to Cap.t Ball of His Majesty's Ship Alexander.

I have the honor to be
My Lord
Your Lordship's
most obedient and
most humble Servant
Wm Hamilton

P.S. I have received from Malta a Letter dated Tigre off Malta Dec.r 11th 1798 in which Sir Sydney Smith tells me that He left England the 15th November and arrived at Gibraltar the Eighth day and having staid four with Lord S.t Vincent arrived at Malta the 26th day since his departure from England having been only 21 days under Sail, and that the Night of the date of his Letter He proposed sailing for Constantinople.

I have the honor of inclosing a few of the Queen of Naples's last Letters to Lady Hamilton which strongly express the strength of Her Majesty's mind and the perfect and gratefull Confidence the Royal Family had in the protection of His Majesty's Squadron under the Command of the Humane and Brave Lord Nelson, during their heavy distresses.

WH.

Lady Hamilton begs the favor of Your Lordship that the Queen's Letters may be returned to her when she arrives in England.

SICILY

Letters and Papers from Sir William Hamilton at Palermo, Naples and Palermo, Consul Locke at Palermo, and others; to the Secretary of State: with Drafts to Sir W: Hamilton.

From January 3rd 1799 to December 22nd 1799

1) Palermo January 3^d 1799

My Lord
(Since I wrote my Dispatch of the 28th of December N. 40) Accounts have been receiv'd from Naples of the 30th of Dec.r but no Letters from Gen.l Mack. This Court however has had certain accounts of fresh disgraces in Abruzzo, and that two Columns of the Enemy had penetrated, one as far as Isernia and Venafro, and the other to Mola di Gaeta both of which are about fifty miles from Naples. At Naples all was quiet, but complaining greatly of the desertion of the Court & which they lay chiefly to the charge of Gen.l Acton. One circumstance that an officer who arrived here yesterday in His Majesty's Frigate Alcmene told me gives me but a very bad opinion of the Loyalty of Marshall Pignatelli[102] and those to whom His Sicilian (*sic*) has confided the Government of the Capital and Kingdom of Naples during his absence. Capt. Yakings late of the Fox Cutter, told me that he was at the great Opera of St. Carlo's at Naples the 30th of Dec.r and saw represented in one of the Baletti a ludicrous representation of the hasty flight of their Sicilian Majesties and the English from Naples, and which was received with the greatest applause. The Neapolitan Gun boats that were drawn out in the Bay of Naples and one Corvette sunk during the great Storm and as the Marquis Nizza writes to Lord Nelson that it is impossible to put the rest of His Sicilian Ships of War in Sailing Order it is probable that they are all burnt by this time and that the Portugheze Squadron will be in this Port in a few days.

The great fatigue I have undergone of late both of body and mind has occasiond a feverish complaint and confined me to my bed for two days but am now thank God much better but unable to write as fully as I cou'd have wished to Your Lordship at this most interesting period.

I have the honor to be
My Lord
Your Lordship's
most obedient and

most humble Servant
Wm Hamilton

P.S. I have the honor of inclosing a Copy of His Sicilian Majesty's instructions to the Marquis Gallo on his departure from Naples December 20th the day before Their Sicilian Majesties left Naples & which strongly shews the Confusion of the Neapolitan Cabinet at that moment.

2) Palermo January 7th 1799

My Lord
The Neapolitan Messenger that was to have been dispatched the 28th of Dec.r from hence to Vienna and London has been detain'd untill this day but I flatter myself that Your Lordship will have already received my important Dispatch N. 40) (a duplicate of which I have the honor to transmit to Your Lord.p now) through the channel of Lord S.t Vincent.

The latest News received here from Naples was of the 4th instant A Column of the Enemy, said to be about eight Thousand strong, had made an attempt on Capua, but were repulsed. The Head of Quarters of Genl. Mack was at Caserta. The Neapolitan Nobility did not manifest any great attachment to Their Sovereigns, but rather to the contrary. The people appear'd to be violently against the french and loyal to their Sovereigns. General Mack to gain time had endeavor'd to get an Armistice but the french Commander had refused to treat with any but the People and City of Naples. Mareshall Pignatelli in whose hands the chief Command of Naples was left by Their Sicilian Majesties on their leaving that Kingdom, was said to be treating with the Enemy for an Armistice. From what has always happend on like occasions and trusting to french Treaties, it is plain to me that this business must end very ill for Their Sicilian Majesties, and I look upon the loss of Naples as certain.

The Dispatches I have just receiv'd and forward by this occasion to Your Lordship from M.r Wyndham shew that the present State of Tuscany is nearly as desperate as that of the Kingdom of Naples – and all the Consequence of half Measures, mixed with Treachery and Cowardice.

The Chev.r Bouligny, The Spanish Charge d'Affaires at Naples, is I hear very busy Negociating to get the Sovereignty of the Kingdom of Naples for the Son of the Duke of Parma now at Madrid.

Lord Nelson is indefatigable in pushing on with vigor and Activity the blockades of Malta and Alexandria and at the same time affording every assistance and protection in the power of the King's Squadron under His

Lord.p's Command to the Courts of Sicily and Tuscany and it realy Seems as if Great Britain alone dared even to look the proud perfidious Enemy in the face. When the particulars of what has passed rapidly within the last Month in the Kingdom of Naples and in Tuscany, and when the real Numbers of the Enemy and of the Troops that were, or might have been opposed to them, shall have been ascertain'd, it must astonish all Europe, but what it is to be done when Treachery, Corruption and Cowardice had infected the whole of His Sicilian Majesty's Army and Navy.

Their Sicilian Majesties and Royal family are a little recover'd from Their fatigues and the Behaviour of Their Sicilian Subjects is most loyal and praise worthy. My health, tho' much better, is by no means such as to be able to write to Your Lordship as fully as I cou'd have Wished.

I have the honor to be
My Lord
Your Lordship's
most obedient and
most humble Servant
Wm Hamilton

3) Downing Street January 4th 1799

Sir,

I am directed by Lord Grenville to inform You that, in consequence of the Navigation of the Elbe being entirely obstructed by the Ice, no Mails from the Continent have been received here since the 16th of last Month; and Mr. Grenville having proceed as far as the Mouth of that River, has been obliged to return. An attempt is however now made to open a Communication with the Continent by the Island of Nordeney near the Mouth of the Ems; and if this Experiment should Succeed, the Mails will be transmitted hither by that Course until the Navigation of the Elbe shall again be open.

4) Palermo January 14th 1799

My Lord

I find that the Neapolitan Messenger that was to have gone from hence for Vienna and London the 28th of Dec.r is still detain'd here as this Court wished to know more of the fate of Naples before they dispatched him. Commodore Mitchel in one of the Portugheze Ships of War arrived here Yesterday, having left the Bay of Naples at 12 o' clock the 12th instant, when, it being the King of Naples's Birthday, the Neapolitan Colours were flying as Usual on all the Castles of that City, but in direct contradiction to the Orders left by Lord Nelson with the Marquis Nizza, the Commander of the Portugheze Squadron, when His Lordship brought off Their Sicilian Majesties & Royal Family from Naples, all the Neapolitan Ships of War and Gun Boats had been burnt or destroy'd by that Squadron, under a false Supposition of the Enemy having been on the point of taking possession of Naples, when on the Contrary the Accounts received by this Government are that the french have been repulsed at Capua and that Gaeta had been retaken by the Neapolitans and One thousand five hundred french Prisoners sent to Naples, but to my sorrow I observed in the Official Accounts from Naples to this Government that two of the Nobility, The Prince Migliano and the Duke of Gesso, had been sent to the french head Quarters at Caiazzo, to treat with the Enemy, not in the Name of His Sicilian Majesty, who disavows that measure, but of the City of Naples in order to prevent it's being plunder'd, and it is easy to conceive from what has constantly happend elsewhere, what will the case if the french once get any any kind of footing in the Capital of the Kingdom of Naples and I still think that His Sicilian Majesty is betray'd and that The Kingdom of Naples will be lost, altho' at this moment the Court seems to be in high Spirits on the good News lately received from Naples.

Yesterday Commodore Mitchel brought here the inclosed Letter from M.r Wyndham under a flying Seal and directed to Your Lordship but this Court has received fresher Accounts from Florence, saying that General Victor on receiving a Messenger from the Emperor of Germany had retired his Army from Pistoia and the Tuscan State, by which Tuscany was releived from it's impending danger.

This Court has received Accounts from Corfu that a Messenger had arrived there from Constantinople with an Account of the Total Defeat of Buonaparte and his Army in Egypt by the Grand Signor's Army, and that the Russian and Ottoman Squadrons had made great rejoicing at Corfu on the Occasion.

I have the honor to be
My Lord
Your Lordship's
most obedient and
most humble Servant
Wm Hamilton

5) Palermo January 16th 1799

My Lord

The News received from Naples the night before last proves clearly to my Mind that His Sicilian Majesty is betray'd and that the Kingdom of Naples is now or will be soon at the Mercy of the french Directory.

The Mareschall Pignatelli who was left Vicario Generale at Naples on their Sicilian Majesties and Royal Family leaving that City has now, with the advice of the Neapolitan Nobility, Solicited and obtain'd from the french General Championet an Armistice of two Months, and for which he has made the Shamefull Conditions of paying him Two Million and a half of Neapolitan Ducats, half of which was to be paid yesterday and the other half in three days more, besides ceding immediately to the french Army the important Fortress of Capua, Gaeta and all the Country in a line from that City on the Mediterranean to Manfredonia and Barletta on the Adriatick, including the fertile and rich Country of Foggia in Puglia and from Whence alone Naples can now be Supplied with Corn and Cattle.

General Mack who did not accede to this Armistice retired with his Army to Aversa half way between Capua and Naples. Their Sicilian Majesties and their Ministry here are enraged at the treacherous and pusillanimous behaviour of Mareshal Pignatelli and the Neapolitan Nobility and mean to disavow all that has been done, to remove Pignatelli and Name General Mack Vicario Generale in his room, but before these orders can reach Naples and be put in Execution the Conditions of the Armistice will have compleatly taken place at Naples; this day accounts have been received of the Arrival of the french Commissaries at Naples to collect the two million and a half Ducats and that their Arrival had caused some fermentation among the Lazzaroni or populace of that City and whih the Nobility were endeavouring to calm.

Your Lordship has long been acquainted with my private Opinion that if the french Army ever came within reach of Naples all wou'd be lost, as few there were pure in their principles, or realy attached to Their Sicilian Majesties, and that there was an Universal Complaint of a total want of Justice and good Government throughout the Kingdom of Naples and that the Provinces were in the most extreme Want and Misery so that few, shou'd it come to the trial, wou'd think such a Government worth the fighting for[103].

Their Sicilian Majesties and Royal Family in this Island, with every protection that Great Britain so generously affords Them will not be in a perfect State of Security when the french are in possession of the Calabrias and few remaining Provinces of the Kingdom of Naples, and which will probably take place soon particularly as they seem to do little or Nothing here to place this Island in a true State of defence relying chiefly on the continued Assistance of Their most powerfull Ally.

I have the honor to be
My Lord
Your Lordship's
most obedient and
most humble Servant
Wm Hamilton

P. S. January 17th 1799
Yesterday Captain Horn in the Mutine Brig arrived here from Naples, from whence he sail'd the 15th inst. in the Afternoon. At that time the Populace of Naples had risen against the Vicar General Mareshall Pignatelli and the Nobility saying that they had betray'd their Sovereign by making an Armistice with the french without consulting them; and that they were determined to defend the City against the french in the Name of their Sovereign whom they hoped wou'd return; and they actually had forced their way into the Arsenal The Castles of St. Elmo, del Ovo, and Carmine before the Mob came away and were in possession of them and the flag of His Sicilian Majesty was flying every where. The french Commissaries who came to Naples from the head Quarters of Mons.r Championet the french General in the Royal Palace of Caserta, for the two Millions and a half of Ducats escaped with difficulty the rage of the people and returned to Caserta without the Money. This Court has been immediatly informed of all these recent Events, and surely, with a proper Leader the Spirit of the Neapolitan populace might be improved and perhaps being well directed prevent the approaching Revolution at Naples. – but Alas! I have long experienced that there is nothing like Energy or decision in this Government, and it will probably end in the Nobility of Naples calling the french Army into Naples to quell the populace and save their persons, and the Revolution will be hasten'd by an Event which well Conducted might have rescued the Kingdom of Naples from its impending Ruin.
Your Lordship can not fail making certain reflexions on the Singularity of the inclosed printed Edit, being the only one that has been published since the arrival of His Sicilian Majesty in this Capital[104].
WH.

6) Palermo January 18th 1799

My Lord
Last Night General Acton Sent to Lord Nelson Copies of all the Official papers relative to the Infamous Armistice agreed upon by the Mareshall Pig-

natelli and of His Sicilian Majesty's Proclamation sent to be published at Naples entirely disavowing and disapproving of what His Vicar General had done.

Lord Nelson has sent the above mention'd Papers directed to Lord Spencer through the channel of Lord S.t Vincent so that Your Lordship will soon see them and be convinced as I am that Naples will be lost by the basest Treachery.

I have the honor to be
My Lord
Your Lordship's
most obedient and
most humble Servant
Wm Hamilton

7) Palermo January 19th 1799

My Lord
On our being obliged to fly from Naples, the french and Corsican Emigrants under the pay and protection of His Majesty, and that were left to my charge by Sir Gilbert Elliot on the Evacuation of Corsica and Porto Ferraio, have been by my care transported here, but an Order from this Government obliges all french and Corsican Emigrants to quit this Kingdom immediatly, part of them have desired to go to Tangiers and others to Trieste; Lord Nelson has been so good as to provide a large Transport for those that go to Tangiers and they Sail this Evening under the Convoy of His Majesty's Frigate the Alcmene Capt. Hope. The Emigrants desirous of going to Trieste will have a Transport and a Corvette to convoy them provided by this Government.

I have this day given to the Order of Mr. Abraham Gibbs Ten Sorts of Bills, as specified in the Margin, dated Palermo the 19th of January 1799 on the Lords Commissioners of His Majesty's Treasury, ammounting to the Sum of One Thousand Seven Hundred forty Pounds, Eight Shillings and Seven Pence, at 30 days Sight and to ballance the french and Corsican Emigrant account to this day, and may I beg the favor of Your Lordship to give the proper Notice to the Lords of the Treasury of my having thus drawn upon them.

The News from Naples of yesterday was very bad and there is every Symptom that the Revolution, under the french direction, will be complete in that Kingdom, and in a very short time. How long Their Sicilian Majesties and Royal Family may be Secure here, amidst such accumulated Treachery, God only knows. Mareshall Pignatelli is arrived here, and General Mack deserted by the Neapolitan Army is said to have disappeared.

I have the honor to be
My Lord
Your Lordship's
most obedient and
most humble Servant
Wm Hamilton

8) Palermo January 26th 1799

My Lord

The Messenger that was to have been dispatched by this Court from hence the 28th of December is only this day going off for Vienna and London but fortunately I have had opportunities of forwarding some of my Dispatches to Your Lord.p through the channel of S.t Vincent, and which I flatter myself Your Lord.p will have received long before this Messenger reaches London. The last Authentic News from Naples was of the 18th instant. The Deputies for the internal Tranquillity of that City having insisted as Your Lordship will see by a Copy of their Letter to the Mareshal Pignatelli inclosed N. 1) that His Excy shou'd resign the Power left in his hands by His Sicilian Majesty, and make it over to them, and the remainder of the Neapolitan Army having given up their Arms to the people, the Mareshall thought it high time to embark secretly on board an Imperial Vessel and arrived here, as mention'd in my last, but Their Sicilian Majesties justly irritated at the infamous Armistice which His Excy had made with the french General Championet, has now been suffer'd to come on Shore and as I beleive be sent to a Castle at Girgenti.

Your Lordship will see by the Copy of the Duke della Salandra's Letter to Mareshall Pignatelli inclosed N. 2) that General Mack has disappeared and left under the Duke's Command the poor remains of the fine Neapolitan Army reduced to two thousand five hundred discontented men, without provisions, forrage, or Money; and Now at Naples there is not a trace of a Soldier left having all sold, or given up their arms, to the people. No one can guess where General Mack is going. General Championet is lodged in the Queen of Naples's magnificent apartment in the Royal Palace of Caserta, and has already, in the Style of His Sicilian Majesty, given a grand Hunt in that Neighbourhood.

On Mareshall Pignatelli's leaving his Post of Vicar General of Naples, The Deputies for the internal order and security of the City of Naples, and at the request of the People, nominated the Prince Moliterno, a brave ambitious but inexperienced young Man, Commander in chief of the Urban Militia, as Your Lord.p will see by the Copy of their Act inclosed N. 3). As soon as the Prince Moliterno had accepted that Command He issued a Paper a Copy of which is inclosed N. 4) and in which Your Lordship will Observe there is not the least mention of the name of His Sicilian Majesty. This Court has not received any Official Accounts from Naples since the Arrival of Mareshall Pignatelli at Palermo, and he left Naples the 18th ins.t but the Commander of a Ragusean Vessel that left Naples the 19th and arrived here yesterday has deposed that the Neapolitan Troops from Leghorn, under the Command of Genl. Naselli, were arrived at Naples and that the People had disarmed them and Seized upon the Armed Corvette that Convoy'd them from Orbetello, and that every thing was in Confusion when he left Naples on account of the people's opposing the desire of Prince Moliterno to admit the french into that City.

My Opinion has been long fixed that the Kingdom of Naples was nearly ripe for a Revolution and that all wou'd be lost if the french were not kept at a distance. The Neapolitan people do not certainly love the french, but if by their means the price of bread and Oil cou'd be lower'd in the City they wou'd become their friends immediatly, for a true Patriotic Spirit does not I beleive exist in Italy[105].

Cardinal Ruffo of a Calabrian Family has been appointed with full Powers as His Sicilian Majesty's Vicar General, to go to Calabria to put those Provinces in a proper State of defence[106].

Your Lordship may well imagine the Anxiety of this Court and particularly of the Queen (who has a great deal of feeling) kept in a constant State of Suspence by the different reports from Naples. The Shamefull Armistice appears to me to have sufficiently decided the Ultimate fate of the Kingdom of Naples, let the Revolution take place a day sooner or later.

I fear the Mesdames of France have not yet got from Puglia to Trieste as the Neapolitan Frigate that was to have gone from Messina for them is still in that Port, the Sailors having deserted the Ship saying their Officers were Jacobins.

The Greek Vessel with the Corsican Emigrants under the King's protection, supposed to be lost on their passage from Naples put into Lipari and they are coming in here daily from that Island.

Reports say that Corfu has surrender'd to the Combined Squadron of Turks & Russians and by my last Letters from Mr. Spencer Smith at Constantinople of the 23[d] of Nov.r it appears certain that Berthier with Sixty Officers and all the french Garrizon at Cairo, had been Massacred and

Buonaparte retired with only five thousand of his remaining Army towards Alexandria.

    I have the honor to be
My Lord
Your Lordship's
most obedient and
most humble Servant
Wm Hamilton

9) Palermo February 3ᵈ 1799

    My Lord
The Entreprenante Cutter was on the point of Sailing this Morning with Lord Nelson's Dispatches to Lord St. Vincent, when just in time to Communicate the important but Melancholy News from Naples to Your Lordship, I received a Billet from General Acton, from which The following is an Extract.

"I return You my Cordial thanks for Lord St. Vincent's Paragraf which I immediatly translated for His Majesty: it is the only comfort that they may receive and the only one truly Serviceable to Support Them in their most Critical times: The King is extremely gratefull and feels most Sensibly His Obligations to the British Court and to their brave Navy, in these Moments especially. I hope that You will be so kind as to present to Lord St. Vincent Their Majesties Sincere Gratitude. Their Hope is only depending on the English. You are surely acquainted that Wednesday last 3000 french Entered in Naples with the Support of 12 thousand Jacobins of the Town who invited them. The people had killed many of the last and was fighting. Thursday however the infamous Tree was to be hoisted, 2 french men only came to Procita and the Island agreed to the Democratisation. At Ischia they opposed and sent away all those who thought in that same way. This report is of the Sicilian Chebec¹⁰⁷ sent for Information who anchored at Procita and Ponza Wednesday and Thursay last"

    I have the honor to be
My Lord
Your Lordship's
most obedient and
most humble Servant
Wm Hamilton

10) Palermo February 7th 1799

My Lord

Since my last This Court has not received any Official Accounts from
Naples but by the Governor of the Island of Procida and some Officers who
have made their Escape from Naples, We are assured that on the 27th of last
Month The french and Jacobine party of the Neapolitans, with the Prince
Moliterno at their head, had completely got the better of the Lazaroni, or
Neapolitan populace, who fought bravely in defence of the City, Men Women
and Children for three days, and that no less than Eleven thousand Lives on
on side or other, had been lost in the Conflict. They add that Immediatly on
the Arrival of the Three Thousand french Troops at Naples, a regular Government took place which plainly proves that there has long been a perfect
Understanding between the Neapolitan Jacobin Party and the french General.

It is now certain that General Mack went off with his Etat Major, Horses,
Equipages, Baggage, etc. through Rome with the Passport of General Championet, which has not a good appearance, but it is also certain that before he
took this Step his Army had deserted from him to a man, and that his life
was in danger from the rage of the people who have actually grievously
wounded the Duke of Salandra mistaking him for General Mack[108].

Before the french were call'd in to Naples by the Nobility and Jacobin
party the people had committed many Excesses. They dragged the Duke
della Torre, his brother and a Priest out of his Palace, shot them in a public
place and burnt their bodies on suspicion of their favouring the french Party.
The Island of Procita was so ripe for the Revolution that it took place immediatly on the Arrival of only two french Priests as The Governor himself told
me here.

On the Arrival of His Majesty's Ship Belerophon with a Convoy of Merchant Vessels from Gibraltar, Lord Nelson hoisted His Flag on board her, and
has sent the Vanguard to Malta to assist Capt. Ball in bringing matters there
to a Conclusion. The horrid News from Naples which cou'd not possibly be
kept from the Valette will naturally encourage the french Garrizon to resist
as long as it can, but there is every reason to hope, as it's Wants are so great
and the Port so well blocked up that it must Surrender very Soon.

All I can say as to the Security of this Island is that the french are in general detested by the Sicilians, yet there are discontents here also, and Extreme
poverty and Misery among the common people and therefore in my Opinion
the best and only Security wou'd be keeping the french at a distance. Shou'd
they get possession of the Calabrias, this Island wou'd be in great danger,
Notwithstanding the powerfull protection afforded it by His Majesty's
Squadron under the Command of our Brave Lord Nelson.

I have the honor to be
My Lord
Your Lordship's
most obedient and
most humble Servant
Wm Hamilton.

11) Palermo February 13th 1799

My Lord

According to Custom the Neapolitan Messenger intended to carry the
Dispatches from this Court to that of Vienna, having been detain'd much
longer than wa expected, I have an Opportunity of adding to what I had the
honor of writing to Your Lordship in my last Number, in the hands of the
same Messenger, that I have seen a Letter from the Cardinal Ruffo to Their
Sicilian Majesties dated the 7th ins.t from Pizzo in Calabria Ultra, in which
His Eminency gives Their Sicilian Majesties little hopes of there being a possibility of preventing the Calabrias from following the example of the Capital; that Calabria Citra had already errected the Tree of Liberty, and Monte
Leone and some other Towns of Calabria Ultra had likewise acknowledged
the Neapolitan, now called the Vesuvian Republic, under the french protection. There is no saying where this frenzy will Stop, and altho' the Sicilians
certainly hate the french, yet there are already Symptoms in several parts of
this Island, particularly at Messina, Catania and Trapani, of discontents
fomented probably by Agents of the french Republic, and as in all appearance The Whole Kingdom of Naples will very soon be compleately Republicanized, some sort of Change of Government may naturally be expected to
take place in this Island.

I have the honor of inclosing a Copy of a Dispatch I received the day
before Yesterday from General Acton, and Lord Nelson received One from
His Excy to the same purpose and which was the first Official Notice We
have received of the Monarchy having been destroy'd at Naples and that
Government declared to be a Republic under the protection of the french.

Yesterday His Majesty's Ship the Vanguard and Dorothea Frigate returned
here from Malta which place they left the 11th instant having on board some
Maltese Commissaries sent to His Sicilian Majesty to implore Provisions and
Succours to carry on the Siege of the Valetta with more vigour. As the Season
advances the harbour of Malta will be more closely blockaded by His Majesty's
Ships, and the distresses of the french Garrizon, already great must increase,
but still they are said to have Corn and Oil for some months longer. I am sorry

it is not in my power to give Your Lordship more Satisfactory Accounts from this Quarter, but I must own that every thing here appears to me to wear a gloomy aspect – and I even suspect that in a short time Their Unfortunate Sicilian Majesties and Royal Family may have no other resource than to take refuge again on board His Majesty's Ship the Vanguard, but as I have been far from Well ever since I left Naples I may perhaps see things in too melancholy a View.

This Court has not receiv'd any Letters from the Court of Vienna since the Month of Nov.r last, which is very Extraordinary.

I have the honor to be
My Lord
Your Lordship's
most obedient and
most humble servant
Wm Hamilton

12) Palermo February 17th 1799

My Lord
Finding that I am still in time to write to Your Lordship by the same Messenger mention'd in my last going from this Court to that of Vienna and London, I have only to add that this Government having little hope of saving the Calabrias is seriously occupied in endeavouring to put this Island in a proper State of defence and particularly the important Fortress of Messina.

This Government not having a thorough Confidence in the Troops that Garrizon Messina and having a strong Suspicion of there being many Jacobine Emissaries there from Naples have with with Lord Nelson's assistance sent off Yesterday in one of the Portugheze Ships of War five hundred chosen Men from this Garrizon to reinforce that of Messina from whence all Suspicious persons are to be sent off immediatly.

The Supplement of a Roman Monitor inclosed will shew Your Lordship that General Mack did realy escape through Rome under the protection of the french General Championet.

I have the honor likewise to inclose the last Palermo Gazette in the Supplement of which Your Lordship will observe that they flatter themselves here greatly with the hope of a powerfull assistance that may come to them from the Emperor of Russia.

I have the honor to be
My Lord

Your Lordship's
most obedient and
most humble Servant
Wm Hamilton

13) Palermo 6th March 1799

My Lord

Letters from Cardinal Ruffo of the 21st of February give hopes that the Calabrias may be recover'd as His Eminency's Army increases daily, and the Tree of Liberty that had been planted (in consequence of an Inflammatory Paper a Copy of which is inclosed N. 1) at Monte Leone, and Polistene, had been already taken down. This Court has also received accounts of very considerable Risings in Puglia, and particularly at Lecce, in favor of Their Sicilian Majesties, and in opposition to the french and New Neapolitan Republic. In Abruzzo The Duke of Andria, One of the most enraged of the Neapolitan Jacobin Nobility has been killed by the people. By fresh Accounts from Naples General Championet and his Army in that Capital are by no means at their ease, the Common people Shewing evident and frequent marks of detestation and it is said that at least five hundred french have been murder'd at Naples, mostly by the Women. The french Army at Naples by all accounts does not exceed Six Thousand men, and the New Neapolitan Army intended to be rais'd by the Republic is to be Twenty Thousand, but We hear that General Championed retards that Operation as much as he can. The Prince Moliterno and the Duke of Angri are gone as Embassador's to Paris to return the thanks of the Neapolitan Republic to the Directory for the Assistance given them in planting the Tree of liberty at Naples.

If there was a chance of any Succour coming from the Emperor of Germany or Russia, in the present State of Affairs, Your Lordships sees there might still be a hope of His Sicilian Majesty's recovering the Kingdom of Naples, and of Tuscany being Saved, but We are totally in the dark on that point.

Three Commissaries are come to this Court from the Maltese Insurgents to Sollicit a further Supply of provisions and Ammunition, which by Lord Nelson's and my support has been immediately granted to them, and as the Maltese were desirous of a demonstration of their fighting under the protection of Great Britain as well as that of the King of Naples It has been agreed that the British Flag shou'd for the future be planted with that of His Sicilian Majesty in all the places recover'd from the french in that Island. A Copy of the Maltese Commissaries Letter to me on that Subject is inclosed N. 2). Capt. Ball of His Majesty's Ship Alexander has likewise by the desire of the Maltese and the consent of His Sicilian Majesty been appointed by Lord Nelson to the Chief Command of the blockade of the Port of Malta and Siege of the Valetta.

N. 3) is a Copy of a Curious Proclamation of General Buonaparte with an intercepted Letter from a french Officer at Alexandria, which Lord Nelson has given me to communicate to Your Lordship, and which His Lord.p received lately from Captain Troubridge.

The whole Confidence of Their Sicilian Majesties and of Their Subjects in this Island, entirely reposes on the protection of His Majesty's Squadron commanded by Lord Nelson, and in gratitude for the important Services He has already render'd to this Island His Lordship has been in form presented with the freedom of this City, an honor never conferred before to any foreigner, except to Louis the 11th King of France.

As yet no good effects have been felt from the expected Cooperation of the powerfull Squadrons of Turks and Russians, consisting of twenty Sail of the Line, and as many Frigates that have hitherto kept constantly to the Harbour of Corfu, whilst Lord Nelson is obliged to divide His Squadron for the very important Services (left to Him alone) of blocking up Alexandria and Malta and of protecting Their Sicilian Majesties and the Great Duke of Tuscany besides occasionally providing Convoys for the Trade of Great Britain so I can assure Your Lordship that not a Ship or Vessel belonging to this Squadron has a moment of repose.

It is probable that in the Course of Next Month Some Ships of this Squadron may be going down to Gibraltar, in which case I mean to profit of the King's Gracious permission to go home to look after my private Affairs, particularly as I am enabled by the Arrival of M.r Charles Lock, to do so without prejudice to His Majesty's Service as I shall put M.r Lock in the Way of carrying on the Correspondence with Your Lordship's Office during my Absence; indeed, My Lord, my health has sufferd very Considerably from so many Years of continued Anxiety of Mind, and my shatter'd Constitution now calls for some little repose and relaxation.

I have the honor to be
My Lord
Your Lordship's
most obedient and
most humble Servant
Wm Hamilton

14) Palermo March 7th 1799

My Lord

After having made up my packet of Yesterday's date for Your Lordship a Vessel arrived from Corfu with a Messenger from Mons.r Ludolaf, His Sicilian Majesty's Minister at Constantinople, who has brought the Treaty of Alliance lately agreed upon between this Court and the Grand Signor. The same Messenger brought from the Russian Ambassador at Constantinople a Packet for Lord Nelson, containing a letter in His Imperial Majesty's own hand writing congratulating His Lordship on His Glorious Victory over the french Squadron on the first of August and desiring His Lordship's acceptance of a Snuff box with His Picture (richly set with large Diamonds) as a small token of His remembrance.

The diligent and Indefatigable M.r Spiridion Forresti His Majesty's Consul at Zante profited of this opportunity of sending me His Dispatches for London under a flying Seal and which I have the honor of inclosing. In the last of those dispatches Your Lordship will have convincing proofs of what Lord Nelson and I have long suspected, that the Court of Russia has further Views in these Seas, than merely to assist the Turks and Cooperate with them and Great Britain in the Common Cause.

Lord Nelson having written fully to Lord Spencer upon the Subject of the Blockade of Malta by the same Vessel (The Dorothea Frigate) that is to Sail this Afternoon with Our Dispatches to Lord S.t Vincent, I need not say more on that subject.

I have the honor of inclosing a Palermo Gazzette in which Your Lordship will see the Account of Lord Nelson's being honor'd with the freedom of this City, as mention'd in my last. M.r Smith's last Letter to me from Constantinople is likewise inclosed.

I have the honor to be
My Lord
Your Lordship's
most obedient and
most humble Servant
Wm Hamilton

P.S. May I beg the favor of Your Lordship to forward the inclosed to the Lords of the Treasury.

15) Palermo March 22ᵈ 1799

My Lord

Last Week We were agreably Surprised by the arrival of Sir Charles Stuart in His Majesty's Frigate Aurora, having with him as many Troops as He cou'd possibly Spare from the Garrizon of Minorca. After his having conferred with Lord Nelson and me I had the honor of presenting the General to Their Sicilian Majesties and all the Royal Family who expressed the greatest gratitude to Sir Charles for the very unexpected aid that He had brought them and which cou'd not fail of contributing greatly to the putting this Island in a State of Security. It was agreed immediately with this Government that Sir Charles Stuart shou'd have the absolute and entire Command of the important Fortress of Messina and with full Powers from His Sicilian Majesty. He went in three hours after his arrival at Palermo on horseback to Messina as he wished to see himself the Nature of this Country. The Transports with the Troops sailed from here the same day for Messina and Yesterday this Court had Notice of the General's and Troops being safely arrived there and to the infinite satisfaction of the inhabitants of Messina. Sir Charles when he left us proposed to return here to make his report to His Sicilian Majesty and then go back to Mahon, leaving the Command of Messina to one of his Officers.

His Majesty's Ships The Zealous, Culloden and Swiftsure are arrived here from Alexandria, Capt. Hood having left the command of the blockade of Alexandria with Sir Sidney Smith. As Lord Nelson makes his report to Lord St. Vincent by the Bull dog Bomb Vessel that is to Sail to Night, it is unnecessary for me to touch upon the Marine Subject. I can not help however expressing to Your Lordship my astonishment and Satisfaction at seeing The King's Ships after such long and hard Services in such good Order, and their Crews in such perfect health and Spirits.

Lord William Stuart in His Majesty's Brig Il Corso returned here yesterday morning fromCorfu. His Lordship had been sent from hence with Lord Nelson's Dispatches to the Turkish and Russian Admirals and with the Chev.r Micheroux having His Sicilian Majesty's Commission to Sollicit the speedy aid of the Turks and Russians to releive Him from His present most distressed Situation. I am assured that the Answer given to His Sicilian Majesty's Minister was most favourable & Satisfactory and as Your Lordship will see by the inclosed packet from M.r Spiridion Forresti (and which He desires me to forward to Your Lordship) that Corfu has Capitulated, it is probable that a portion of the Turkish and Russian Fleets may be already on the Coast of Puglia in the Adriatick.

Cardinal Ruffo's Army in Calabria is increased to the Number of Fourteen Thousand men, and by the last Accounts His Eminency was advanced as far as Cosenza in Upper Calabria. This Court has also received good Accounts from Lecce and the Province of Abruzzo where there are very considerable risings of the people in favor of the Monarchy. This Court has not received any Letters or Dispatches from Vienna since the 14th of November inst., and has not had as yet any account from the Marquis Gallo who was sent to Vienna on an important Commission before Their Sicilian Majesties left Naples.

We hear from Naples that the Lazzaroni continue to manifest their hatred to the french and attachment to His Sicilian Majesty, that the City is ill Supplied with Provisions and that the french are laying heavy Contributions on both Friends and Foes, so that if the promised foreign Succours realy do arrive and the Emperor of Germany shou'd Awake from his lethargy, and with the Assistance of the King's powerfull Squadron under the Command of the truly Brave Lord Nelson, a very favourable Alteration may reasonably be expected to take place, and very soon, in favor of Their Sicilian Majesties and Royal Family. I can assure Your Lordship that Their Sicilian Majesties are most truly sensible of the Obligations They have to The King, and Express Their heartfelt gratitude on every Occasion, particularly as it is from Great Britain alone that They have as yet received any Assistance or Comfort in their heavy Distress.

I have the honor to ber
My Lord
Your Lordship's
most obedient and
most humble Servant
Wm Hamilton

16) Downing Street March 25th 1799

Sir

Your Dispatches to N. 6 of this Year have been received and laid before the King with the exception of N. 5 which by some accident has not yet reached me.

His Majesty is pleased to direct that you should express in His Majesty's Name to Their Sicilian Majesties the lively Interest which His Majesty takes in their present (but as He trusts, temporary) misfortunes, and that you should assure their Majesties that the Events which have happened far from diminishing His Majesty's friendship towards Their Majesties will only make Him more anxious to take every opportunity of proving it by His Conduct.

In conformity to these Dispositions on His Majesty's Part, I am to inform you that His Majesty has determined to ratify the Treaty of Alliance (signed by you at Naples) precisely on the same principle on which it was concluded. The necessity of any, even the smallest change, in the Stipulations of that Treaty arises solely from a mistake (as I imagine) of Monsieur de Circello to whom I have explained the Circumstances and who, as I apprehend, is now fully aware of the difference which exists between the Treaty in the form it was signed at Naples and the principle on which His Majesty was pleased to agree in October last, that it should be concluded, if His Sicilian Majesty on a review of all the Circumstances of his Situation should think Himself under the necessity of commencing Hostilities in Italy.

The proposal of the Court of Naples, and the answer given to it, as is distinctly and repeatedly stated in my dispatch to you N. 6 of last Year, were that the Convention of 1793 should be taken as the Basis of the new Engagements to be concluded between the two Courts, and no Events that have since occurred can have the effect of inducing His Majesty to entertain for a moment the idea of departing from Engagements which under more properous Circumstances as with respect to the Situation of His Ally, His Majesty then authorized His Minister to conclude. If therefore in framing the Treaty of Alliance the Convention of 1793 had been strictly adhered to nothing would have been necessary but a pure and simple Ratification of the Alliance nor would that Ratification have been delayed even for the smallest time. But you will find on a careful examination of the two Instruments, that in the main point of the Engagements to be mutually taken respecting the conclusion of Peace by common consent, and the Guarantee of the respective Dominions of the two Sovereigns a difference is introduced, which altho' it may at first sight appear purely verbal, is of real and substantive effect and tends considerably to change the nature of the intended Stipulations.

In the 2nd Article of the Convention of 1793, the Two Sovereigns guaranteed to each other their Dominions against the Common Enemy and engaged not to lay down their Arms (*unless by common Consent*) without having obtained the entire restitution of the Territories which belonged to them before the War and which the Enemy might take during the War.

Either Sovereign might therefore under that Stipulation make Peace

1st By obtaining for His Ally the Restitution above mentioned, in which case he was free from the obligation of procuring the Consent of His Ally to the Conclusion of Peace; or,

2dly By obtaining the consent of His Ally to make Peace on terms short of the entire Restitution to such Ally of all his Territories as aforesaid, in which Case he was freed from the Obligation of procuring such Restitution.

And, 3dly it followed of necessity that if such Ally were totally disabled of carrying on the War on His Part and from thereby performing his Share of the Obligations of the Alliance his consent to a Treaty short of such entire Restitution can not in good faith be refused and even if not expressly given must under such Circumstances be presumed.

But by the present Treaty the Parts of this Engagement (which by that of 1793 were thus connected and made dependent on each other) are divided in Two Articles, each of which contains a positive and substantive stipulation: the first, that the Two Sovereigns will in no case make Peace but by common Consent – the second, that they will in no case make Peace without obtaining for each other the Restitution of their Dominions as aforesaid.

The mere statement of this difference is sufficient to shew it's importance[109]. I perceive that in adopting it you were misled by the extract which you have sent me of Monsieur de Circello's dispatch; but I am perfectly persuaded that this Minister had no intention of introducing into the Negotiation any Principle differing from that on which he admits that both proposal and the answer were grounded: He did not indeed seem to be aware of the consequence of the Change when I remarked it to him, nor did it seem that his attention had been much directed to it. He has however now undertaken to state the Circumstance to his Court. I have not yet received His Majesty's Commands as to the precise Mode in which the necessary Alteration shou'd be made so as to be most consistent with the Forms to be observed in the Ratification of an Instrument already signed, and as I expect that I shall shortly have an occasion to write to you again by another of His Majesty's Ships I reserve myself to enter more fully into this Point by that Opportunity. All therefore that will be necessary for you to do is to explain in the most distinct and unequivocal manner that it is not the King's intention to depart by the slightest degree (on account of the present difficulties of the King of Naples) from the Principles of the Convention of 1793; and that if the present Treaty had been framed in the same Terms with that Instrument it would instantly have been ratified, and that the King so far from meaning to abandon the King of Naples in his present distress will perform exactly and fully towards Him all the Duties of a faithful and intimate Ally.

Monsieur de Circello has in consequene of his late Instructions renewed with the utmost urgency the Application which he had before been directed to make on the subject of pecuniary Aid. With respect to any Subsidiary Engagements I could only refer him to my former answer, adding, that while it remained uncertain what the Issue of His Majesty's Negotations on the Continent might be, I should only deceive his Court if I were to hold out expectations which His Majesty might be totally unable to fulfill; and I reminded him that when the War was renewed by the King of Naples, it was under an express declaration, as stated to you in my N. 6 abovementioned, that no such Aid could be afforded by His Majesty. But I have been authorized to say that without entering into such Engagements or holding out any further expectation, the King is desirous of enabling His Sicilian Majesty to make such immediate exertions as may lead to the assembling and arming a Force in Calabria to be ready to take advantage of the first Moment when the French may be obliged to withdraw their Force towards the north of Italy and to re-establish His Sicilian Majesty's Government in the Neapolitan Provinces with the least possible delay or confusion. With a view to this object, His Majesty has taken Measures for remitting to Sicily the Sum of One Hundred Thousand Pounds, which will sent in Specie as expeditiously as its distribution amongst the different Ships of War bound for Lisbon and the Mediterranean will allow.

The King does not annex any precise Conditions to this supply, which is to be considered rather as a mark of His Friendship towards His Sicilian Majesty than as a part of any Subsidiary Engagements. But His Majesty entertains the fullest confidence that it will be faithfully applied to the object the most interesting to the Common Cause, and he is desirous of pointing out in a particular Manner the infinite importance of the Service abovementioned, which He considers as being paramount to every other.

It is therefore the King's Pleasure that you should earnestly endeavour to direct the unremitted Attention of His Sicilian Majesty's Ministers to this point, and that you should also converse with Lord Nelson upon it, and desire him to use to the same end all the Influence which is so justly due to His Councils and Suggestions[110].

17) Palermo April 8th 1799

My Lord

As we have no regular Post from this Island to the Continent I can only hazard writing to Your Lordship through the Channel of Lord S.t Vincent when Lord Nelson sends a Vessel down to Gibraltar or through that of Sir Morton Eden when this Court sends a Messenger to that of Vienna. The last Dispatch I had the honor of receiving from Your Lordship was of as old a date as the 23d of November last.

By a Messenger of the Cabinet now going from hence to Vienna I have the honor of informing Your Lordship that General Sir Charles Stuart returned from Messina to this port last Week in the Dolphin Frigate, but as the extraordinary fatigue He had undergone had brought the Gout into both his feet He was not able to come on Shore but wrote me a Letter with the Observations He had made on the Coast of Sicily in His journey from hence to Messina, offering His Opinion as to the putting Messina and this Island in a proper State of defence. The General has left Collonel Stewart with the command of the Fortress of Messina but I find he wou'd not trust any of the Neapolitan Officers or Troops in the Citadel which is Garrizond with the British Troops and Sicilian Militia only.

The King and Queen were so sensible of the important Service that General Stuart had render'd that Their Majesties did him the honor of going on board the Dolphin on the 28th of March to pay him a visit and return Their thanks in person and on the 30th the General sailed with a fair wind to Minorca.

The reports from Cardinal Ruffo's Army in Calabria continue to be favourable as are also those from the provinces of Abruzzo, Lecce and Salerno where there are very considerable Risings in favor of His Sicilian Majesty and former Government. If the promised, and much wished for Russian Succours do but arrive soon at Brindisi or any part of the Coast of Puglia on the Adriatic, it is possible that the risings in favor of the Monarchy will be general. As such an happy Event may now be daily expected Lord Nelson has thought proper (and according to the wish of this Court) to send from hence a powerfull Squadron of five Ships of the Line, some Frigates and a Bomb Vessel under the Command of Captain Troubridge to take possession of the Islanda of Ischia, Procita and Caprea by which the Bay of Naples will be completely blocked up and the french who are detested by the Common people of Naples and are not Numerous in that City will not dare, whilst they are threaten'd with such a formidable Maritime Force, to detach any of their Troops into the Provinces. This Detachment from His Majesty's Squadron under the Command of Lord Nelson Sailed from this Port the 31st of March.

Lord Nelson having received a Letter by Express from M.r Lucas His Majesty's Consul at Tripoli expressing a desire of a Ship or Frigates being sent to Tripoli to oblige the Bey to conform to the Orders of the Porte and not protect the french or hold any Communication with General Buonaparte which he lately has done, Lord Nelson detached immediately His own Ship the Vanguard under the Command of Cap.t Hardy with a very proper and Spirited letter to the Bey of Tripoli, and which had the immediate and desired Effect, for in Eleven days from his departure from Palermo Capt. Hardy brought back the Bey's most Submissive Answer and Assurances in writing and with His Signature of his joining most heartily for the future in the good Cause against the french, having thrown into Slavery all the french at Tripoli and taken possession of three of their Vessels in that Port before the Vanguard left but as Your Lordship will see in Lord Nelson's Dispatches to the Admiralty the particulars of this Transaction and the good consequences that may be expected from it by having shut the door through which General Buonaparte seem'd to be meditating his Escape, I need not enlarge upon this Subject, not being in my department.

Lord Nelson having allowed me the perusal of all the intercepted french Letters and printed papers relative to General Buonaparte and his Army in Egypt (some of which are of as late a date as the 2^d of February) I must own that the Army does not appear to me to be in that distressed Situation as is generally represented, on the Contrary Buonaparte's Plans seem to be all directed towards a permanent Station in that fertile Country and if the printed papers speak the truth He has himself been as far as Suez and settled there the Tariffs for the different Merchandizes coming by the Red Sea; at the same time it must be confessed that the discovery Lord Nelson has recently made of General Buonaparte's intended Negociations with the Porte offering upon certain Conditions to evacuate Egypt, and with the Bey of Tripoli to whom He sent a present of a valuable Diamond, in order to Secure a retreat if Necessary from that Port, does not indicate his feeling himself Secure in his present Situation, however Your Lordship will be able to form a better judgement, when You have Lord Nelson's Dispatches and the intercepted Papers before You.

By the arrival of the Bellerophon from Leghorn a few days ago, and the Letters brought us by Captain Darby from M.r Wyndham there is every reason to beleive that the french are by this time in possession of Leghorn. The Great Duke of Tuscany having determined at all Events to await His fate at Florence M.r Wyndham determin'd also to remain with His Royal Highness, having sent here to my Care on board the Belerophon his most interesting Papers, and valuable Effects. The Bellerophon Sail'd the first of this Month for Minorca, and at present the Marquis Nizza in the Princess Royal is the only Ship in Leghorn Road.

Twenty One Sail of British Merchant Vessels and Victuallers for Lord Nelson's Squadron convoy'd by His Majesty's Frigate the Hyena Capt. Lloyd arrived here three days ago.

Their Sicilian Majesties and Royal Family are in good health and much better Spirits from the prospect of a Speedy and happy change in Their Affairs. Hitherto it has been from Great Britain alone that They have had any Comfort or Assistance, and there is not a day that Their Majesties do not Express Their lively Gratitude for what the King, Our Royal Master, Has done for them

I have the honor to be
My Lord
Your Lordship's

most obedient and
most humble Servant
Wm Hamilton

P.S. Having told Lord Nelson that I had mention'd to Your Lordship the Packet of Letters and Printed papers intercepted in Egypt by Captain Foote of the Sea Horse[111], His Lordship has been so kind as to allow me to transmit to Your Lordship the whole Packet just as He received it.

18) Palermo 9th of April 1799

My Lord
The Minerva Frigate returned here the day before Yesterday from Malta and brought Letters from Captain Ball to Lord Nelson. The Operations of the Islanders against the Valette go on slowly as they are ill fed an (*sic*) ill cloathed and have had a Sickness amongst them, which Communicated to Cap.t Ball's Ship, but by the Captains timely care and having errected an Hospital on Shore, although twenty seven of the Crew of the Alexander were attacked by the disorder only two have died and the Companies of all His Majesty's Ships blocking up Malta, are now in perfect health; it does not appear probable that the Fortess's of the Valette will Surrender, untill obliged by a force of Regular Troops. The Appearance of the expected Three Thousand Russian Grenadiers will probably decide the business immediatly, as the french Garrizon of the Valette is by no means at it's ease, being Sickly and very short of Provisions, but as they are flatter'd with the hope of this Island falling soon into the hands of the french they will naturally hold out as long as they can.

Lord William Stuart, in His Majesty's armed Brig Il Corso, returned yesterday evening from the Bay of Naples with Letters from Captain Troubridge to Lord Nelson informing His Lordship that He had taken possession, in the Name of His Sicilian Majesty, of the Islands of Ischia, Procita and Caprea; that the Inhabitants of those Islands (most of which were loyal to His Sicilian Majesty) had very readily assisted him in cutting down the Trees of liberty and giving into his hands the most Notorious Jacobins employ'd by the french Government at Naples in those Islands, the most conspicuous of which Captain Troubridge had Secured on board the Culloden, and the rest are Confined in the Castle of Ischia. His Sicilian Majesty at the request of Captain Troubridge sends to day a Judge from hence with Orders that the most guilty of the Rebels shou'd be immediatly tried and Executed.

There were no french Troops in those Islands. Capt. Troubridge in order to recover some of his Sailors that were cast away in a boat near Naples, Sent an Officer with a Flag of Truce to General Macdonald at Naples. The report of that Officer, who was treated with the greatest politeness, is, that from what he cou'd learn there were not more than two Thousand french at Naples, that they were in possession of all the Castles, and that the Jacobin Neapolitan Army there consisted of about twenty thousand men, that the Lazaroni, or common people, continued to detest the french and express their love and Loyalty on every occasion for Their Sovereign. The french have already extorted from Naples Contributions amounting in Money to Six Million and a half Ducats. The reports Capt. Troubridge has received from Gaeta are very favourable, the french dare not stir out of that Garrizon, as a part of a very Considerable Army that has been raised in favor of the Monarchy in Abruzzo by an outlaw'd Priest that goes by the name of the Gran Diavolo (a Notorious Murderer and who wishes to obtain a Pardon by his Services)[112] is at the Gate of Gaeta. At the same time the Risings at Salerno in favor of the Ancient Government go on Successfully; of One thousand five hundred french that have been sent from Naples against that body, only three hundred (and most of them wounded) are returned to Naples. The News from the Army of Cardinal Ruffo in Calabria continue likewise to be very good, in consequence of which Capt. Troubridge has sent a Ship to Salerno, and an other to Gaeta in order if possible to keep up a Communication with the well disposed in those parts.

By desire of Capt. Troubridge this Government is sending a quantity of Flour and provisions for the Island of Ischia, Procita and Caprea, that are returned to their Allegiance, and must be supplied from hence. The population of Ischia is about twenty Thousand Souls. The City of Naples depends much on the Sea for it's daily Provision and must soon be greatly distressed by the Bay being blocked up compleatly by His Majesty's Ships. The french and Neapolitan Republic have declared War against the Emperor of Germany and seized all the Vessels with Imperial Colours in the Mole of Naples.

Your Lordship may imagine what a favorable moment this wou'd be for a Counter-revolution at Naples and what a happy Circumstance it will be, if the the Nine thousand promised Russian Troops shou'd arrive soon and be landed on the Coast of Puglia, at Brindisi, Barri, or Manfredonia, and which We have every reason to Expect, Corfu having Surrender'd.

I am happy that by the Neapolitan Messenger's having been detain'd I am able to send Your Lordship this further Important Intelligence.

I have the honor to be

My Lord

Your Lordship's

most obedient and
most humble Servant
Wm Hamilton

19) Palermo April 13th 1799

My Lord

The Europa going down from hence with a Convoy to Gibraltar I seize the
opportunity of transmitting to Your Lordship through the Channel of Lord
S.t Vincent Duplicates of my last two Numbers, which I sent to Vienna by
a Neapolitan Messenger under Cover of Sir Morton Eden I have only to add
that this morning the S.t Leone Armed Brig arrived from the Bay of Naples
with Letters from Captain Troubridge to Lord Nelson dated the 10th instant
by which I see with pleasure that every thing goes on well. Captain
Troubridge has taken possession of all the Islands, Ischia, Procita Caprea etc.
and where the abominable french Trees of liberty have been cut down and
the Flags of His Sicilian Majesty are now flying.

There is the greatest appearance of Loyalty and attachment to the Sovereigns among the people Every where; Cardinal Ruffo's Army from Calabria
now augmented to near thirty Thousand men is advancing to join an other
large body of Royalists assembled near Salerno, and Capt. Troubridge has
sent a Ship into the Bay of Salerno and has already established a Correspondence with the Cardinal. He has likewise sent a Vessel to Gaeta to endeavour to communicate with the insurgents in favor of Royalty from the
Province of Abruzzo commanded by the Outlaw'd Priest called the Gran
Diavolo, said to be in that Neighbourhood.

General Macdonald sent One thousand five hundred men against the
Insurgents of Salerno only three hundred of which are returned to Naples,
and most of them Wounded.

General Macdonald has only about two Thousand five hundred french
Troops at Naples, and they keep possession of all the Castles. The people continue to detest them and call aloud for their beloved Sovereign. If the Russians arrive soon I have no doubt but that Their Sicilian Majesties might be
replaced on Their Throne of Naples as certainly at this moment the appearances are most favorable.

Some Swiss Officers escaped from Naples arrived here this morning in His
Majesty's Brig and have assured me that News has been received at Naples
of the french being in Possession of Tuscany & Porto Ferraio, and that the
Great Duke and His Family were gone to Vienna, That the Pope had been
sent by the french to Besançon.

I have the honor to be
My Lord
Your Lordship's
most obedient and
most humble Servant
Wm Hamilton

20) Palermo April 17th 1799

My Lord
I had the honor of receiving Your Lordship's Letters of the 28th of Nov.r last, with a Congratulory Letter inclosed from His Majesty to the King of Naples on the happy delivery of the Hereditary Princess, and the Birth of a Princess, which Letter I had the honor of presenting to His Sicilian Majesty the day before Yesterday in the Usual form.

I have nothing to add since my last Dispatch but that His Majesty's Frigate The Hyena arrived here two days ago from Malta and brought me a Letter from Capt. Ball of His Majesty's Ship Alexander and as that Letter paints so well the present miserable Situation of that Island and Fortress I can not do better than to forward the Letter itself to Your Lordship with two others from Malta, One directed to His Majesty and the other to Your Lordship.

I have the honor to be
My Lord
Your Lordship's
most obedient and
most humble Servant
Wm Hamilton

21) Palermo April 29th 1799

My Lord
I had the honor of receiving last Week by the Lord St. Vincent Cutter Your Lordship's Dispatch of the 25th of March N. 1) The Contents of which having been immediat

ly communicated by me to Their Sicilian Majesties and General Acton afforded Their Majesties and Their Minister more Consolation than They had yet experienced under Their heavy Misfortunes, and Their Majesties desired me to express through the channel of Your Lordship Their heart felt gratitude to The King and His Ministry for the constant marks of Friendship and powerfull Aid His Majesty has been pleased to afford them whilst hitherto They seem to have been abandoned by all Their Friends and near Connections. The Pecuniary Supply which Your Lord.p says His Majesty has commanded to be remitted to Sicily, being much wanted, seem'd to give great Satisfaction to Their Sicilian Majesties, and the more so as I had never been authorized to give Them the smallest hope of any such Aid[113].

Your Lordship will certainly be told by the Marquis Circello to what degree Their Sicilian Majesties were affected by this fresh mark of the King's Friendship towards Them, and Their Majesties repeat it to me daily.

I did not fail to explain in the most distinct and Unequivocal manner that it was not the King's Intention to depart in the slightest degree from the Principles of the Convention of 1793 and that if the late Treaty of Alliance Sign'd by The Marquis de Gallo and me, at Naples in December last, had been formed in the same terms with that Instruction it wou'd have been ratified immediatly. Your Lordship having pointed out very clearly the difference in the wording of some Articles of these Treaties, Their Sicilian Majesties and General Acton were sensible of it, and, as They wish The Treaty to be ratified as soon as possible, are impatiently waiting for it, with any Alteration that The King may have thought proper to make as They had an entire Confidence in His Majesty's Friendship. It was certainly much against my inclination that I allowed of any variation from the former Treaty, but as I had the honor to inform Your Lordship at the time, it was an extract of a Letter from the Marquis Circello to the Marquis Gallo that induced me to acquiesce to that deviation.

A large Swedish Ship arrivd here three days ago from Leghorn having on board M.r Wyndham, The Neapolitan Russian and Portugheze Ministers at the late Court of Tuscany, as also The Great Dukes Secretaries of State Messieurs Serrati and Manfredini. All the french and Corsican Emigrants under the protection and pay of Great Britain, that resided in Tuscany, are likewise come to Palermo for refuge, so that my Bills on the Treasury for their maintenance will be considerably increased, and I have the greatest Difficulty in getting permission of this Government for any of the french Emigrants to come on Shore, that Nation being universally detested in this Island. However I hope that I shall be able to procure some place in the neighbourhood of this city for their present Security. I can assure Your Lordship that I have had more trouble with the Emigrants both at Naples and here than can be Expressed but I have had patience, and acted I hope with a proper humanity towards these Unfortunate people, and certain it is that without the protection and Subsistance so generously afforded them by Great Britain they wou'd have been driven long ago into the utmost State of misery and despair; most, but not all of them, are truly sensible of it and express their Gratitude on every occasion.

The late Revolution in Tuscany is a fresh proof of the bad faith of the french Directory, but as M.r Wyndham's Dispatches will give Your Lordship authentic information on that Subject it is unnecessary for me to touch upon that Subject.

Yesterday His Majesty's Frigate The Emerald arrived here from Minorca and brought Collonel Graham who is to take the Command of the Citadel of Messina in lieu of Collonel Stewart, who returns to Maiorca. I have had the honor of presenting the Collonel, my Nephew, to their Sicilian Majesties who were pleased to receive him very Graciously.

Last Night a Neapolitan Corvette brought Letters from Capt. Troubridge to Lord Nelson, by which it appears that the french Troops were quitting the City of Naples with the utmost expedition, in consequence, as it was said at Naples, of their having received the News of the Emperor's Army having beaten completely the french near Verona and the Adige. The same News M.r Wyndham had heard at Leghorn. Unless the french mean to evacuate entirely the Kingdom of Naples, They will probably make their Stand at Capua, but as the Cardinal Ruffo is advancing from Cosenza with his Army of thirty thousand Men, to join a large body of Royalists at Salerno (Capt. Hood of the Zealous having succeeded in driving the Enemy out of Salerno and garizond that City with his Marines) and on the other side of Naples the outlaw'Priest called the Gran Diavolo has a very considerable body of Troops near Gaeta and has promised Captain Troubridge(having been on board the Culloden) to take the City of Gaeta immediatly, there is every reason to expect to hear from one moment to another of a Counter Revolution at Naples in favor of His Sicilian Majesty.

The Lazaroni, or common people of Naples, are loyal to a man, and the Jacobin Neapolitan Leaders have no Confidence in their Civic Guard, many of whom are suspected to be still inclined to Monarchy. Shou'd the Emperor's Army in Italy continue Successful, there can be very little doubt but that the french, who are Universally hated, will in a very short time be driven out of Italy.

Lord Nelson and I expect daily to hear from Captain Troubridge that it is thought Necessary for His Sicilian Majesty to shew Himself in the Bay of Naples; if so it is probable that his Sicilian Majesty's Standard will be hoisted again on board the Vanguard. It wou'd be glorious indeed if Their Sicilian Majesties cou'd be replaced on Their Throne of Naples without any other foreign Aid than that of Great Britain, and as We have no certain accounts of the Russian Troops, such an happy Event may take place.

I have the honor to be

My Lord
Your Lordship's
most obedient and
most humble Servant
Wm Hamilton

22) Palermo April 30th 1799

My Lord
As M.r Wyndham's Messenger has been detain'd on account of His Sicilian Majesty's Letters for England not being ready I have the opportunity of
sending to Your Lordship the inclosed Moniteurs and curious printed papers
which Captain Troubridge has got from Naples and sent to Lord Nelson and
have been communicated to this Court.
I have the honor to be
My Lord
Your Lordship's
most obedient and
most humble Servant
Wm Hamilton

23) Palermo May 10th 1799

My Lord
I profit of the Opportunity of His Majesty's Ship The Harleem that sails
from hence this day for Gibraltar to inform Your Lordship that the News We
receive from Genoa relative to the Operations of the Austrian Armies, both in
Italy and Germany, continues to be most brilliant, and every where successfull.
The inclosed Gazette published here by Authority contains the particulars of
the great News already received; and as by Letters received yesterday from
Capt. Troubridge from the Bay of Naples, in which he says the french were
plundering and evacuating Naples, it is natural to imagine that they have been
called for to oppose the progress of the Imperial Army in Italy. We have had
reports of Austrian and Russian Troops having driven the french out of Tuscany and taken possession of Leghorn, but such reports want confirmation.
As we have no accounts of the body of Russian Troops that have been
promised to His Sicilian Majesty and were expected to land in Puglia, until
they arrive, His Majesty's Ships can do no more than continue to block up
the Bay of Naples and protect the Royalists which are very Numerous in the

Islands and on the Coast of Sorrento and Salerno. Shou'd the french retire from the Neapolitan and Roman States it is most probable that a Counter revolution wou'd take place immediatly at Naples, The populace being quite ripe for it, and as We are informed have actually marked the Houses of the principal Jacobins for destruction.

His Majesty's Ship the Lion Capt. Dixon returned here from Alexandria the day before yesterday, and as I hear Sir Sidney Smith having been called off for some other Service, several of the french Frigates have escaped from that Port and are supposed to be gone to Toulon or Ancona.

The inclosed periodical printed papers from Naples will shew Your Lordship how very artfully the french endeavour to blind the Neapolitans with respect to the late Successes of the Emperor's Army in Germany and Italy.

I have the honor to be
My Lord
Your Lordship's
most obedient and
most humble Servant
Wm Hamilton

24) Palermo June 5ᵗʰ 1799

My Lord
As no Messenger has been sent lately from this Court to Vienna and we have no establish'd Post to the Continent and the french and Spanish Fleets being in the Mediterranean, all communication with Great Britain has become more difficult than ever. Lord Nelson has assembled in this Bay most of the Ships of His Majesty's Squadron under His L.p's Command, where I suppose they will remain until His Lordship shall have some tidings of the Enemy's Fleet from Lord S.t Vincent. Unfortunately also the last Neapolitan Messenger from Vienna having been chased by a Vessel in the Adriatic (supposed to have been an Enemy altho' it proved to be a friend) threw all the packets of Letters overboard and I fear that some of Your Lordship's Letters to me, sent to Sir Morton Eden, may have been of the Number.

It is amazing with what amazing expedition Lord Nelson collected his force here consisting (including three of the Portugheze Ships) of Eleven Sail of the Line, besides the Harleem, The Lion and several Frigates, having left the Sea Horse, a Bomb ketch and several Armed Vessels to protect The Islands in the Bay of Naples that continue loyal to Their Sovereign. The Alexander & Goliath have also been sent back to continue the Blockade of Malta.

Yesterday, The King's Birth Day was celebrated to the hearts content of all His Majesty's good and loyal Subjects and indeed to the Satisfaction of every well thinking Neapolitan or Sicilian at Palermo. I had the honor of having Lord Nelson and all the principal Officers of His Lordship's Venerable Squadron at my Table to dine and drink the Healths of His Majesty and all The Royal Family (whom God may long preserve) and His Sicilian Majesty having heard that Lord Nelson intended to give a Fete and Ball in the Evening on board The Vanguard in honor of the Day desired as a particular favor of His Lordship to permit Him as a public demonstration of His Gratitude and attachment to the King to give such a Fete and Illuminations at the Royal Palace and to which His Majesty invited all the King's Subjects of distinction and every Officer of the Squadron whose duty did not require their particular attendance on board of their Ships. Nothing cou'd exceed the brilliancy of the Fete nor the abundance of refreshments except the very particular attentions that Their Sicilian Majesties and Royal Family themselves were pleased to Shew to every one of Their British Guests.

I can not resist the pleasure of inclosing to Your Lordship for His Majesty's perusal the joint Letter of the Queen and Young Royal Family with which Lady Hamilton was honourd Yesterday just before our Dinner.

The Royal Salute of Such a respectable Squadron as that of His Majesty drawn up in Line of Battle and decked with Colours opposite to this City afforded such a Sight as was never seen or will ever be forgotten at Palermo.

The french have Evacuated the Cities of Rome and Naples and the Presidia of Tuscany, probably owing to the great and continued Successes of the Imperial Troops, Austrians and Russians in Italy. Four hundred french Troops have however remained in the Castle of S.t Elmo at Naples. The Royal Party there is certainly very Numerous and the Republican party Shew every mark of the greatest Apprehension Several of their Chiefs having fled and there can be no doubt of their Submitting to their lawfull Sovereign shou'd even a Small (but regular) land force approach the City.

Two Russian Frigates have landed a few men at Brindisi in Puglia, but We have not any acc.t of the Nine Thousand Auxiliary Russian Troops promised to the King of Naples by the Court of Russia, nor of the three thousand Grenadiers intended for the Garrizon of the Fortress of Malta.

I can not think of profiting of His Majesty's Gracious permission to return home, whilst I feel my presence here Necessary for His Majesty's Service, altho I am much worn and my private affairs in South Wales are suffering by my long absence. The Satisfaction I feel in doing to the utmost of my Ability my duty to the King and my Country at such a Critical Moment, amply repays me for all personal inconveniencies.

I have the honor to be

My Lord
Your Lordship's
most obedient and
most humble Servant
Wm Hamilton

25) Downing Street June 6th 1799

Sir,

Your Dispatches marked N. 14, 15, 17 & 18 were at length received here on the 30th of last Month with the Intelligence of the Evacuation of Naples by the French Army: an Event upon which you will not fail to offer to their Sicilian Majesties the warmest Compliments of Congratulation in His Majesty's Name.

The present will be accompanied by the Ratification of the Treaty which has been executed in the Spirit & Terms of the Convention of 1793.

The Motives which determined His Majesty to adhere to the Form of the original Treaty, and to reject the Variation which appeared to have been inadvertently introduced into it, have been already detailed to You in My Dispatch of March 25:th. It appears from Yours that the Justice of the Distinctions there stated has been admitted by His Siclian Majesty, & that at the same Time, great Impatience & Anxiety had been expressed for the Arrival of the Treaty in any Form, or with any Alteration which His Majesty might think fit to introduce. The Ratification has therefore been expedited in its present Form; and You are directed to assure His Sicilian Majesty, that as it is concluded in the Terms of the Treaty of 1793, so it will be acted upon in the same Spirit, & with the same good Faith and good Will which has distinguished His Majesty's Conduct towards all His Allies.

A Representation has been made by the Marquis de Circello of the Inconvenience which would arise from a strict Construction of the Casus foederis, as applied to the present Situation of Spain accompanied with a Request that an additional Article should be inserted in which the Case of Spain as it stands at present should be excepted. The Fairness of M. de Circello's Demand was admitted in so far as regards the present War only and it was therefore agreed that You should at the Time of exchanging the Ratifications deliver in a formal Declaration in His Majesty's Name, that the Treaty is to be constructed as not applying to the case of Spain, in the present War, but that if at any time after the Conclusion of Peace a War should arise between His Majesty & the King of Spain by the Aggression of the latter, the Treaty should then have its full Force & Effect.

26) Downing Street June 11th 1799

Sir,

The King having been pleased, upon the Ratification of the Treaty of Alliance between the Two Courts, to order that a Snuffbox with His Majesty's Picture enriched with Diamonds should be given to the Plenipotentiary who signed the Treaty with You, I am to desire that You will present to that Minister, in His Majesty's Name, the Box which I now send to You for that purpose.

His Majesty has also been pleased, as a particular mark of His Satisfaction with the Conduct of Monsieur de Cercello, His Sicilian Majesty's Minister at this Court, to direct a similar present of a Snuffbox and Picture to be made to Him on this Occasion.

His Majesty has also been pleased to Order the usual present of £ 500 for the Neapolitan Department for Foreign Affairs, which Sum You are Authorized to pay on the exchange of the Ratifications.

27) Palermo June 16th 1799

My Lord

The Royalist Army under the Command of Cardinal Ruffo from Calabria, joined by about five hundred Russians, and Seventy Turks, from on board the Russian and Turkish Frigates at Brindisi, having Succeeded in making themselves Masters of all the Provinces on the Adriatic, and being advanced within twelve Miles of Naples whilst the Outlaw'd Priest, called the Grand Diavolo with his Army from Abruzzo has cut off all Communication between Rome and Naples, and taken possession of the high grounds, even within a mile of the City, and destroy'd the Acqueducts that supplied Naples with Water, His Sicilian Majesty requested of Lord Nelson to present Himself before Naples with the whole of the Squadron under His Lordship's command and to take with him The Hereditary Prince of the Two Sicilies on board the Foudroyant, in which Ship his Lordship's Flag is now flying, by which His Majesty flatterd Himself that the General attack of the City, intended to take place on the 17th instant cou'd not fail of Success. Lord Nelson having consented to shew at least for a short time His Majesty's Squadron in the Bay of Naples at so interesting a moment, altho' He cou'd not venture the risking any of His Majesty's Ships to be damaged whilst so formidable a Marine Force of the Enemy was in the Mediterranean, Two thousand regular Troops with a small train of Artillery were embarked on board His Majesty's Ships and the Hereditary Prince of the Two Sicilies went also on board The

Foudroyant on Thursday last the 14th inst. and I had the honor, at the particular request of The King of Naples, signified to me in writing by General Acton, to accompany His Royal Highness on this Expedition.

The Squadron set Sail the same morning with a fresh and favorable Wind for Naples, and We had before the Evening performed a third part of the Voyage, when His Majesty's Ships the Belerophon and Powerfull join'd Us and brought Letters from Lord Keith to Lord Nelson dated the 7th of June in which Lord Keith informs Lord Nelson that Lord S.t Vincent had been obliged to return to Minorca on account of the bad State of his health, that he, (Lord Keith), with the Fleet now under His Command had looked into Toulon where there were only two french Ships of the Line refitting, and some of the Ships taken from Venice, that having had intelligence that the french Fleet from Brest had only remaind six days in that Harbour and was gone towards Genoa He had follow'd them as far as Monaco, and that some of the Frigates of His Fleet had actually been near enough to ascertain their Number to be Twenty two Sail of the Line and many Brigs, that His Lordship not thinking that it woud be prudent for him to proceed further to leave Minorca exposed He had determind to send the Powerfull and Belerophon to reinforce Lord Nelson's Squadron and bring him the Intelligence of the Enemy's Fleet which was between Monaco and Cape del Mell[114] Steering Eastward on the 7th of June.

Lord Nelson having receiv'd this important Intelligence and communicated it to the Hereditary Prince of the two Sicilies, it was decided that it wou'd not be proper to proceed further and the Squadron tacked about instantly and came again to an Anchor in this Bay Yesterday opposite to the City. The Hereditary Prince, The Troops and Artillery were immediatly disembarked, and Orders were given for the King's Squadron to prepare for Sea directly, and most probably it will be at Sea Tomorrow.

Lord Nelson's Intentions can not be known, but Common Sense must Suppose that a Squadron very inferiour to that of the Enemy will not go in Search of that Enemy. Shoud the Russian Squadron from Corfù expected hourly at Messina fortunately arrive and join the King's Squadron under Lord Nelson's Command then indeed Their combined force wou'd be equal to any thing the french Republic cou'd oppose to them in these Seas.

Considering that the Maritime Force of Great Britain must naturally be increasing daily in the Mediterranean, I can not help thinking that the french Squadron will not venture to proceed so far as Naples, Sicily or Malta, but profit of the present moment, whilst the Squadrons of the King's Fleet are employed in protecting Minorca, The two Sicilies and Malta to compleat their Rapines in Italy by the Plunder of Genoa, Tuscany and Leghorn and return, with the Booty in their Ships, into the Port of Toulon. I beg Your Lordship to excuse the liberty I take in having troubled you with my Conjectures.

Yesterday General Acton shew'd me a Letter from The Chevr. Micheroux dated from Brindisi the 7th of June in which he says "This moment We have received the positive Account of Ancona's having been taken by Assault by the Russian Squadron, and that all the Jews in that City had been put to death."[115]

I find this Government has every reason to beleive that the intended attack upon the City of Naples by the Royalists, without and within, the City, and protected by the King's Frigate, the Sea Horse with the Armed Brigs, Bomb Vessels and Gun Boats left in the Bay of Naples by Capt. Troubridge, will still be attended with Success, but the appearance of Lord Nelson in the Bay of Naples wou'd have surely put it beyond all doubt.

Every thing that Collonel Graham has requested from this Government through my Channel in order to put the Citadel of Messina in the best State of defence has been immediatly granted, and I am happy to assure Your Lordship that this able and diligent Officer is already greatly beloved and respected in this Country.

I have the honor to be
My Lord
Your Lordship's
most obedient and
most humble Servant
Wm Hamilton

28) To The Right Honble. Lord Keith KB.   Foudroyant Naples Bay
                                                  June 27th 1799

My Dear Lord
Having detailed my proceedings to the 16th of June by the Telegraph Brig I have now to go on with my movements on the 17th the Alexander and Goliath joined me off Malta leaving to look out in that Quarter three Sloops of War[116] the Force with me was now 15 Sail of Two decked Ships English and three Portuguese with a Fire Ship and Cutter on the 20th the Swallow Portugese Corvette brought me your Lordships dispatches of the 17th acquainting me with the near approach of the Squadron under Sir Alan Gardiner and that Lord Keith was going in Search of the French Fleet as I had now no prospect of being in a Situation to go in Search of the Enemys Fleet which at least is 25 Sail of the line and might be reinforced with two Venet-

ian Ships altho' I was firmly resolved they should not pass me without a Battle which would so Cripple them that they might be unable to proceed on any distant Service. I determined to offer myself for the Service of Naples where I knew the French Fleet intended going, with this Determination I parted for Palermo and on the 21ˢᵗ I went on Shore for two Hours saw his Majesty and General Acton who repeated to me what the General had wrote (but which I had not received) to request that I would instantly go into the Bay of Naples to endeavour to bring His Sicilian Majestys affairs in that City to a happy Conclusion. I lost not one moment in Complying with the request and Arrived in the Bay of Naples on the 24ᵗʰ where I saw a Flag of Truce Flying on Board His Majestys Ship Seahorse Capt. Foote and also on the Castles Ovo and Novo having on the passage received letters informing that an infamous Armistice was entered into with the Rebels in those Castles to which Capt. Foote had put his Name I instantly made the Signal to annul the Truce being determined never to give my Approbation to any Terms with Rebels but that of unconditional Submission the Fleet was anchored in close line of battle NW by N and NE by S from the Mole Head 17 Miles Distant flanked by 2 Gun and Mortar Boats which I recalled from Procida – I sent Capts. Troubridge and Ball instantly to the Cardinal Vicar General to represent to His Eminence my Opinion of the Infamous Terms entered into with the Rebels and also Two Papers which I enclose, His Eminence said that he would send no papers that if I pleased I might break the Armistice for that he was tired of His Situation, Captain Troubridge then asked his Eminence this plain Question, if Lord Nelson breaks the Armistice will your Eminence assist him in his attack on the Castles His Answer was clear I will neither assist him with Men or Guns, after much Communication His Eminence desired to come on Board to speak with me on His Situation, I used every argument in my Power to convince him that the Treaty and Armistice was at an End by the Arrival of the Fleet, but an Admiral is no match in talking with a Cardinal I therefore gave him my Opinion in Writing Right Rear Admiral Lord Nelson who arrived in the Bay of Naples on the 24ᵗʰ June with the British Fleet found a Treaty entered into with the Rebels which he is of Opinion ought not to be carried into Execution without the Approbation of His Sicilian Majesty – Earl S.t Vincent – 30ᵗʰ June 1799

Lord Keith under this Opinion the Rebels came out of the Castles which was instantly occupied by the Marines of the Squadron – On the 27ᵗʰ Captains Troubridge and Ball with 1300 Men landed from the Ships united with 500 Russians and a body of Royalists half of whose Officers are, I have every reason to believe, Rebels – Cowards they have already proved themselves. Our Batterys are Open on St. Elmo and a few Days will I hope reduce it.

The Alexander and another are just going to resume their Station off Malta which I am confident will very soon Surrender now all Hopes of Relief are cut off. I shall not fail to keep up a constant communication with your Lordship and Have the Honor to be with the Greatest Respect

Your most Obedient

Faithfull Servant

(signed) Nelson

NB. Carraciolo (*sic*) was Executed on Board His Sicilian Majestys Ship Minerva on the 29th June 1799

29) Captain Foote's Justification for Signing the Infamous Treaty with the French and Rebels at Naples
To Lord Nelson 27 June 1799

I shall not take any Notice of the various letters which I received from the Cardinal at Procida they prove how very little he knew about the Force that was under my Orders or what is possible to be done by a few small Ships of War and that he kept Advancing without any fixed Plan, or Project, trusting entirely to the Chapter of Accidents.

On the 9th of June I received a Letter from the Cardinal in which he mention'd that on the 13th and 14th he should be at the Tour del Greco and he gave me some Signals by which I was to know when the Royal Army reached that Place and I promised to give him all the Assistance in my power by Sea Accordingly on the 13th I stood into the Bay & perceived that the Coast from Portici to Castelamare was in a State of Insurrection but saw no Signals.

Innumerable requests were made to me for Assistance but no one could tell me for Certain where the Cardinal was I supplied the Chief of the Tour del Greco with Powder musquet Balls & Cannister, and Observing the French and Neapolitan Republican Colours flying on the Fort of Granatelli, I immediately stood for it (having the Neapolitan Frigate Sirena and two Gun Boats with me) this Fort is close to Portici, and had in it upwards of two hundred Men who kept up a constant Fire on a party of Royalists who were in the Kings Palace and which they returned from One Field piece and small Arms when within Musquet Shot of this Fort I fired a few Shot and the Tri Coloured Flags were struck and the Royalists rushed in putting the whole Garrison to the Sword Shortly after a certain D. Constantino de Filippis came on board the Seahorse and informed me that he Commanded about 4000 Royalists that those at Portici were part of them and that he would attack Villena the next day when I promised to assist him by Sea. The Cardinal I have since learnt instead of being at his Rendezvous was at Nola for as to any direct Information I had none not receiving any Letter from him between the 9th and 17th of this Month.

Some Country people informed me that the Republicans had a Camp of 800 Infantry and and 120 Cavalry near the Tour dell Annunciato (*sic*) which was protected on the sea side by ten Gun Boats and two Mortar Boats. I had written to the Count de Thurn for three Galleys which were not much wanted at Procida but instead of their coming I only received excuses about the Weather which no doubt was at one time very threatening but it afterwards cleared up which induced me to write a positive Order and the Galleys were sent; but the Count de Thurn at the same time informed me that his Instructions were quite independent of my Orders and that he could not receive any but from His Sovreign or those who were his Superiors, reference may be had to my letters on this Subject but I do not wish it to be renewed as I am perfectly Satisfied the Count meant no insult to me, and that the evil originated in his having secret Instructions, which if I had not acted with caution might (in Consequence of my being directed to consider all the Neapolitan Ships and Vessels as under my Orders) have been attended with very fatal Consequences.

On the Evening of the 13th the Cardinals Troops (or rather the Russians) took the Fort of Villena and the Pont di Maddalena during which time Carracciolo Gun Boats annoyed them a good deal the Weather preventing my approaching sufficiently close with the Frigates but had the Galleys been with me I should have taken some of them or forced them to retreat.

On the 14th the weather was bad and it was not until the 15th (the Day the Galleys joined me) that I could venture so deep into the Bay as the Forts of Revigliano and Castelamare which Capitulated with me on terms mentioned in my letter Book which I considered of the utmost Consequence, for if their Garrisons and Friends amounting to about 1000 Men had availed themselves of the Opportunity to concert with the Republicans at annunciato (*sic*)[117] and make an attack on the Cardinals Rear, his enterprize must have inevitably failed.

On the 17th I informed the Cardinal that I should immediately join the Gun Boats & Mortar Boats at Piedi Grota with a view of attacking Castell del Uovo and on the 18th I sent Captn. Oswald (of the Perseus) with a Letter to the Commandant of that Fort in the Hopes of its opening a way to a Negociation.

On the Night of the 17th I had sent an Officer to the Cardinal who told him that the Rebels and the French but particularly the latter had refused to capitulate to an Ecclesiastic, that his Force was not sufficient to reduce determined and Obstinate People and that he wished me to try what I could do with them. I made the Cardinal acquainted with the very insolent verbal

Answer which I received from the Commandant of Castell del Uovo and told his Eminence it was my Intention to attack it by every means in my Power to which I received the following Answer "that it was no longer time to hearken to Capitulation but that it became necessary to think seriously of attacking Fort St. Elmo." The next day (the 19th) to my great Surprise I had a letter from the Cardinal requesting me to cease hostilities, and not to renew them whilst the Flags of Truce were flying as a Negociation had taken place: the same Night I sent an Officer to the Cardinal to acquaint him that the British were not accustomed to to grant so long a Suspension of Arms and that as my Sovereign was a principal Ally of the King of the two Sicilies I claimed a right to be made acquainted with wha as going on and the answer I received from His Eminence was that the Cavalier de Micheroux conducted the Treaty and that he had sent him my letter that he might inform me what was going on but not receiving a line from this Gentleman I informed the Cardinal that I thought nothing could be more prejudicial of the Interests of His Sicilian Majesty than the having such a Multiplicity of Chiefs and that I knew no other man than his Eminence to be Specially Charged with the Interest of the King of Naples & that I could act with no other.

The Cardinal then told the Officer whom I had sent that he knew nothing of what was going on, that he stood in great need of the Russians that he would not give them the least ground to Complain and that it was the Russians who Conducted the Treaty.

On the 19th I received a project of Capitulation already signed by the Cardinal and the Chief of the Russians with a request that I would put my name to it, in answer I informed the Cardinal I had done so because I considered him as the Confidential Agent of his Sicilian Majesty and that some Advantage would result from the Capitulation otherwise I would not have signed it, but that I could not say I approved of such a manner of treating and that I could not be answerable for its Consequences, I also made some Observations relative to St. Elmo's Capitulating which may be seen in my Letter Book. At length on the 22nd I received a letter from the Chevalier de Micheroux with the Capitulation in form already signed by the Cardinal and the Chief of the Russians I replied to the Chevalier de Micheroux that I had signed where he had pointed out but that I protested against every thing that could be in the least contrary to the rights & Honor of my Sovereign & and the British Nation. I signed this Capitulation least on a reverse of Fortune or the Arrival of the Enemys Fleet it might be asserted that my refusal was the cause of such Misfortunes as might occur and because I considered that the Cardinal was acquainted with the Will and intention of his Sovereign and that the Count de Thurn had told me that the Chevalier de Micheroux was authorised to act in a Diplomatique Character.

The result of all this is that with a very small Force I have had to conquer Difficulties which were only got the better of by that tenor which the British Flag inspires, and that I never was consulted by the Cardinal relative to the Capitulation, and that I had neither Instructions or any Document whatever to assist or guide my Political Conduct[118].

(Signed) Edw.d Jas. Foote

30) Observations on the Armistice concluded between the Cardinal and the French and Rebels
24 June 1799

The Armistice I take for granted is that If the French and Rebels are not releived by their Freinds in 21 days from the signing the Armistice then they shall evacuate Naples, in this infamous manner to His Sicilian Majesty and triumphant to them as stated in the Articles.

All Armsties signifies that either party may renew Hostilities giving a certain notice fixed upon by the Contracting parties, In the present instance I suppose the Cardinal thought that in 21 Days he had not the power of driving the French from the Castle of St Elmo or the Rebels from the Lower Castles of Uovo and Nuovo. The French and Rebels thought that if they could not be releived in 21 days, they could when unable to remain any longer covenant to be removed to a place where they may be in a Situation to renew their diabolical schemes against His Sicilian Majesty and the peace and happiness of His faithfull Subjects, and their removal to be at the expence of His Majesty, and those Enemys and Rebels to be protected by the Fleet of His Sicilian Majestys faithfull Ally the King of Great Britain, Therefore evidently this Agreement implies that both parties are supposed to remain in Statu quo – but if either parties receive releif from their Situation then the Compact of course falls to the ground and is of no effect, for if one party can be liberated from the agreement it naturally implies the other is on the same state. And I fancy the question need not be asked whether if the French Fleet arrived this day in the Bay of Naples whether the French and Rebels would adhere one moment to the Armistice. No! the French Admiral would say I am not come here to look on but to act. And so says the British Admiral and declares on his honor that the Arrival of either Fleet British or French destroys the compact for neither can lay Idle.

Therefore the British Admiral proposes to the Cardinal to send in their joint names to the French and Rebels that the Arrival of the British fleet has completely destroyed the Compact as would that of the French if they had the power (which thank God they have not) to come to Naples.

Therefore that it shall be fixed that in two hours the French shall give possession of the Castle of St Elmo to His Sicilian Majestys Faithfull Subjects and the Troops of His Allies on which condition alone they shall be sent to France without the Stipulation of their being prisoners of War.

That as to Rebels and Traitors no power on Earth has a right to stand between their Gracious King and them they must instantly throw themselves on the clemency of their Sovereign for no other terms will be allowed them nor will the French ever to name them in any Capitulation. – If these terms are not complied with in the time above mentioned Viz. two hours for the French and instant submission on the part of the Rebels such any favourable Conditions will never be again offered.

(signed) Nelson
Foudroyant Naples Bay
24 June 1799
Read Explained & Rejected by the Cardinal

31) Summons sent to the Castle St. Elmo

His Britannic Majestys Ship Foudroyant
Naples Bay 25th June 1799

Sir

His Eminence the Cardinal de Ruffo and the Commanding Officer of the Russian Army having sent you a Summons to Surrender, I acquaint you that unless the terms are acceded to within two hours, you must take the Consequences as I shall not agree to any other

I am Sir
Your most obed. Servant
(signed) Nelson

32) Declaration sent to the Neapolitan Jacobins in the Castles of Ovo & Novo

Rear Admiral Lord Nelson K. B. Commander of His Britannic Majestys Fleet in the Bay of Naples acquaints the Rebellious Subjects of His Sicilian Majesty in the Castles of Ovo and Novo that he will not permit them to

embarkl or quit those place. They must Surrender themselves to His
Majestys Royal Mercy

His Britannic Majestys Ship
Foudroyant Naples Bay
25th June 1799
(Signed) Nelson

33) Proclamation Issued at Naples June 29th 1799

Horatio Lord Nelson Admiral of the British Fleet in the Bay of Naples
gives Notice to all those who have served as Officers Civil or Military in the
Service of the Infamous Neapolitan Republic that if in the space of 24 Hours
for those who are in the City of Naples and 48 Hours for those who are
within five Miles of it they do not give themselves up to the Clemency of the
King – to the Commanding Officer of the Castles Uovo & Novo that Lord
Nelson will Consider them as still in Rebellion & Enemy's of His Sicilian
Majesty

Foudroyant Naples Bay
June 29th 1799
(Signed) Nelson

34) On Board the Foudroyant
Bay of Naples July 14th 1799

My Lord
As Lady Hamilton was very particularly requested by The Queen of
Naples to accompany me and Lord Nelson on this Expedition, and was
charged by Her Majesty with many important Commissions at Naples, and
to keep up a regular daily Correspondence with Her Majesty, I have found
the Queen's Letters to Lady Hamilton so very interesting, doing so much
honor to The Queen's Understanding and Heart, and throwing such Clear
light on the present Situation of Affairs at Naples, that I have prevail'd on
my wife to allow me to entrust to Your Lordship the most interesting of
Her Majesty's Letters, but not without a Solemn promise from me that
They shou'd be restored to her by Your Lordship on Our Arrival in England, of which I now See a near prospect, as We mean to profit of the first
Ship that Lord Nelson sends downwards, after that Their Sicilian Majesties
shall have been happily reinstated on Their Throne of Naples, having had,
as Your Lordship knows, in my pocket. for more than two Years, The

King's gracious permission to return home for a short time to look after my private Concerns.

Your Lordship will receive this packet from the hand of Lieutenant Parkinson charged with Lord Nelson's Dispatches to Lord Spencer, as I do not wish this Letter to be consider'd as Official and The Queen's Letters are entrusted only to Your Lordship's well known discretion.

The Queen's Letters inclosed are Twelve N°s 2. 3. 5. 6. 7. 10. 12. 15. 16. 17. 21. and 22. Your Lordship will surely admire the just remarks of Her Majesty, written in Her own hand, opposite the Articles of Cardinal Ruffo's infamous Capitulation with the Neapolitan Rebels, and inclosed in N. 5.

I have the honor to be

My Lord

Your Lordship's

most obedient and

most humble Servant

Wm Hamilton

35) On Board The Foudroyant

Bay of Naples July 14th 1799

My Lord

Since my last Dispatch to Your Lordship through the Channel of Lord St. Vincent of the 21st of June I have been chiefly at Sea with Lord Nelson and have not had any opportunity of informing Your Lordship of what is passing in the Two Sicilies.by the means of the King's Messenger M.r Sylvester who joined us here, and is returning with Lord Nelson's Dispatches to England I have the singular satisfaction of acquainting Your Lordship of the infinite Services the presence of His Majesty's Fleet under the Command of Lord Nelson, has render'd to Their Sicilian Majesties by placing Them again, as I may almost say, on Their Throne of Naples.

The rapid Successes of the Austrians and Russians in the North of Italy, affording a fair prospect of it's being soon deliver'd from the Hord of Robbers with which it has been infested for some Years passed, obliged the french Directory to withdraw most of their Troops from Naples and Rome to reinforce their Army in the North of Italy having left only weak Garrizons in the Fortresses of Naples, Capua and Gaeta as in the Castle of S.t Angelo at Rome. Profiting of this Circumstance Cardinal Ruffo's Army from Calabria having been joined by about five hundred Russians, and Eighty Turks, taken out of some Russian Frigates and a Turkish Vessel that arrived at Brindisi from Corfu, was encouraged to push on towards this Capital and having also been joined by many parties of Royalists on their March carried all before them, and actually got with the assistance of the Lazaroni and Royalists possession of this Capital on the 13th of last Month. The french having retired into the Castle of St. Elmo and the Jacobins into the Castle Nuovo and the Castle del Ovo and into that of the Carmine, where they were besieged by Cardinal Ruffo's Army. Lord Nelson after his return to Palermo and having disembarked The Hereditary Prince and the Sicilian Troops, as mention'd in my last, proceeded with His Squadron to Maritimo on the Coast of Sicily towards Malta to look after the french Fleet, but having had certain advice that Lord S.t Vincent's Fleet had been very considerably reinforced and that the french Brest Fleet had been seen steering a different Course from that of Sicily, His Lordship return'd to Palermo the 19th of June. Their Sicilian Majesties having received allarming Accounts from Naples, that the Calabrese Army after their Entry into Naples was plundering the houses of that City, and setting them on fire under the pretence of their belonging to Jacobins, and that Cardinal Ruffo, Elated with his Unexpected Successes, was taking upon Himself a power, far beyond the possitive Instructions of His Sovereign, and was actually treating with His Sicilian Majesty's Subjects in Arms, and in open Rebellion against Him, earnestly entreated of Lord Nelson that He wou'd go immediatly wih His Majesty's whole Squadron to Naples, and prevent if possible the Cardinal from taking any Steps or coming to any terms with the Rebbels, that might be dishonorable to Their Sicilian Majesties and hurtfull to their future Government and to assist in the reduction of the french Garrizons in the Castle of S.t Elmo, Capua and Gaeta, and in bringing the Jacobin Rebells to Justice. Lord Nelson readily undertook to go and do all that was possible for the Service of Their Sic.n Majesties, having had, as His Lord.p said, full instructions so to do from The King Our Royal Master and Their Majeties most Singular and faithfull Ally. The King of Naples entreated me also to accompany Lord Nelson which might be of great Service to His Majesty, having been so many Years acquainted with Naples, and particularly as Lord Nelson was not accustom'd to the language of the Country. Accordingly on the 20th of June We set Sail from Palermo with the whole of the Squadron, Nineteen Sail of the Line, including the Portugheze Ships, and were four days on our passage to the Bay of Naples. We received from the Governor of Procita just before we got into this Bay a Copy of a most shamefull Treaty that Cardinal Ruffo had made with the french and His Sicilian Majesty's Rebellious Subjects, who were by that Treaty to march out of the Castles of Naples with all their property and the full honors of War, and at their option either to return to Their own homes or be transported to Toulon at His Sicilian Majesty's expence. As a Copy of this Treaty is inclosed Your Lordship will see that had not His Majesty's Fleet arriv'd in time, and the Treaty been carried into execution, all the Chiefs of the Rebellion wou'd have escaped and others wou'd have remain'd unmolested in the Kingdom to propagate at their leisure the same pernicious Maxims that have brought this Kingdom to the brink of destruction, and the Honor of Their Sicilian Majesties wou'd have remain'd for ever Sullied by so unwarranted a Stretch of Power of Cardinal Ruffo, Their Vicar General, whose Ambitious Views were certainly to favor the Nobles, put himself at their head, reestablish the feudal System and oppress the People, which is Diametrically opposite to Their Sicilian Majesties Intentions, who wish to make the Nobles feel their indignation for their late Treachery ingratitude and disloyalty, and to cherish and reward the people+e by whose Loyalty and bravery, and with the aid of Their good Allies The Kingdom of Naples has been so speedily recover'd.

When We Anchor'd in this Bay the 24th of June The Capitulation of the Castles had in some measure taken place. Fourteen large Polacks or Transport Vessels had taken on board out of the Castles the most conspicuous and Criminal of the Neapolitan Rebells, that had chosen to go to Toulon, the others had already been permitted with their property to return to their own Homes in this Kingdom and Hostages selected from the first Royalist Nobility of Naples had been sent into the Castle of St. Elmo, that Commands the City of Naples where a french Garrizon and the flag of the french Republic was to remain untill the News of the safe arrival of the Neapolitan Rebells, (always called Patriots by the Cardinal), at Toulon, and who were agreable to the Cardinals Treaty to have been convoy'd by a British Marine force.

Lord Nelson on our first Interview with Cardinal Ruffo told His Eminency without any reserve, in what an infamous light he view'd the Treaty, and how disgracefull it wou'd be to Their Sicilian Majesties, whose Opinion and Intentions We both knew were directly contrary to such a capitulation Treaty, which if carried into execution wou'd dishonor Their Majesties for ever. The Cardinal persisted in the Support of what was done as His Eminency said to prevent the Capital from becoming a heap of Stones.

There was no time to be lost for the Tramsport Vessels were on the point of Sailing for Toulon, When Lord Nelson order'dall the boats of His Squadron to be mann'd and Armed and to bring those Vessels with all the Rebells on board directly under the Sterns of His Ships, and there they remain, having taken out and secured on board of His Majesty's Ships, the most guilty Chiefs of the Rebellion. Lord Nelson assured the Cardinal at the same time that He did not mean to do any Act contrary to His Eminency's Treaty, but as that Treaty cou'd not be valid untill it had been ratified by His Sicilian Majesty His Lordship's meaning was only to Secure His Majesty's

Rebellious Subjects untill His Majesty's further pleasure shou'd be known. Admiral Caracciolo The Chief of the Rebels of His Sicilian Majesty's Marine, not having been comprized in the Cardinal's Treaty, but having been taken endeavoring to make his escape by land, was by Lord Nelson's orders tried on board the Foudroyant by a Court Martial composed entirely of Neapolitan Marine Officers, was condemn'd and hung up at the Yard Arm of the Neapolitan Frigate (the very same Ship he had with the Gunboats of the Neapolitan Republic under his Command fired upon near Procita) at five o' clock in the evening of the same day, where he hung untill the Setting of the Sun, to the great satisfaction of His Sic.n Majesty's loyal Subjects, thousands of which came off in boats with loud applause of so speedy an Act of Justice for this happen'd the day after the King's Squadron came to Naples. His body was afterwards thrown into the Sea. We found on our arrival into the Bay a general discontent of the People and of His Sicilian Majesty's most loyal Subjects of the higher Class, complaining of the rapine and plunder committed daily at Naples by the Calabrese and of the evident partiality shewn by the Cardinal to the Jacobine party, whilst the Royalists and loyal people were brow beaten and denied access to His Eminency at his head Quarters at the Ponte Maddalena in the Suburbs of Naples; not that they accused him of being a Traitor but that His Eminency was surrounded by Jacobins and Venal Evil Counsellors – in short Your Lordship can have no conception of the Anarchy and Confusion at Naples. Lord Nelson by sending immediatly a Garrison of British Marines into the Castle del Ovo and an other of Sailors under the Command of Capt. Hood of the Zealous into the Castle Nuovo immediatly restored Tranquility to the distracted Capital, and that such of His Sicn. Majesty's Rebel Subjects who according to the Cardinal's Treaty might escape might not do so with impunity, Lord Nelson publish'd at Naples a printed Notification, a Copy of which is inclosed, and which The Cardinal had declined publishing.

The Cardinal finding soon that the whole Confidence of the people was withdrawn from him and reposed entirely on Lord Nelson and His Majesty's Fleet, endeavor'd to throw the whole weight of Affairs on His Lordship and by that means cause inevitable Confusion, but We contrived to keep every thing going on decently, by supporting The King's Vicar General untill We had Answers from Their Sicilian Majesties at Palermo, to whom We had painted Exactly the State of Affairs and the confusion at Naples, preventing at the same time His Eminency from doing any essential Mischief, and recommending to Their Sicilian Majesties in the strongest manner to shew temselves in the Bay of Naples as soon as possible, by which means, and by that alone, all wou'd be calm'd and the Cardinal's dangerous power die of a Natural death.

By the return of the Vessel that carried our Letters to Palermo, Lord Nelson received a Letter from the King of Naples in His Majesty's own hand writing in which He thank'd His Lordship for having saved His Honor, approved of all that had been done and sent Letters with full powers to appoint a New Government and even to arrest the Cardinal and send Him to Palermo in a British Ship if Lord Nelson shou'd think it Necessary to come to that Extremity. His Majesty acquainted us also that He was coming Himself directly with General Acton and the Prince Castel Cicala into the Bay of Naples according to our Advice. His Sicilian Majesty embarked the 3^d instant on board the Sirene One of His own Frigates accompanied by The King's Frigate The Sea Horse but having a numerous Convoy by bringing with Him from Sicily One Thousand four Hundred Infantry and Six Hundred Cavalry, and meeting with Calms His Majesty did not arrive in this Bay untill the 11th instant in the Afternoon, and wou'd not suffer His Royal Standard to be hoisted untill He got on board the Foudroyant, when it went up to the Main Mast head and was immediatly Saluted by the King's whole Fleet and by the Castles at Naples in our power, which, with the multitude of boats covering the Sea and Surrounding the Ship all full of loyal Subjects calling the King their Father, was such a Sight as never can be forgotten, at the same time Captain Troubridge and Captain Holwell that Lord Nelson had detached with all the Marines of the Fleet the five hundred Russians and some Portugheze Artillery were keeping up a heavy fire of Mortars and battering Cannon against the Castle of S.t Elmo, into which Strong Fortress the only remaining french had taken refuge in Number about Eight Hundred, and the only Castle at Naples on which the french Republican Flag was flying. The next morning at day break Captain Troubridge unexpectedly open'd a New masked Battery within less than two hundred yards of the Walls of the Castle which in two hours obliged the french to hang out a flag of Truce and about Eleven o' clock yesterday morning His Sicilian Majesty had the compleat Satisfaction of seeing from this Ship His own Flag Triumphant on the Castle of S.t Elmo. Inclosed is a printed Copy of the Capitulation and which, as Your Lordship will observe is a compleat Contrast to the Cardinal's Capitulation with the Castles del Ovo, and the Castle Nuovo.

As His Sicilian Majesty Himself writes to the King by this Messenger it is not necessary for me to say any thing of the Gratitude expressed daily by Their Sicilian Majesties, Their Royal Family and their Loyal Subjects for the Signal Services that have been render'd to them by the King's Fleet under the Command of the Incomparable Lord Nelson, and particularly for the last, which as to all appearances has Seated them Again on Their Throne of Naples. Nothing remains to Compleat the business but the reduction of Capua and Gaeta in which Fortresses there are small french Garrizons.

Tomorrow a proper force goes to Capua under the Command of Captains Troubridge and Holwell who expressed to Lord Nelson a desire of being so Employ'd and as Gaeta is closely pressed both by Sea and land all our business in this Quarter will probably be compleated, and Satisfactorily, in a few days; in the mean time His Sicilian Majesty holds His Councils with His Ministers on board the Foudroyant for the Police and better Government of this Capital & Kingdom. Your Lordship may well conceive the labour that Lord Nelson and I must have Undergone in the space of time between the Arrival of the King and the Cardinal His Vicar General's having declined all business.

I have thus given Your Lord.p as well as I can recollect the Substance of what happen'd during the Seventeen days that We have been at an Anchor in This Bay[119].

I have the honor to be
My Lord
Your Lordship's
most obedient and
most humble Servant.
Wm Hamilton

36) On board The Foudroyant
Bay of Naples July 19th 1799

My Lord
Yesterday I had the honor of receiving Your Lordship's Letter N. 2) of the 10th of June by the Marquis Circello's Messenger with The King's Ratification of The Treaty Sign'd at Naples by the Marquis of Gallo and me in December last, and I shall not fail, according to Your Lordship's Directions, at the time of Exchanging the Ratifications, to deliver in to this Government my formal Declaration in His Majesty's Name that the Treaty is to be Construed as not applying to the Case of Spain in the present War, but that if at any time after the Conclusion of a Peace a War shou'd arise between His Majesty and The King of Spain by the Aggression of the latter then have it's full Force and Effect.

I can assure Your Lordship that when His Sicilian Majesty and General Acton (who as You will have seen by my last Dispatch are on board this Ship) heard of the arrival of the Ratification of a Treaty which they had so much at heart, They expressed the highest Satisfaction and gratitude, and only regret the impossibility of Their profiting of this early opportunity to return His Sicilian Majesty's Ratification of the Treaty The Great Seal being in the Secretary of States Office at Palermo but Your Lordship may be sure that it will be executed as soon as possible, and forwarded by the next safe opportunity. The Snuff box with The King's Picture enriched with diamonds I have deliverd to General Acton desiring of His Excy to send it in His Majesty's Name to The Marquis of Gallo, who is at Vienna. I likewise acquainted Gen.l Acton that The King, as a particular mark of His Satisfaction with the Conduct of Monsieur Circello, had order'd a like present to be made to him on this Occasion.

As to the settling by Order of His Majesty the Usual present of 500 £ for the Neapolitan department for Foreign Affairs it has been agreed between General Acton and me that His Excellency shou'd order the value of the present of 500 £ to be paid to The Neapolitan department for foreign Affairs here at the same time We request of Your Lordship to give in His Sicilian Majesty's Name the Sum of 500 £ to the British Department for Foreign Affairs.

I flatter myself that in a very few days, as I had the honor of mentoning fully in my last to Your Lordship that by the fall of Capua and Gaeta Their Sicilian Majesties will be again happily and Securely Seated on Their Throne of Naples.

I have the honor to be
My Lord
Your Lordship's
most obedient and
most humble Servant
Wm Hamilton

37) On Board the Foudroyant
Bay of Naples August 4th 1799

Here have We been, My Dear Charles[120], since the 24th of June when our Line of Battle under the Command of my incomparable Friend Lord Nelson consisted of no less than 19 Ships of the Line including Portugheze and the Lion of 64. This respectable British Force under such Commanders has been attended with the most compleat Success, and Their Sicilian Majesties may now be said to be firmly Seated on Their Throne of Naples; The King's Fleet having prevented the most Serious Anarchy & Confusion in the Capital & reduced the Castle of S.t Elmo & the Fortress's of Capua & Gaeta, in which were found abundance of Artillery & Ammunition & more than Six Thousand french, all of which are embarked for France and more than 1000 of the Principal Neapolitan Rebells, many of which of the first Nobility, have been put into the King of Naples hands, all of which wou'd have escaped justice had the King's Fleet come into the Bay of Naples One day later, Lord Nelson's Dispatches go hence Tomorrow by Capt. Oswald – You will then see the difference in the Capitulations of Capt. Troubridge for the Castle of S.t Elmo, Capua & Gaeta & the most Shamefull One of Cardinal Ruffo for the Castles del Ovo & Nuovo at Naples, before our Arrival, the Mischief of which we prevented – You will wonder at The Cardinal's being left Captain General at Naples after what he did – But you know This Country never comes to a decisive point, but always Half Measures altho' I every moment Quote to this Government Pontano's advice to his Countrymen, & to whom he left on his Sepulchral Stone in a Chappel at Naples This Inscription – Audendo Agendoque, Res Publica crescit, non iis Consiilis que Timidi Cauta apellant. It will be Their own fault now if they do not establish a better Government in this Kingdom than it was ever blessed with – yet I dread these half measures – The King by our advice came here from Palermo the 10th of June[121] & has remained on board the Foudroyant is most amiable & daily acknowledges his utmost Gratitude to The King & Lord Nelson and has thank'd often Emma & Me seeing that without us L.d Nelson wou'd have been at the greatest loss – I am now amply repair'd for my Constancy in not abandoning Their Sicilian Majesties altho' I sufferd so much by it in Mind body and Estate. When I wrote last I still hoped to return in time before Winter set in, but as We have been delay'd here necessarily for without us The two Sicilies wou'd probably have been lost again – I begin to depair of coming home until next Spring – The Brest Fleets coming into the Mediterranean had nearly unhinged us, & if Ld. Nelson had implicitly obey'd L.d Keiths orders Their Sic.n Majesties were undone – however Ld. Nelson has not neglected Minorca having detached by degrees Six Sips of the Line to that place, besides two to Malta & 2 – towards Genoa – I admire Lord Nelson more & more every day – but it requires some temper to stem the torrent of his impetuosity, even against his best Friends, & in that respect he is just enough to own that I have been of infinite Use to him. In short L.d Nelson & I with Emma are the *Tria Iuncta in Uno* that have carried on affairs to this happy crisis – Emma is realy The Queen's bosom Friend, I am steady with the King & Acton & have much more of the Queen's Confidence than formerly – You may imagine then that when We three agree, what real business is done – but still The Cursed System of half Measures cross us and this Country was such in a State of total Corruption that I beleive the only hopes of a perfect reform must remain for the Next Generation – it is this moment resolved that We return Tomorrow Night to Palermo The King having completed his business for the Government of Naples untill He shall think proper to return with The Queen and Royal Family. L.d Nelson leaves Trobridge in the Culloden wth some few Ships – and such is the Confidence the people have in the English that I am convinced all We be kept quiet untill the 11 Thousand Russians sent to the King of Naples by the Treaty for 4 Years, shall arrive and they were said to be at Ferrara 15 days ago.

I dare not think of my loss of the Colossus- but I see you are taking every precaution to save as much as you can from the Wreck, and to your Friendship alone I trust – Never did or will exist such an other collection & realy as near as I can recollect it had Cost me Six Thousand Pounds, and my Collection of pictures on board the Samuel & James Transport at Palermo I value still more – All these I intended to sell & clear my debts, for what pleasure can one take in the Arts with the thought of such an incumberance as I have before me constantly – My House at Naples the most compleatly & Elegantly furnished as imagination coud make to one has been torn to pieces, What furniture I left in the hurry of our retreat, stolen by the french who likewise took my Horses & three English Carriages – Untill I came here I never received a letter from my Maitre d'Hotel & he kept all my Servants at full wages whilst a french Commissary lodged in my house and made use of them – I have now cut that matter short as you will see if you ask Ross[122] to show you the letter I wrote to him this morning –

I am infinitely obliged to you for the friendly Conversation you held with Lord Grenville on my Account. As to ever bringing in a Bill to Government on acct. of my losses and the Extraordinary Expences brought upon me by Prince Augustus's living so many years at Naples, and The King's Ships frequenting these Seas during these last years, and the losses suffer'd by the Revolution of Naples – I can not bring myself to it. Thanks to my first Wife I never can want the comforts of life & have in my power to provide for Emma – I glory in the Hospitality I have had in my power to show to Lord Nelson and almost all the Hero's of the Nile – it will be the pride of rest of my days to have been intimately acquainted with such a valuable set of men – But if Government does not think of me I will do myself the justice, when I return home, to lay the whole state of my Circumstances before The King who I have reason to think has not forgot (as he never forgets) the many years I passed with him in his early days – It comes to a very simple operation by laying Ross's books before him for my accounts are in that house since the Year 1747. As to Wales I am convinced that you have done, & are doing great things & Milford Haven[123] must one day be treated as such a Glorious Harbour deserves – but Years, Rheumatisms, and Bilious Complaints remind me, that I have no time to lose, and that repose begins to be the most Necessary object for me, and to find myself embarassed in my Circumstancs in my latter days wou'd be the very devil – I realy know not my present Circumstances but I have no debts but what Ross is acquainted with – In short My Dear Charles do what you please for me with Ministry except to beg, which I will never Submit to – I do not mean to resign, but to go home on leave but I fear not until next Spring, and when at home I shall see & Consult with my Friends what is best for me – but to keep an Inn as I have done for 35 Years – it is impossible for me to go on, even with Emma's assistance & which is infinite – but then a Comely Landlady calls more company than I coud wish to my House – as they do not as in other Public Houses fatten the Landlord –

Adieu My Dr. Charles

At least I shall finish my Diplomatical Career gloriously – as you will see by what the King of Naples writes from this Ship to His Minister in London owing the Recovery of His Kingdom to the King's Fleet, & Lord Nelson & me

Yours ever
most affectionately
Wm Hamilton

38) On board The Foudroyant
Bay of Naples August 5th 1799

My Lord

I have the satisfaction of acquainting Your Lordship that the Siege of Capua carried on Under the direction of Captains Troubridge and Holwell, has been attended with little loss and the most complete Success; that Fortress having Surrender'd to the Arms of His Sicilian Majesty and of His Allies on the 28th of July. A printed Copy of the Capitulation is inclosed N. 1). The french Garrizon, consisting of more than two Thousand Men, were immediately embarked and Sent prisoners on their parole to Toulon. Lord Nelson and General Acton wrote a Letter to the french Commander at Gaeta acquainting him of the Surrender of Capua and that Brigadier General Girardon, late Governor of Capua and his Superiour, had sign'd the Capitulation for Gaeta, a printed Copy of which Your Lordship will find inclosed N. 2). Lord Nelson having sent Capt. Lewis in the Minotaur to take possession of Gaeta, The french Commander after some little altercation, complied with the terms of Mon.r Girardon's Capitulation, and the french Garrizon, consisting of Sixteen hundred men, were immediately embarked for France. The Garrisons of S.t Elmo, Capua and Gaeta, have proved to be much stronger than was expected, upwards of Six Thousand french men having been embarked for France from these three Fortresses only; and both Capua and Gaeta were found abundantly furnished with Artillery and Amunition and Notwithstanding that Brigadier Girardon had given his word of honor that all his Sicilian Majesty's rebellious Subjects shou'd be deliver'd up at Capua, about four score were detected in french Uniforms, and secured as they were embarking for France from the Mole of Naples.

As there is not now a french man left in the Kingdom of Naples and His Sicilian Majesty having sufficient time to settle a temporary Government at Naples, untill His Majesty shall think proper to return with the Queen and His Royal family to this Capital, His Majesty has desired Lord Nelson to carry Him back to Palermo in this Ship, and We are to Sail for Sicily, accompanied by a Portugheze Ship, The Prince Royal, Commanded by the Marquis Nizza, this Evening.

Your Lordship will naturally be surprised after the extraordinary conduct of Cardinal Ruffo to find that His Eminency is now appointed, with a Giunta, Captain General to govern Naples during The King's absence; both Lord Nelson and I, sensible that without some Explanation of so extraordinary a Measure, and so contradictory to the reports We had made relative to the Cardinal to our Superiours at home, in our Dispatches of the 14th of July, sent from this Ship; We applied to General Acton to explain to us this Aenigma, and which His Excellency has done very fully and Candidly in a confidential Letter to Lord Nelson a Copy of which is inclosed N.3) accompanied with a Copy of the Cardinal's present appointment N. 4) and a Copy of His Sicilian Majesty's Instructions to the Giunta di Stato N. 5) for its' Guidance huring His Majesty's absence − Your Lordship will observe that the Cardinal is tied up, as tight as possible, but neither Lord Nelson or I, can be brought to relish such half measures which generally prove the Worst altho' the only in vogue in this Country. General Acton's Letter is so clear and fair that I need say no more on this subject. The Army brought by Cardinal Ruffo from Calabria to Naples, consists now of upwards of Six Thousand men, The Lazaroni, or populace of Naples, and that are said to have hidden Arms, are more than Twenty Thousand − of His Sicilian Majesty's regular Troops brought from Sicily or raised here lately, There are not more than Three Thousand, therefore, untill the Eleven Thousand Russians (promised to the King of Naples for Eight Years, if His Majesty pleases, by the late Treaty with Russia) shall arrive, This Government can not be looked upon as very Secure − These Russians are said to be (on their way here) at Ferrara.

My former Dispatches to Your Lordship have painted sufficiently the abominable, and general Corruption of this Country, and it has not been improved by the french Republican Government of Seven Months.

Lord Nelson sends off Captain Oswald with his dispatches for London this Evening and I profit of the opportunity and have entrusted to Capt. Oswald (who has done himself great honor at the Sieges of S.t Elmo & Capua) His Sicilian Majesty's Ratification of our late Treaty in a box, the key of which is here inclosed, and have taken the liberty to send by him also a tin Box containing three drawings One of His Majesty's Fleet in Line of Battle at Anchor in this Bay, and two views relative to the Siege of S.t Elmo and which I beg of your Lordship to present to The King most humbly in my Name.

I do not enter into any Naval Operations, as Lord Nelson will have given a full and satisfactory account of his own proceedings, but I must say that had his Lordship detached any Ships from his Squadron soon after our arrival in this Bay, in all probability the two Sicilies wou'd have been lost. Their Sicilian Majesties, Their Ministers, and all Naples are convinced of this truth, and there are no bounds to the gratitude they daily express towards The King, the British Nation, and to the incomparable Lord Nelson, and the rest of the Brave Commanders of this His Majesty's Invincible Squadron, and by which Their Sicilian Majesties are now replaced on Their Throne of Naples, and more than Seven hundred of their most Rebellious Subjects, that woud have escaped, have been secured, and are now lying at the mercy of His Sicilian Majesty.

I did not fail to obey Your Lordship's Commands at the moment when I exchanged with General Acton the Ratification of our last Treaty, having given in to His Excy a Solemn Declaration in the King's Name, a Copy o which is inclosed N. 6). Your Lordp. will also find N. 7) a Copy of General Acton's Answer to that Declaration, the Original of which is in the box with His Sicilian Majesty's Ratification of the Treaty.

I congratulate Your Lordship on the Surrender of Mantua, the certain News of which was brought last Night to The King of Naples from Leghorn in a Letter dated from thence the first of August.

Altho' I have not enter'd into Lord Nelson's department I know that His Lordship has sent a considerable Naval force on the Coast of Genoa, to assist Marshall Suwarrow[124] in his Operations against General Moreau, and a still greater force, to Minorca, the Safety and protection of which, His Lordship keeps ever in View.

I have the honor to be My Lord
Your Lordship's
most obedient and
most humble Servant
Wm Hamilton

39) Palermo August 17th 1799

My Lord
His Sicilian Majesty arrived here in three days from the Bay of Naples in the Foudroyant, the 8th instant in the afternoon, when the Queen of Naples,

The Hereditary Prince, and all the Royal Family immediatly came on board to welcome His Majesty on His happy and Triumphant return to this Capital. In the Evening Lord Nelson and I had by their own desire the honor of attending Their Majesties and Royal Family in the barge of the Foudroyant to a Superb Landing place errected, and decorated for the purpose, on the Shore of this City. Their Majesties were received with the loudest acclamations of Joy, and with a General Salvo from the Castles of Palermo and from all the Ships in the Harbour. The Royal Family proceeded directly in great State to the Cathedral where a Solemn Te Deum was Sung and the whole City was Illuminated for three Nights on Account of Their Majesties having happily recoverd their Throne of Naples, and the french having been compleatly beaten, and driven out of that Kingdom.

As the Fetes of S.ta Rosalia the tutelar Saint of this City, had been deferred untill His Majesty's return, they have now taken place and We are in the midst of Fireworks, Illuminations and Prcessions every Night; for the particulars of these uncommonly Superb Fetes I refer Your Lordship to the printed Relation inclosed N. 1) His Siclian Majesty, on quitting the Foudroyant, made a present to Capt. Hardy of His picture on a Snuffbox, richly set with large Diamonds, and of a valuable diamond Ring, and an other diamond ring was presented in His Majesty's Name to M.r Tyson, Lord Nelson's Secretary. A few days after our return The Duke of Ascoli One of His Sicilian Majesty's Gentlemen of the Bed Chamber presented to Lord Nelson in His Majesty's Name a Gold Sword, richly set with Diamonds with a Letter of His Majesty's Own Hand writing, a Copy of which with the Translation is inclosed N. 2) The same day Lord Nelson received from the Prince Luzzi, Secretary of State in the Foreign Department, by order of his Sicilian Majesty, a Dispatch, a Copy of which with the Translation is likewise inclosed n. 3) acquainting His Lordship that His Sicilian Majesty had been pleased to Create Him Duke of Bronte, with the rich Estate, or Feudo, of that Name, at the feet of Mount Etna, which, as I am credibly informed is of the clear value of Eighteen Thousand Ducats per Ann.m, altho' its' Nominal Value is Twenty four Thousand Ducats.

On our late Expedition His Sicilian Majesty and His Ministers were more than a Month on board the Foudroyant, The goodness and singular affability of His Majesty was such as to Enchant every Officer and Sailor on board; On quitting the Ship at Palermo, His Majesty left a present of Two Thousand Three hundred Ounces[125], to be divided among The Admiral Lord Nelson's Servants, and the Ship's Company. The King of Naples having remarked Lady Hamilton's Zeal for His Service and the trouble She took in receiving the Neapolitan Ladies that came on board the Foudroyant to pay their Court to His Majesty, during our stay in the Bay of Naples, and in keeping up a contant Correspondence with The Queen of Naples at Palermo, was Graciously pleased to preent her with His Picture richly set with Diamonds on our return to Palermo, and The Queen of Naples has done Lady Hamilton the honor to make her a present of Her Majesty's picture and hair set with Diamonds in bracelets, with a pair of Ear rings of Diamonds and Pearls, with an Aigrette[126], and Her Majesty's Cypher in Diamonds & with a compleat dress of the finest point lace. I know also that magnificent presents are preparing for all the Captains of Lord Nelson's Squadron that were Employ'd on the Sieges of S.t Elmo, Capua & Gaeta. The Strongest Expressions of Gratitude to the King, His Majesty's Ministers, The British Nation, and to Lord Nelson who has so completely Executed the Benificent intentions of His Majesty and the Nation towards Them, are repeated in publick daily by Their Sicilian Majesties, and will certainly never be forgotten, and of which The King of Naples's Letter to Lord Nelson with the Sword of His Royal Father, is a sufficient proof.

Three Russian Ships of the Line and a Frigate are arrived here from Gibraltar the Crews of which are very unhealthy, and the Ships very foul.

The Russian and Turkish Squadrons from Corfu are arrived at Messina, with the intention of proceeding to the Bay of Naples.

Cardinal Ruffo has been order'd with his Calabrese Army to proceed to Rome, the Vanguard of that Army has already taken possession of Frascati, and a body of Austrians are said to have advanced as far as Viterbo, on the other side of Rome.

Lord Nelson is doing all in his power to bring the long winded business of Malta (owing to the want of land forces) to a a happy Conclusion an has his Eye also on the reduction of Civita Vecchia and Ancona, besides the assisting as far as He is able Marshall Suwarrow in His operations against Moreau's Army at Genoa. His Lordship has also at the request of the King of Sardinia order'd the Foudroyant to leave Malta & proceed to Cagliary to carry His Majesty and Royal Family from thence to the Continent. Brigadier General Ross, charged with Letters from England to the King of Sardinia arrived here this morning, and Lord Nelson will forward him this Evening to Cagliari in the Perseus so that His Sardinian Majesty will have timely Notice to prepare for the arrival of The Foudroyant.

From the present most favourable appearances thare is every reason to hope that by the end of Next Month the miscreant french will be compleatly driven out of Italy.

From Letters received by Lord Nelson this day from Sir Sidney Smith and dated from on board the Tyger off Cypruss July 16th We find that General Buonaparte after prodigious losses, raised the Siege of Acri in the night of the 21st of May having left all his Artillery behind him, and was retreating towards Cairo, so Surrounded by hords of Arabs that it was judged impossible for him to reach Cairo. An advice boat from Alexandria, bound to Constantinople assured Sir Sidney Smith that Damietta, Rosetta, and Aboukir, were already in the hands of the Turks, and Alexandria near Surrendring all Communication with Cairo having been Cut off.

I have the honor to be
My Lord
Your Lordship's
most obedient and
most humble Servant
Wm Hamilton

40) Downing Street August 20th 1799

Sir
Your dispatch marked N. 22 containing an account of the Surrender of the Fort of S.t Elmo and of His Sicilian Majesty's return to the Bay of Naples has been received and laid before the King.

You will not fail to convey to His Sicilian Majesty the expression of the sincere satisfaction which has been occasioned by these interesting and important Events. His Majesty's Answer in return to the letter of the King of Naples will be forwarded to you by the next Opportunity.

41) Palermo August 24th 1799

My Lord
The Neapolitan Messemger having been detain'd here untill this day I have an opportunity of inclosing the Palermo Gazette of Yesterday which contains an exact List of the Russian and Turkish Squadrons that are taking in Provisions at Messina, and propose to proceed to the Bay of Naples.

Your Lordship will observe that This Fleet has not any land forces on board except One Thousand four hundred Albanese at the disposition of His Sicilian Majesty

I have the honor to be
My Lord
Your Lordship's
most obedient and
most humble Servant
Wm Hamilton

42) Palermo September 7th 1799

My Lord

As we have not any regular Post establish'd as yet to the Continent I take advantage of every opportunity that offers to keep up my Correspondence with Your Lordship: I forward this Dispatch by means of Capt. Duns in the Incendiary, that Lord Nelson sends down to Gibraltar this Evening.

Since my last sent to Vienna by a Neapolitan Messenger We have had the glorious News of Marshall Suwarrows Victory over Jauberts and Moreau's Army, at Novi, by a Letter His Excellency wrote himself to Lord Nelson from Asti, where He was waiting to attack the french reinforcement expected from Grenoble.

The Russian and Turkish Squadrons from Messina are arrived here and at the desire of His Sicilian Majesty are to proceed directly to the Bay of Naples. They are all fine Ships particularly The Turks, but the Russians are not Copper bottom'd, and both Admirals declare that their Ships are not in a condition to be able to keep at Sea in Winter.

Marshall Suwarrow hearing of Lord Nelson's compleat Success at Naples has detain'd the Eleven Thousand Russians destin'd by Treaty for Naples, not reflecting that His Sicilian Majesty can as yet have no great dependance on His own Troops and that altho' the french have been driven out of the Kingdom of Naples the pernicious Maxims they have left behind them will require force and a watchfull Eye, and that Their Sicilian Majesties do not think it safe to return to Their Throne of Naples untill there shall be a strong Garrison of foreign Troops that They can depend upon to ensure the Police and good Order of Their Capital. The Russian Minister here has been desired by this Government to represent the circumstance in the strongest light to the Marechall, but I fear untill the french shall have been compleatly driven out of Italy, The King of Naples has not any chance of seeing the Russian Land forces at Naples, and therefore the quiet of that City must depend upon the Squadrons of Russians and Turks going to Naples under the Command of Admiral Usacon, and which have not any regular Troops on board. Lord Nelson has been obliged to detach most of the Ships of His Squadron down to Gibraltar Minorca and on the Coast of Genoa except The Foudroyant and the three of His Majesty's Ships of the Line employ'd with the Portugheze Ships against Malta, which We flatter ourselves can not hold out much longer.

The Austrians are coming on in Numbers, and with hasty strides to take possession of Tuscany, the Praesidii, and of as much of the Roman State as they can. It is to be hoped that Admiral Usacon will assist as far as He can His Sicilian Majesty's Calabrese Army going under the Command of Cardinal Ruffo into the Roman State – but unfortunately We hear that the Vanguard of the Calabrese Army has met with a Considerable check from the french and their Roman Partizans at Frascati, and been obliged to return as far back as Sora in Abruzzo.

The Whole and Sole Confidence of Their Sicilian Majesties appears to be reposed in Lord Nelson. Their Majesties are not easy if His Lordship is absent from Them one moment and as Lord Nelson seems to think that my going home at the moment wou'd distress him, I have let the Goliath go down to Gibraltar without me, altho' Capt. Foley was so good, and as he said by the directions of Earl S.t Vincent, to offer me and Lady Hamilton a passage home in the Ship under his Command. My own Interest or Conveniency Shall never weigh with me when The King's Service or that of His Sicilian Majesty is any way in Question, of which I hope I have given sufficient proofs already, and indeed I have been amply repaid by the very great honors received from Their Sicilian Majesties, who were pleased to see my poor Endeavors for Their Majesties' Service in the most favorable light.

I have the honor to be
My Lord
Your Lordship's
most obedient and
most humble Servant
Wm Hamilton

43) Palermo 22^d September 1799

My Dear Charles
The Goliath Capt. Foley had orders from Lord S.t Vincent to carry us home as you know he is a Neighbour in Wales and a very worthy man he had prepared all for us and seem'd happy to have such orders – However when it came to the point I weighd all Circumstances and found it impossible to quit Lord Nelson who does not understand any language but his Own & fairly said that if We went he coud not stay here – The Court also was much alarmed at our going – The Season is advanced & We shoud probably not arrive untill Winter had set in – and my health is realy but indifferent – Plagued with bilious Complaints and Diarrhea continually owing to the intense heats & damp of this Climate; I was well on board of the Ship in the Bay of Naples. In short I must go on untill next Spring altho' at an Expence I can by no means afford as it is now a year that Lord Nelson has lived with us & of Course all the numerous train of Officers that come to him upon business – Besides all Foreigners and the Nobility of this Country flock to our House my House with some Servants goes on at Naples also, & I can not

give it up untill January – As I told you in my last I will not apply to Government for some indemnification for the losses I have Sufferd & the very extraordinary Expences I have been at – This Court has made us all handsome presents I have got a ring I suppose of 1000 £ value this and two boxes with the Kings Picture for signing two Treaties is all I have had from this Court since I came to Naples in 1764 & I shall bring them home in the state I received them – Ross's books in which are all my accounts for 50 Years passt will shew what I was worth when I left England 35 Years ago & how much poorer I return not that I have any idea of the present State of my own Affairs – I will submit all this to the King and His Ministers at home – and they may do what they please if they do nothing I hope I shall have enough to retire into some warm Corner and die quietly when my hour shall come – No one has taken more pains than I have for these seven years pass'd nor labour'd harder in the good Cause than I have and withou vanity I may safely say that my labours have been more than once of Essential Service & They know it at home but I have never yet had the smallest encouragement or word of approbation from my Superiours at home – but still I have the inward Satisfaction of feeling that I have done my duty well & that Satisfaction they can not rob me of – You see I am not in good humour This is a damn'd World & no matter how soon you get out of it – Neither Emma or Lord Nelson have been well lately the Thermometer generally at 85 in our house & sometimes 90. M.r Cadogan has also been ill –

As to Politicks they seem to go on well and We may now flatter ourselves that all is drawing towards a happy Conclusion – As I had stay'd so long here that was an other reason to defer my journey untill next Spring before which probably a Storm might have taken place, I fear that many Pictures & Books that have been on board a Transport ever since We were driven from Naples may suffer by damp I took out two trunks of Cloaths & they were very damp indeed – In short God knows what I shall get home out of the General Wreck – As to my Vases being recoverd from the Colossus I give that up.

Adieu My Dear Charles I will not tire you any longer with my bad humour but hope you will allow I have some reasons for discontent

Y.rs Ever

Wm Hamilton

P.S. This Court indeed has expressed its Gratitude to us all & I send you an Acct. of a ball & Fete given by The Queen but under the Name of Prince Leopold to commemorate the Services We lately renderd to their Sicilian Majesties, at Naples.

However low we may be at home, here We are respected indeed ! & I finish my Career most Gloriously, and I am sure my Name will ever be rememberd in the Two Sicilies –

44) Palermo September 22^{d} 1799

My Lord

I have had the honor of receiving Your Lordship's Letter N. 3) dated August 20th by the Marquis Circello's Messenger, and immediatly according to Your Lordship's instructions had the honor of expressing to Their Sicilian Majesties and Their Ministers the very sincere Satisfaction with which the late most important and interesting Events at Naples had been received at the Court of St. James's, and by the British Nation in general.

Whilst His Sicilian Majesty remain'd on board the Foudroyant in the Bay of Naples the method of proceeding against the Rebel prisoners was settled with Cardinal Ruffo & the Giunta of State, and as I heard They were to be divided into three Classes The most Guilty to suffer death the next imprisonment for life & the third Banishment or imprisonment for a certain term of years. There have been many executions of the lower Class but few of the Nobility have sufferd death The Count Ruvo Duke of Andria one of the most guilty has however been hang'd at Naples and a Son of the Prince Stigliano and an other of the Duke Cassano Serra have been beheaded. The Prince La Tonella and the Duke Riardo, the Heads of two of the first Families at Naples have been sent for life into a Subterranean Prison in the Island of Maritimo off Sicily, a punishment worse than death. There were more than Eight Thousand persons confined as Jacobines and Rebels in the Naples' Prisons ten days ago, but as I understand many have been since removed to Capua & Gaeta, and it is to be hoped that when a sufficient number of Examples shall have been made, and the most inveterate & noxious Rebells shall have been either shut up or banished from the Kingdom, His Sicilian Majesty will grant a general & sincere pardon – and return to Naples where the immediate presence of the Court is much wanted, and without which the discontents in that City will be increasing daily. The Russian Squadron under the Command of Admiral Usacon that is gone into the Bay of Naples will however be sufficient to keep the City in order for the present. Capt. Troubridge and Lewis with some Frigates that were left in the Bay of Naples have been order'd by L.d Nelson to quit that Bay as soon as the Rusian Squadron shall appear and to go and attempt the reduction of Civita Vecchia, and there is every reason to hope that this little Expedition may prove successful.

The Turkish Squadron under the Command of Cadir Bey has been obliged to return to Corfu, owing to the riot and fray that took place last Sunday Sennight between some of The Turkish Sailors and the people of Palermo, and in which above 100 Turks & 15 Palermitans lost their lives. It is imagined, and We beleive not without foundation, that the Second Turkish Admiral who is very popular and desirous of the Command in Chief encouraged The Turkish

Crews on board the Ships to mutiny as they did against Cadir Bey by insisting either to be allowed to revenge themselves at Palermo or to return directly to Constantinople. The Turkish Ships are realy fine Ships kept clean & in good order of french Construction & all Copperd, which Advantage the Russian Ships have not – The departure of the Turkish Squadron appears to me to be rather a fortunate circumstance for this Country – They had no Troops on board and as they have no idea of going to Sea in Winter, They must either have remain'd in this port or that of Naples, from which their numerous wants must have been constantly Satisfied. Admiral Usacon told Lord Nelson also that His Ships were not in a condition to keep the Sea in Winter. It is with infinite Satisfaction that I have been witness for Seven years passd that when the Service required it a British Ship never lost a moment or regarded the Season of the year, or waited for a favorable Wind. She was out in an instant & the business was done whereas The Turkish & Russian Squadron lay 15 days at Messina waiting for a favourable Wind before they came to Palermo, where they might have got out of the harbour of Messina any Evening when the land Wind Constantly prevails in higher Summer.

I have taken the liberty of giving this day my draught on Your Lordship for the Sum of Three Hundred and Six Pounds payable at Twenty days Sight to the order of Abraham Gibbs Esq. Your Lordship will be pleased to remember that I was authorized by Your Lordship to supply to the extent of One Hundred Pounds Sterling the extreme wants of M.r. Wm England His Majesty's Consul who had been obliged to fly from Malta with the loss of most of his property, & which I have done. I flatter myself that upon reading the inclosed Letters of Lord Nelson to me N. 1. 2. 3. that Your Lordship will not disapprove of my having exactly complied with His Lordship's request with respect to Mess.rs Harryman & Burns, and M.r Wyndhams receipt to me for Eighty Pounds inclosed N. 4 will enable Your Lordship to charge the Said Sum to his account Mons. de Tayllerand having never brought in his account to me as promised by M.r. Wyndham

I have the honor &c

P. S. Lord Nelson has just receivd a Letter from Cadir Bey with a Copy of his journal since he left this harbour with the Squadron under his Command, by which We find that He had passed the Straights of Messina in pursuit of the Ship of the Admiral Second in Command and another of his Ships that had ran away from him in the night time. It appears also that a general Mutiny had taken place on board The Turkish Squadron in this harbour & that Cadir Bey had been forced to Sea contrary to his intentions which were not to separate from the Russian Squadron. The Copy of Cadir Beys journal is inclosed & will inform Your Lordship of all the particulars We know of this most unfortunate Affair.

45) Downing Street October 4th 1799

Sir,

Your Dispatch marked N. 23 with its Inclosures containing an Account of the Capitulation of the Fortresses of Capua and Gaeta has been received and laid before the King.

I have at the same time to acknowledge the receipt of the Ratification accompanied by a Copy of the written Declaration made by You in His Majesty's Name agreeable to the Instructions contained in my Dispatch N. 2 relative to the Casus foederis as applied to Spain.

You will receive together with this Dispatch a letter from the King, a Copy of which is inclosed, in answer to the one received from His Sicilian Majesty, which You will present in the usual form and accompanied by suitable Expressions in His Majesty's Name.

I have the Satisfaction to conclude by conveying You the expression of His Majesty's Satisfaction at the Zeal and judgement with which You appear to have acted during the whole course of the momentous and interesting period of which the detail is related in your last Dispatches.

46) Palermo October 14th 1799

My Lord

Captain Hardy in His Majesty's Ship The Foudroyant returned to this Harbour the 3^d instant, having Executed the Commission given him by Lord Nelson to carry the King and Queen of Sardinia with Their Royal family from Cagliari to Leghorn; which service was performed in three days, and to the compleat Satisfaction of Their Sardinian Majesties.

The Foudroyant having compleated her Water sailed from hence on the 5th inst. with Lord Nelson on board, for Minorca and it appears to be His Lordship's intention to collect the greatest part of his force at Mahon, except the Ships employ'd in the Blockade of Malta.

Commodore Troubridge in the Culloden had been directed by Lord Nelson to quit the Bay of Naples with the Squadron under his Command as soon as the Russian Squadron under the Command of Admiral Usacon, (and order'd there from hence) shou'd appear in that Bay, and to try if he cou'd reduce Civita Vecchia already blocked up by Capt. Lewis in His Majesty's Ship Minotaur. The Active Commodore has not only oblig'd Civita Vecchia to Capitulate but contrived that Rome shou'd be included in the same Capitulation, and acting in Concert with General Bourcard who commanded His Sicilian Majesty's regular land forces at the Gates of Rome put a strong Garrison of Neapolitan Troops into the Castle of S.t Angelo taking possession both of Rome and Civita Vecchia in the Pope's Name, and His Sicilian Majesty has sent from hence Mareschal Naselli to Command at Rome, with orders that the Flag of the Sede vacante (The Pope being dead) shou'd be put up in all the Fortresses in the Roman State of which His Majesty, with the Assistance of Great Britain, had taken possession. The Austrian General Froelick came into Rome soon after it had been taken possession of by The King of Naples. We understand here that such places in the Roman Sate, and Praesidii of Tuscany, as have possessed by the Austrians remain under the Flag of the Emperor of Germany.

By Commodore Troubridge's account, the french Garrisons of Rome and Civita Vecchia consisted of about Six Thousand men, all of which are either embarked, for France, and sent off directly without being consider'd as Prisoners of War. This Capitulation was made by Mons.r Garnier, the french Commanding Officer at Rome who came for that purpose to Civita Vecchia and settled with Commodore Troubridge on board the Culloden in that Port.

I most sincerely Congratulate Your Lordship on the great Event of the defeat and death of Tippo Saib, and his two Sons taken Prisoners at Seringapatam taken by Storm, which according to the Accounts I have just received from Sir Sidney Smith in a Letter dated from Cyprus Sep.r 9th, happen'd in the Month of May last, and is particularized in the Gazettes of Bombay and Madras, sent to Lord Nelson.

Sir Sidney's Dispatches for Lord Nelson and me were brought to Messina in a Turkish Corvette commanded by M.r England, one of the Lieutenants of the Tyger, and order'd to join Lord Nelson with all speed, but as she wanted repairs, Collonel Graham advised the sending these Dispatches by land to me, but as there is not any British Vessel in this Port at present, and this Government to whom I applied not having an Armed Vessel ready to send to Minorca I was obliged to return the Dispatches to Sir Sidney Smith's Lieu.t at Messina, who in a Letter to me said that he hoped to have the Turkish Vessel sufficiently repaired in a few days, for him to be able to go on to join Lord Nelson at Mahon. By Sir Sidney Smith's Letters to me I find that he does not doubt but that Buonaparte must soon be reduced to the last extremity and take shelter with the remains of His Army in Alexandria, now in a good State of defence, and notwithstanding his having compleatly beaten the vanguard of the Grand Signor's Army (which was at Damascus), consisting of five thousand Men and allowing themselves to be cut to pieces by a small body of french Cavalry without ever daring to look them in the face; The Gun boats however under Sir Sidney

Smith's direction did so much Execution on the Enemy in this Action near Aboukir that He says that two or three such Victories as Buonaparte now boasts of wou'd anihilate his Army.

I mention these circumstances least by chance no fresh accounts from Sir Sidney Smith shou'd have reached England, altho' as I imagine as this Affair of Aboukir happend the 29th of July, such an account must have reached Your Lordship long ago.

The presence of His Sicilian Majesty at Naples appears every day to be more and more Necessary, but I am convinced that the Court will not return to that Capital unless they are protected by a part of the Britih Squadron under the Command of Lord Nelson, for it has no true Confidence in any other Support than that of its Good Ally the King Our Royal Master.

The object that Lord Nelson seems to have principally, and very properly, in View at this moment, is the Reduction of Malta and is in Concert with Admiral Usacon endeavouring to Collect a force sufficient to Awe the Fortress of La Valetta into Submission, before the breaking up of the Season can give the french a chance of throwing in the ample succours they have prepared at Toulon for the relief of Malta.

Unless Lord Nelson shou'd have found it absolutely necessary to go down to Gibraltar His Lordship will probably return to Palermo in the course of this month.

Their Sicilian Majesties heve been both indisposed, and indeed amost all here have been indisposed of late, owing to the excessive and continued heats. I am so reduced with a Diarhea that I am incapable of much application, but the Palermitans console us with the assurance that when the rain comes and cools the Air We shall all be well – As yet the Thermometer at midday in the Shade has seldom been lower than Eighty degrees.

A British Consul being much wanted at Civita Vecchia at this moment I have taken upon me to authorize M.r Richard Bortron to act as such untill Your Lordship's pleasure shall be known. I am not personally acquainted with M.r Bortron but can assure Your Lordship that he bears an excellent Character, and is well known to Lord Nelson and most of the Officers of His Majesty's Mediterranean Squadron, to whom he has renderd essential Services during the Course of this War.

I have the honor to be
My Lord
Your Lordship's
most obedient and
most humble Servant
Wm Hamilton

47) Downing Street October 25th 1799

Sir,

Colonel Mahony formerly Colonel Commandant in the Regiment of Ben-
vick and who has since served in this Country as Lieut Colonel of the Irish
Brigade is unfortunately so circumstanced in consequence of having been
educated in the Roman Catholic Religion as to find himself excluded from
that situation to which his talents and experience would otherwise entitle
him: – It has been in consequence his object to procure some Opportunity of
Foreign Service in which his Zeal and Military knowledge might be displayed with credit to himself and to the Advantage of the Cause to which is
attached by habit and principle.

With this View it was that he was at the Recommendation of the Duke of
Brunswick mentioned by me to Monsieur d'Almeida as a Person well fitted
to hold a considerable Station in the Portugheze Army; – But His Royal
Higness The Prince of Brazil having determined not to make any Addition
to the number of Foreigners employed in the Portugueze Armies, I am
induced to recommend him to your good Offices as a Person who is represented to me to be both in principle and in military talent and experience
likely to be a useful Acquisition to the Staff of the Neapolitan Army.

48) Palermo Nevember 8th 1799

My Lord

On the 21st of last Month Lord Nelson in His Majesty's Ship Foudroyant
accompanied by the Minotaur Capt. Lewis return'd to this Port from
Minorca, having left all well there, but Sir James Erskine expecting Gen.l
Fox daily, did not think proper to comply with Lord Nelson's request immediatly, and afford him One Thousand or fifteen hundred men from the Garrison of Mahon, to go upon the intended necessary Expedition against Malta.
Lord Nelson sent the Foudroyant and Minotaur directly on his return to
block up the harbour of Malta more closely and wrote to Admiral Usacon in
the Bay of Naples to point out to His Excy the necessity of acting directly,
and with vigour against Malta, which never can be reduced without a regular Military Force, and it is to be hoped that the Russian Admiral will send
Three Thousand Russians (that embarked some time ago at Leghorn and
were bound for Naples) to join such forces as can possibly be collected, of
British and Neapolitans, for the Expedition against Malta.

We have not yet received the News of the Surrender of Ancona besieged by Russians, Austrians, and Neapolitans, and said to be in the utmost distress.

His Sicilian Majesty has appointed The Prince Cassaro a Sicilian Nobleman Lugo Tenente at Naples to supply the place of Cardinal Ruffo who is going to the Conclave which We hear is to be held at Venice.

The Trials of the principal Neapolitan Rebels having been carried on without intermission ever since We left the Bay of Naples, many of all Classes have sufferd death, by having been either beheaded or hang'd; among the latter We have seen with regret the name of Doctor Domenico Cirillo, One of the first Physicians, Botanist's and Naturalist's in Europe.

By the last Letters from Mareshall Naselli to this Government Rome was perfectly quiet and seemingly contented.

Our Eyes are anxiously turned towards Holland and Switzerland from whence the most favourable reports circulate here, but from our remote Situation We are the last in receiving any Authentic accounts.

Their Sicilian Majesties are greatly recover'd from The late indisposition and all the Invalides that suffer'd here from the long continued Heats are daily recovering, as a great quantity of rain has fall'n of late and cool'd the Air.

I am desired by the Marquis de Gallo in a Letter dated 11th of Sep.t from St. Petersburgh to entreat of Your Lordship to lay him at the King's Feet and to return his most humble thanks for the Snuff Box with His Majesty's Picture which he has received in consequence of his having Sign'd with me the late Treaty between Great Britain and the Two Sicilies.

A Messenger arrived here a few days ago from Constantinople with Letters for Lord Nelson from the Grand Vizir and Captain Bashaw and a present of a Diamond Emblem or Star set in the European Fashion, in the midst of which is a crescent and Star and which the Grand Signor sent to His Lordship as a most particular mark of His Friendship, desiring that He might wear it on his breast. The passion that the Grand Signor has taken for Lord Nelson is not to be expressed, Every one coming from Constantinople has assured me that He is daily named by His Imperial Majesty with signs of the utmost Veneration Expressing always a strong desire of seeing His Lordship at Constantinople.

I have the honor to be
My Lord
Your Lordship's
most obedient and
most humble Servant
Wm Hamilton

49) Palermo November 12th 1799

My Lord

I profit of Captain Hardy's return to England to send to Your Lordship a Copy of an Italian Translation of Mr. Rose's valuable, and to us most interesting, Publication, on the present State of Great Britain relative to it's Finances Commerce &c and which has been just published here under the Auspices of General Acton.

Since my last We have nothing New except Lord Nelson's having receiv'd certain accounts of the french Squadron consisting of two Venetian Ships of the Line armed en Flute[127], Two Frigates and two Brigantines having Sailed from Toulon. Their destination is supposed to be for the Succour of Malta. Lord Nelson supposes them to have put in to Villa Franca but has dispatched His Majesty's Frigate Penelope from hence to look after them. At present there are no less than Nine Ships of the Line British and Portugheze that block the Harbour of Malta.

This Court has received accounts from Corsica confirming the reports of General's Buonaparte and Berthier having been at Bastia in a Bomb Vessel that escaped from Alexandria. According to these reports they bragged to their Friends of having left the french Army in a prosperous Situation and well fortified both at Cairo and Alexandria. General Buonaparte was struck on hearing of Mantua's having fallen into the hands of the Austrians, but said it wou'd soon be retaken. The Account of the French Commissaries having been assassinated at Radstadt seem'd to afflict him most saying they were his bosom Friends.

I have the honor to be
My Lord
Your Lordship's
most obedient and
most humble Servant
Wm Hamilton

50) Palermo December 6th 1799

My Lord

The Principessa Reale The Ship of the Portugheze Admiral Niza came into this Port the day before Yesterday having been struck with Lightning and most of her Main Mast consumed. The Portugheze Squadron is in a miserable State and has long been order'd home, but the Marquis keeps his Squadron and remains himself at Malta untill the arrival of the Russian

Squadron daily Expected there from Naples, with a considerable body of Russian Land forces. Lord Nelson praises much the Zeal and good Conduct which The Marquis Niza has shewn on every occasion since He has been under His Lordship's Command.

By the last reports from Malta the french Garrison of the Valetta seem'd to be much distressed and as the Russians are probably arrived there by this time, and the King's Ships The Foudroyant and Culloden with the greatest part of the British Garrison of Messina under the Command of Brig. Gen.l Graham are supposed to have already Sail'd for Malta from Messina according to their Orders; We entertain the most sanguine hopes that We may be able to inform your Lordship before the end of this Month of the Surrender of the Valetta, and of Malta's being in the possession of the three Allied Powers – Great Britain Russia and Naples. The poor brave and Loyal Inhabitants of that Island have often been on the point of Surrendering to the french from extreme hunger and Misery, and wou'd have done so if they had not been prevented by the Extraordinary Efforts of Capt. Ball of His Majesty's Ship Alexander, and the small Sums of Money and some little Provisions which Lord Nelson and I obtain'd for them from time to time & with the utmost difficulty from this Government in order to prevent this inconveniency for the future, particularly as this Government refused to advance any more Money or Provisions Solely on it's Account, Lord Nelson The Chev.r Italinski the Russian Minister and myself had a Meeting with General Acton Where it was agreed by word of Mouth that in future the expence of keeping the Loyal Maltese from starving shou'd be placed to the account of the Three above mention'd Power's, and I flatter myself that His Majesty will not disapprove of this Measure which We all thought to be absolutely Necessary and cou'd not suffer any delay.

Shou'd any application be made to Your Lordship by the Marquis Circello concerning five Neapolitan Vessels that have been captured by Algerine Cruizers, notwithstanding their having had Lord Nelson's Passports, the inclosed Copies of the Billet that the Prince Luzzi wrote to me on that subject and of my Answer, will give Your Lordship the fullest information as to the true state of the Case. I can testify that Lord Nelson on every Application from this Government to grant His Passports, alway's declined it, doubting much whether such Passports wou'd be respected, but this Government still Urging His Lordship to put his Name to a sort of protection for certain Vessels employ'd in supplying Naples with Corn, and without which the Masters of those Vessels refused to sail He Complied but with the greatest reluctance, and foretold the Event that has taken place.

By the last Accounts from Rome and Naples all Seem'd to be quiet in those two Capitals, but the Neapolitans are very Anxious for the return of the Court to Naples, which certainly ought to take place as soon as possible.

This is the first time that I have been able to trust my Dispatches to the common Post of Naples which is now open and I hope Secure.

I have the honor to be
My LordYour Lordship's
most obedient and
most humble Servant
Wm Hamilton

51) (Secret) Palermo December 19ᵗʰ 1799

My Lord
I profit of Lord Nelson's dispatching a frigate to Gibraltar to send Your Lordship this Letter through the Channel of General O' Hara, and which allows me to write with more freedom than I cou'd do by the common Post.

Nothing can be more evident than the Necessity of His Sicilian Majesty's speedy return to Naples, the Actual State of the Kingdom of Naples and of the Capital from the account (A copy of which is inclosed N. 1) I have received from one whom I have reason to believe to be well inclined to Their Sicilian Majesties and Their Government is realy deplorable. The Prisons are full and every day fresh prosecutions are began against persons of every class suspected to have been more or less concern'd in the late Rebellion and Revolution or against zealous Royalists that committed some acts that can not legally be justified. No kind of provision having been made for the families and dependants of the principal Rebels that have been executed or banished, or have absconded, and whose Estates and property have been either Sequester'd or Confiscated, there are a great number of people in want of the daily bread. The Nobility having been justly deprived of their feudal power are Silent, but Sulky. The Absence of the Court from Naples causes an Universal languor and of course much discontent and the arrival of the Prince Cassaro from hence, as a Sort of Vice Roy, tho' stiled only, Captain General, confirms the Neapolitans in the opinion that His Sicilian Majesty has not the intention of returning soon to Naples. Lord Nelson and I have spoken our minds very freely on this Subject both to the Queen of Naples and General Acton, who allow of the necessity of the Court's returning soon to Naples, but say that The King will not hear of of it at present. I must do justice to the Queen, by assuring Your Lordship that She often declares her readiness to return to Naples, if thought Necessary confessing at the same time that after the ingratitude and ill usage Her Majesty has met with from the Neapolitans, She never shou'd be happy there. I can well conceive The King of Naples's not liking to return to Naples at this moment, His Majesty is sensible that He cou'd not with propriety lead the same dissipated life there, as formerly and He does not yet see such a Military force at Naples as He can rely on for His own personal Security, and which I have observed always had a great influence upon His Majesty. At Palermo His Majesty diverts Himself much the same as He did at Naples by going from one Country House to an other and by Shooting. His Majesty has been for these last ten days on the Mountains and in the Woods after the Wild Boars and Woodcocks.

In my former Letters I must have more than once mention'd to Your Lordship my observation on the general Corruption of Naples and of the infinity of defects in the Neapolitan Government, and I am sorry to say that I do not see any intention of endeavouring to reform it. At this moment when the most energic Government is wanting there appears to be little or no Government, for the Queen and General Acton are at variance and His Sicilian Majesty being now in possession of General Acton's advice without the Medium of the Queen has withdrawn much of His former attention to Her Majesty. The Prince Belmonte and the Prince Castel Cicala seem to posses most of the Queen's Confidence at present but His Sicilian Majesty having Secured to Himself General Acton now, as to all appearance, takes the whole of Business on His own Shoulders without consulting The Queen. Altho' it is impossible to defend General Acton's conduct throughout, I must own my partiality for him, I think him an honest man, and truly attached to what He thinks to be for the Interest and dignity of Their Sicilian Majesties, and the Two Sicilies. He is the only man of business that I have met with in this Country and altho' a Slave to His Office is reproached by the opposite Party of Undertaking every thing, of excluding every body else and not finishing any thing Himself. I do not say which party is in the right but I lament that there shou'd be such a division at this moment in a government where the utmost temper and Unanimity is requisite, to retrieve the Nation from Anarchy and Confusion and restore to it Peace and good order. I lament that the good heart and excellent head of Her Sicilian Majesty shou'd be so little consulted. The Party in opposition to the Queen allow of Her Majesty's very superiour Understanding, but say that Her Majesty's Passions being very strong, and getting the better of Her judgement, She is but too often led to open her mind, and put Her trust in persons very unworthy of Her Confidence, who deceive and betray Her Majesty, and I fear that The King is of the same opinion.

I sent a Copy of the paper that I received from Naples to General Acton, and Your Lordship will see in His Excy's Answer to me inclosed N. 2) His remarks upon it. It is clear that General Acton's Idea still is to keep down the Nobility and favour the People as much as possible. Was I to be called upon for an opinion it wou'd be that The King shou'd return to Naples immediatly grant himself the General Pardon, and put an end to the Numerous Prosecutions on foot, and apply Himself seriously to the formation of a better Government, inviting the Nobility to assist him in so Salutary a Measure, assuring them that what had pass'd shou'd be entirely forgotten; and that He wish'd to live upon a Friendly footing with them; I am convinced that all wou'd go right, whereas by following the present plan I shou'd fear that Their Sicilian Majesties will meet with more intrigues and opposition from the Barons at Naples than They are aware of, and will never enjoy a moment of Tranquility, and that either the Court of Vienna, or Madrid, will endeavor to profit of these discontents.

Your Lorship will see in Gen.l Acton's billet that the Application I made to His Excy in favor of Colonel Mahony according to the Instructions Your Lordship was pleased to give me in Your dispatch of the 25th of October N. 6.) has been properly attended to and that as soon as His Sicilian Majesty returns from his Shooting Party I shall probably be authorized to send Your Lordship an Official and favorable Answer.

Brig.r General Graham with his detachment from the Citadel of Messina is safely landed at Malta but We have no account of the Russians long expected there from the Bay of Naples – Whatever request Brig.r Gen.l Graham has made to this Government for Artillery, Artillery men &c has been readily Granted.

The Marquis Nizza with the Portugheze Squadron is on the point of returning home according to the Orders He has receiv'd.

Lest Your Lordship shou'd not have heard of the late most important Successes of the Emperor of Germany's Army in Italy, Three Printed Bulletins which I receiv'd the day before Yesterday from Leghorn are inclosed.

I have the honor to be
My Lord
Your Lordship's
most obedient and
most humble Servant
Wm Hamilton

52) Downing Street December 22ᵈ 1799
Sir Wm Hamilton K. B.

Sir,

The present Situation of Affairs in Italy appears to offer an Opportunity for complying with the Wish which You have so frequently expressed of being able to avail yourself of His Majesty's gracious Permission for Your Return to England after the very arduous & laborious Duties in which You have been recently engaged. I have accordingly received His Majesty's Commands to signify to You His most gracious Pemission for this Purpose; I should however but ill satisfy My own Feelings & My Sense of what is due to Exertions so zealously employed and so long and so usefully continued, if I did not express to You the Sentiments which I entertain in common with the rest of His Majesty's Sevants of Your Zeal and Assiduity in the Performance of those Duties and of that Conduct by which You have at the same time so much recommended Yourself to the favourable Opinion of Their Sicilian Majesties, and have so well expressed the Feelings and Wishes of His Majesty's Friendship towards those Sovereigns.

The Memory of those Transactions will I am confident be advantageous to the Reputation and to the future Interests of this Country as connected with the other States of Italy.

As the present State of the Neapolitan Dominions appears however still to require the constant Residence of a Minister on the Part of His Majesty, His Majesty has been pleased to appoint for that Purpose the Honble Arthur Paget with whom I have to request that You will communicate fully upon the Subject of the present internal Situation of the Country and upon such Points of Information as may be necessary for his Instruction and for preventing as far as possible the Inconvenience which might otherwise arise from the Want of that local Knowledge which an Experience of so many Years has enabled You to acquire[128].

CONCLUSION

"What are the textual features of Hamilton's dispatches?" and "What is their documentary value?" are two questions which will be addressed in this final section of the present work in the hope that the answers will give an insight into Hamilton's personality as well as bring new light on some aspects of the Neapolitan Revolution of 1799.

As is well known, a text can fulfil many different functions but the structure of a message depends primarily on the predominant one. Now, one would expect an ambassador's dispatches to be characterized by the almost exclusive predominance of the referential function, or the context, for they are supposed essentially to contain political, military, economic information on the foreign country where the ambassador is living. Yet, strange though it may seem, Hamilton's dispatches strike the reader as being centred, in the first place, on the emotive function (expression of the speaker's attitude) and, in a hierarchically subordinate position, on the directive one (the effect of the words on the addressee). It goes without saying that it is exactly this heterodoxy of Hamilton's dispatches that makes them more interesting and pleasant to read, and it is enough to have but a cursory glance at the classic and formal dispatches by Paget, Hamilton's successor at the Bourbon court of the Two Sicilies, to share that view[129].

The emotive or expressive function is conveyed by a variety of elements ranging from Hamilton's jingoism, which permeates all the dispatches and finds its expression mostly through a fierce hatred towards the French, always spelled with a small letter and invariably seen as morally perfidious robbers and brigands, to the celebration of his own skill at performing his diplomatic tasks, namely his being instrumental in persuading the Neapolitan Court to adopt a pro-Britain foreign policy and his ability to predict important political events, to the help given to the French and Corsican emigrants and, especially all the trouble taken in assisting the king's wayward son, to the hospitality afforded, at a price, to innumerable British subjects, travellers, navy officers and so on, to the crucial role played in restoring the Sicilian sovereigns on the throne of Naples.

These elements also can also be seen as falling within the domain of the directive function – subordinate yet essential- namely the pressure that Hamilton put on the British king and government so that they would give him credit and meet his foremost expectations of a pension large enough for him to settle his debts which spoiled his artistic taste, live quietly in retirement, provide for his wife Emma and buy back, if possible, the art collections he had been obliged to sell[130]. In this regard, Hamilton's two letters to his nephew Charles are insightful and final. Here, in a decidedly melancholy mood, he took stock of the thirty-six years spent in Naples, which he regarded as amply successful since he had ended up by being in terms of intimacy with the King of Naples, Queen Carolina's confidant, Nelson's bosom friend and one of those who had played a leading role in the dramatic events which had been deeply affecting the life of the kindom at the end of the century; for, without his help, the heroic Admiral would have been alone and speechless like an explorer venturing into an unknown land without the indispensable guide of an expert guide.

As for the referential function of the dispatches, which has a more strictly historical interest, one must note that, from what he called a remote corner of the world, Hamilton could only provide first-hand information on what was going on in the Kingdom of Naples since all the intelligence about Italian events, which he got from his correspondents in Rome, Florence, Milan, Venice, etc., and from the Court, most probably through Acton and the Queen, was often out of date[131].

But despite such limits, Hamilton's dispatches do furnish some useful information about Britain's foreign policies in the Mediterranean at the end of the 18th century and, obviously in greater measure, on the foreign policy of the kingdom of Naples, which, like an earthenware pot between solid metal containers, at a certain point in its history, found itself involved in the French revolutionary wars; as a result, Southern Italy was awaken out of its state of lethargy, its age-long slow pace was forced to change when the king had to flee to Palermo and the Republic was soon after proclaimed in Naples.

Beyond question, Hamilton's dispatches are most interesting when dealing with that revolutionary period which was followed by a ruthless, bloody counter-revolution led by Ruffo'army with the help of the British fleet and the violent mob of the *Lazzaroni*. They shed light on two issues which are central to the present work. The former concerns the role played by Hamilton in persuading the Neapolitan court to wage a disastrous war on the French in Rome, and the latter is the role played by the English in the bloody repression that followed the restoration of the monarchy in Naples in mid-1799.

In April 1796 Napoleon had started his campaign of Italy and Naples was soon obliged to make peace with France: Great Britain thought it would be better for Naples to stay neutral rather than be occupied by the French troops. An armistice was concluded in June and a peace treaty signed on the 10th of October, according to which only four ships from countries at war with France would be admitted into the Neapolitan ports and all the French political prisoners were to be set free. Peace was therefore a logical strategy: in Hamilton's view, Naples had better stay neutral until the occasion for a successful attack on the French supported by the British fleet and the Emperor's land forces should arise. To this purpose, the British minister set out on a propaganda campaign aimed at showing how necessary it was for the kingdom to take action for the common cause against the detrimental, contagious disease of the French revolution, and favour Britain by making its ports accessible to the British ships and trade. In Hamilton's words, the French were just notorious robbers and plunderers whose only interest lay in imposing heavy financial contributions, perfidious traitors who thought treaties were nothing but scrap paper, and, above all, staunchly opposed to monarchical rule. In doing so, Hamilton resorted, more than once, to the rhetorical device of Pontano's lines, which had appeared in one of his dispatches of the previous year. The following year saw the defeat of the Austrian forces by the new type of French army capable of incredibly intense attacks and led by remarkably skilled generals, and England obliged to oppose to the *Armée d'Angleterre* by itself. Hamilton's dispatches clearly mirror the British government's three main worries: the danger of an invasion, the cost of the war and the issue of internal dissent. The first two, which keep cropping up in the 1797 and 1798 dispatches, go a long way towards accounting for Great Britain's reluctance to give Naples naval assistance and a much-sought-for financial aid, while the third one, which seems to be the main reason for the behaviour of the British triad in repressing the Jacobins, makes itself felt in the 1799 dispatches. The French occupied Rome on 10 February 1798 and on 6 March Hamilton informed Lord Grenville of his intention to leave Naples, volunteering to plead for the common cause at the Court of St. Petersburgh. Although the French danger was looming large at the border of the Kingdom, the Neapolitan court did not seem to bother about it, which aroused both Hamilton's outrage and suspicion of

a secret agreement between Naples and the French. There was Hamilton
thundering on at the usual Neapolitan half measures out of which no good
would come, arranging for Prince Augustus's flight and his own, and
secretly informing the Foreign Office of the Queen's intention of leaving
Naples. Prince Augustus left Naples on 8 May and on 15 May Hamilton
was still waiting for certain news of the British fleet's arrival into the
Mediterranean to the rescue of the kingdom of Naples before deciding on
his departure for England once and for all. On 22 May Hamilton received
Lord Grenville's dispatch with the news of the imminent arrival of a
Squadron commanded by Lord Nelson. Emboldened by that news, Hamilton pointed out to Marquis di Gallo that the fleet would remain in the
Mediterranean on condition that only the British fleet was given unlimited access to the Neapolitan ports and supplied with all sorts of provisions. All of a sudden Hamilton seemed to change into a strategic expert;
he now needed a consul to deal with the red tape because the presence of
the British ships of war was offering the longed-for opportunity to drive
the French out of Italy and his help would be crucial. Hamilton's meta-
morphosis, which led him to overestimate the Neapolitan armed forces
and underrate the enemy, could be accounted for by his vaulting ambition
to become a front-line diplomat capable of having an impact on events on
a par with his colleagues at the important courts of Madrid and Vienna,
or by that trait of his personality[132] which would lead him to show enthusiasm for anything that could relieve him of the boredom of everyday life,
and to take a lively interest in novelties. On 18 June 1798 Nelson's fleet
made its appearance in the Bay of Naples and Troubridge came on shore
to make sure Britain's demands had been met with. Reassured by Acton
and Gallo, Nelson sailed again in search of the enemy while Hamilton
strongly advised the court to take action using Pontano's lines against half
measures. After Nelson's victory at Aboukir Bay, negotiations for a treaty
between the courts of Naples and London began. Nelson was given an
incredibly hearty welcome in Naples and the Queen Carolina went that
far as to express the desire of having a picture of Nelson on a wall of her
bedroom. On 3 October Downing Street sent Hamilton the necessary
instructions for the treaty, emphasizing, in no uncertain terms, the impossibility for Naples to obtain the financial aid for which Marquis Circello
had been applying for in London, going back to the topic in a subsequent
message. On 9 October Hamilton acquainted London with the arrival of
general Mack, the new commander of the Neapolitan army as well as with
Nelson's intention and his own of leaving Naples if the Neapolitan government did not resolve to make an attack on the French with the support
of the Imperial arms.

On 16 October Hamilton, in a secret letter, informed London that 36,000 Neapolitan troops were ready to march into the Roman State against the French. At St. Germano, in Abruzzo, Hamilton, Nelson and Acton, after watching the military manoeuvres of the army and being impressed by them, agreed that action was to be taken and that the army would get moving on 23 November. Three days later, the Neapolitan army was near Rome while Nelson sailed for Leghorn with 6,000 Neapolitan soldiers in order to bar the French troops' way. On 2 December Hamilton wrote to Lord Granville that the treaty had been signed but the Queen and Marquis Gallo had been insisting on a financial aid because the money collected for the war was barely sufficient for six months' military operations. Hamilton told Marquis Gallo again that the court of London was not in a position to grant the aid, but added, with a great deal of cunning, that the chances, if any, of obtaining it depended on the king's continuing the war against the French. Moreover, Hamilton agreed on a an article without Lord Grenville's authorization. Hamilton's subsequent dispatches of 11, 19 and 28 December tell of the shameful defeat of the Neapolitan army, due, in Hamilton's words, to the cowardly, treacherous behaviour of officers and soldiers alike, and of the king's flight to Palermo.

These are the main facts and they seem to suggest that since as late as 2 December the Queen and Marquis Gallo were still asking for money, Hamilton must have let the court hope for a financial aid from Britain though he perfectly knew that Britain was not in a position to grant it on account of the heavy war expenses which had resulted in higher taxation on British people. However, bent as Hamilton was on talking the court of Naples into making war on the Fench, he probably knew that lack of money would be a sound reason for Naples not to attack the French and try to come to an agreement instead – in this case, with the wisdom of hindsight, the course of events would certainly have been different. In addition to that, Hamilton had a first-hand knowledge of the real state of the Neapolitan army since he had more than once in his dispatches mentioned desertions, demoted officers, poor organization, epidemics due to bad food and unhealthy accommodation. Hamilton knew all of this and much more since he had been a soldier, had fought against the French in the Seven Years War[133], and, even if he was hoping that the Neapolitan army might be successful with the support of the Austrians, he could not ignore that the Neapolitan army by itself was doomed to utter failure as had already happened at the Toulon siege[134]. After thirty-six years pleasantly and expensively spent in Naples between dinner parties, vases and Vesuvian observations, Hamilton knew all about the Kingdom, especially the lack of training and skill of the army led by foreign officers and made up of soldiers with little or no patriotic spirit, which Bourbon misgovernment could not inspire and keep alive. With no support from Austria and no financial help, the kingdom did not have a ghost of a chance in spite of the fine manoeuvres attended by Hamilton and Nelson. Perhaps the British minister trusted in numbers, thinking that 36,000 Neaplitam soldiers would be enough to defeat the enemy. But there is more to war than mere numbers as pointed out by Diamond when dealing with the conquest of the Incas empire by Pizarro[135]; for numbers cannot make up for the organization, valour and, above all, solid military tradition that characterize a good army. Experiments in history are not possible, so there is no knowing what would have happened if Ferdinand IV had not made war. What is known for sure, anyway, is that Hamilton, though warned by Lord Grenville that an attack without the Austrian support would be hazardous, played a major role in causing a war without which subsequent events would have been different.

As far the role played by the British triad in the bloody aftermath of the counter-revolution in Naples is concerned, three documents appear to be of some relevance: 1) Captain's Foote justifications of 27 June, 2) Nelson's observations of 24 June and 3) Hamilton's long dispatch of 14 July 1799. However, they express subjective, fragmentary, apologetic, if not reticent, views and do not settle the crucial issue of whether Nelson made a play of changing his mind, "matching Ruffo's finesse with some of the British variety"[136].

1) In Foote's justifications two elements seem to suggest that Nelson's decision to cancel the pact and hold back the Jacobins, who were expecting to be carried to Toulon in the polaccas, was made by the British admiral only.

Foote wrote he had signed the treaty because he regarded Cardinal Ruffo, albeit lacking in the most elementary knowledge of military tactics, as being His Sicilian Majesty's legitimate representative, which shows there had been no official document issued by the king that deprived the Cardinal of his authority as Vicar General. Besides, Foote had received no instructions about the conduct to follow, which confirms the fact that Ferdinand had made no decision about Ruffo's allegedly arbitrary behaviour. It was Nelson who had lost no time and rushed to the bay of Naples to do his own justice.

2) In his observations of 24 June Nelson clearly stated that the arrival of the British fleet had invalidated the pact made with the rebels and the French and that he had been authorized to make decisions but failed to mention any official document that deligitimized Ruffo, the King's Vicar

General and alter ego[137]. The point is that Nelson did not regard Russo's army as a regular one since it had been collected with money and prayers, nor did he recognize the cardinal as a real Vicar General. Because of his own lack of land forces, Nelson had had to recognise, albeit with bad grace, Ruffo's military successes and the reconquest of Naples, but he could not bring himself to accept an agreement with the rebels which sullied the honor and dignity of the Bourbon monarchy and actually acknowledged the Neapolitan patriots. In this respect, it is worth noting that the financial aid kindly granted by Great Britain was to be only used to organize a regular army for the reconquest of the kingdom.

3) In his dispatch of the 14th of July 1799 Hamilton wrote that Nelson had received complete instructions from the British governement about the course of action to follow in the circumstances. Accordingly, he had assured the Cardinal, who had signed the pact with the rebels with the only aim of preventing the city of Naples from being destroyed, that he would respect the pact until he learnt about the king's intentions.

Well now, in this respect, a new document, which the writer found at the National Archives in Kew, London[138], incontrovertibly shows that, by the time the so-called Nelson's volte-face took place, Ruffo had already received official orders from the Neapolitan king not to negotiate with the rebels, and, even if a pact had been signed, to wait for the king's ratification. It can therefore be reasonably argued that Nelson did not act of his own accord, but, if anything, cleverly followed Ferdinand's instructions to the letter.

Lastly, Hamilton's letters can also be read in the light of the role of chance and necessity in history, as brilliantly exemplified by Jared Diamond in a chapter of his remarkable *Guns, Germs, and Steel*.

Necessity in the Neapolitan events which saw the British triad play a major role could lie in the structural differences between Great Britain and the Kingdom of Naples, two models of monarchy which were similar only nominally. In Diamond's opinion, human societies which are centrally governed and nonegalitarian, at best, "do good by providing expensive services impossible to contract for on an individual basis (e. g. the military defence of the territory). At worst, they function as kleptocracies, transferring net wealth from commoners to upper classes. The difference between a kleptocrat and a wise statesman, between a robber baron and a public benefactor is merely one of degree: a matter of just how large a percentage of the tribute extracted from producers is retained by the elite, and how much the commoners like the public uses to which the redistributed tribute is put. Diamond goes on to ask why the commoners tolerate the transfer the fruits of their hard labour to kleptocrats. He answers that kleptocrats throughout the ages have resorted to a mixture of four solutions:

1) Disarm the populace, and arm the elite.

2) Make the masses happy by redistributing much of the tribute received, in popular ways.

3) Use the monopoly of force to promote happiness, by maintaining public order and curbing violence[139].

4) The remaining way for kleptocrats to gain public support is to construct an ideology or religion[140] justifying kleptocracy.

Whether Great Britain was being ruled by statesmen or kleptocrats at the end of the 18th century is not relevant here, but it is an undisputed fact that the kleptocrats ruling Naples did not enjoy everyone's support, but only that of the Lazzaroni, who represented, as it were, the tribal section of the kingdom's society. Unlike the British kingdom, which had been deeply transformed by the combined effects of the industrial revolution and the political revolution of 1688, the kingdom of Naples, owing to a variety of problems, was not in a position to enter what is commonly referred to as modernity. Without resorting to all that has been said by scholars who have been dealing with the problem of the backwardness of Southern Italy, what Hamilton wrote about the topic in his dispatch of December 1799 would seem to offer an insight, though obviously biased, into the real conditions of the kingdom of Naples in the period concerned: 1) misgovernment; 2) upper classes indifferent to education, politics and art of war; 2) lack of industrial organization which goes hand in hand with lack of cooperative spirit[141]; 3) an army mostly commanded by foreign officers and made up of soldiers with no patriotic spirit and little or no military training.

It is indeed these substantial structural differences that could account for the enormous amount of power enjoyed and put to use by the British triad during the so-called Jacobin triennium with its necessary consequences.

Chance is instead represented by the presence in Naples of a British ambassador who retained his position for as many as 36 years allured by climate, ancient art and Vesuvius. Deeply engrossed in his love of vases and natural phenomena, he did not show much interest in, and talent for, the art of diplomacy. Then, suddenly finding himself at the centre of action in the aftermath of the French Revolution, he thought, in a burst of vaulting ambition, that the time had eventually come for him to make a name for himself also as a diplomat. But all he achieved was to persuade

Ferdinand to go to a ruinous war against the French, thus precipitating the much-dreaded revolution in Naples. All things considered, to Hamilton, who did remarkably well in fields other than diplomacy, but who is nonetheless usually remembered as the complaisant paranymph of his own wife Emma, the famous phrase "Englishman Italianate Devil Incarnate" would seem to be appropriate with the substitution of Neapolitanate for Italianate" for the sake of better precision, as well as the so-called "Peter Principle" formulated by Lawrence Peter in his 1968 book of the same name and stated as 'in a hierarchy every employee tends to rise to his level of incompetence'[142].

APPENDIX

An unpublished letter from Ferdinand IV to Cardinal Ruffo

1) Copia di Lettera Scritta dal Re al cardinale Ruffo da Palermo nel 25. Giugno 1799.

Eminentissimo mio. Dopo la mancanza di notizie direttamente da Voi, che non poca maraviglia mi faceva, finalmente due Lettere Vostre al Generale Sono pervenute questa mattina, l'una del 20, l'altra del 21. Tutto quanto avete fatto fino al vostro arrivo in Napoli, è Stato prodigioso, è degno di tutta la mai gratitudine e riconoscenza: non vorrei però che ora perdeste tutto il ben fatto, e merito che vi Siete acquistato con me, e colla nazione, come l'onore, e gloria verso l'Europa tutta. Mi dite in quelle Lettere che Si Sta trattando un Armistizio, e Capitolazione, ma non che lo State trattando: Io non conosco che Voi per mio Vicario Generale, dunque non So chi altro possa Star trattando. Voi avete le mie Istruzioni che vi Sono State confermate colle ultime mie Lettere, ed esse Sono chiare, e non prolisse, ne confuse. Sento alcunché che Siasi accordato 20. giorni di Armistizio ai Francesi di S. Elmo, e Si preparino dei Bastimenti per rimandare liberi in Francia tutti i Patrioti che Si Sono battuti con tanta ostinazione contro le mie Truppe Sotto i Vostri Ordini, ed i Realisti, e tutti quelli che Si Sono rifugiati nei Castelli, anche i più Scellerati. Io non conosco Patrioti, ma Ribelli, non conosco Dolcezza, ma Clemenza, ed in conseguenza voglio eseguite alla Lettera le mie Istruzioni, e con Speditezza; per ciò poter'eseguire anche con piacere ho veduto costì andare il degno, e bravo Nelson, col quale in tutto ve l'intenderete, e per tutto Su quest'assunto ve l'intenderete, le mie Istruzioni prescrivendo Deportazioni fuori dei miei Domini per i Subalterni, e meno Rei; a morte poi i Rei diffamati, e Capi di qualunque Genere, qualità, Sesso essi Siano. Avete fatto benissimo di non permettere l'unione delle Piazze, perché qte non devono più esistere, ne nemmeno nominarsi. Per i Soggetti che avete impiegati (mi figuro come interini fino ad attendere la mia risoluzione, o

approvazione) devo prevenirvi che dovete nominare, proporre, ma non met-
tere per fisso nessuno, Senza che io lo Sappia perché sarete ingannato, come
lo Siete Stato, non essendo a giorno di tutto, come lo siamo noi, mercè tutti
gl'infami Stampati, ed altri fogli che abbiamo avuto. Bisognio Sappiamo noi
come debolmente Si è condotto per lo passato, e Navarro benché non Si Sia
mostrato cattivo, è tutto per la Nobiltà, e creatura della Casa di Cassano. Di
Novi, e degli altri già vi ho Scritto; Pedrinelli è poi infame essendovi dei
Stampati col Suo Nome. E nemmeno ce n'era di bisogno, essendoci Logerot
che già da me avea ricevuta la firma per gli affari di Guerra. Tutto quanto vi
ho Scritto Sull'Affare dell'Armistizio, e dolcezza coi Ribelli, è per pura pre-
venzione, mentre non lo posso credere vero, conoscendo pur troppo la Vostra
esattezza nell'eseguire i miei Ordini, e l'impegno perché tutto Si termini con
l'onore, e decoro che Si conviene, e coll'assicurare la futura tranquillità dei
miei Stati, quale mai potrà ottenersi Senza estirpare fino all'ultimo Seme
questa infernale razza. Il Signore vi conservi come di tutto Cuore ve lo
desidera il vostro Affezionato

　　Ferdinando

Replico che non credo mai possibile che con Ribelli possa capitolarsi,
come Si farebbe con Truppa di altra Potenza, ma quando Siatene fatta, nulla
Sia Senza mia Ratifica. Per li Tribunali mi Sovvengo avervi detto in fine delle
mie Istruzioni, che questi Si sarebbero da me destinati: non capisco poi come
abbiate potuto fare Reggente della Vicaria Bisignano, quando questa Carica
era Stata da me abolita.

English Translation

　　Eminency,
　　After I did not hear directly from you for some time, which was very surprising indeed, the General has at last received two letters from you this
morning, one dated 20 and the other 21. All you did before arriving in
Naples was prodigious and worthy of my gratitude and appreciation: but I
should not want now that you should forfeit either the good reputation and
merit you won with me and the nation or the honour and glory you acquired
across Europe. You write in those letters that an armistice and a capitulation
are being negotiated, but you do not state that you are conducting these
negotiations. I recognize in you no person other than my Vicar General, so I
fail to understand who else might be negotiating on my behalf. You have my
instructions which were confirmed in my last letters in clear, concise and

quite explicit terms. I hear that a twenty-day armistice has been granted to the French in St Elmo and that some ships are being fitted out to send back free the Patriots who fought so obstinately against the troops under your command and against the Royalists, and all those who took shelter in the castles, even the most wicked villains. I do not recognize any Patriots, I only know rebels; I do not know gentleness, I only know clemency. For this purpose, too, it was with great pleasure that I saw the worthy, brave Nelson set sail for Naples, with whom you shall find an understanding to fulfil my instructions, according to which junior officers, or minor offenders, shall be deported beyond my dominions, while ill-famed offenders and leaders irrespective of kind, quality and sex shall be put to death. You did well not to let the Piazze[143] meet because they must cease to exist and never be mentioned again.

As for the subjects that you have employed (on a temporary base, I imagine, pending my final decision and approval) I feel obliged to warn you that you may appoint, propose but under no circumstances may you employ anyone permanently without my knowing because you are bound to be deceived, as you have been, lacking the intelligence that we can gather from the infamous printed matter and papers that we receive here. Bisognio, we know how weakly he has been behaving in the past, and Navarro, though he did not behave nastily, is completely in favour of the Nobility and a creature of the Cassano family; Novi and the others, I have already written to you about. Pedrinelli is a villain, too, his name appearing on certain printed matter. There was no need to appoint him either as Logerot had already been authorized to sign on my authority for the War Affairs. All I have written to you about the Armistice and supposed gentleness towards the Rebels is simply for the sake of warning you since I cannot believe that can be true, knowing only too well how accurately you carry out my orders and how hard you will be trying to end all matters with proper honour and decorum and guarantee the future tranquillity for my dominions, which cannot be achieved unless this hellish race has been eradicated to the last seed. God keep you as your affectionate Ferdinand wishes with all his heart.

I repeat that no Capitulation is possible with the Rebels as could be agreed with troops from another Power; and even if it has been agreed on, it shall be void and null without my ratification. I remember telling you in the final part of my instructions that I would make a decision about the courts of justice. I cannot understand how you could appoint Bisignano Regent of the Vicaria although I myself had abolished the position.

The letter above seems to be unpublished as there is no mention of it in the vast literature about the Neapolitan Revolution of 1799. The original is in the National Archives of London where it was found and copied[144].

The document can shed new light on the events that took place between the Treaty of 19 June 1799 and the trick that Lord Nelson, Sir William and Lady Hamilton supposedly played to persuade the Jacobins to evacuate the castle of St Elmo[145]. There are two elements in the king's letter that can help consider from a different angle the behaviour of Lord Nelson and Sir William Hamilton, who have repeatedly been accused of ignominiously breaking the agreement with the patriots.

The first element is the letter's date which can be defined as a *terminus post quem* sine it precedes the Jacobins' evacuation of the castle on 26 June 1799, Hamilton's letter to Ruffo of 26 June as well as the letters written by Ferdinand IV to Nelson (missing), by Acton to Hamilton and by the queen to Lady Hamilton[146].

The date refutes the claims made by Sacchinelli and Giglioli, and in particular the latter's assertion that the only reference to an official order given by the king to Ruffo went back to 29 April[147].

In the letter of 25 June there seems to be absolutely no question of any pardons being given, and the king's determination not to negotiate with the rebels is also shown by the instructions in the post-script.

The second element is the post-script itself in which the king stated that even if an armistice had been signed, it was not valid without his ratification. Thus, if this long-standing Nelsonian controversy is based upon the fact the British *tria juncta in uno*[148] pretended to agree on the armistice so that the patriots should evacuate the castle, the two elements above clearly show that Nelson simply obeyed to the letter the king's orders, which Ruffo must also have received before the fatal date of 28 June. Therefore, given that Nelson was a British admiral whose task was to protect His Majesty's ally, the Bourbon king, and that he certainly knew about the explicit orders for Cardinal Ruffo, it goes without saying that he could not have disobeyed them without failing to do his duty as an officer and without following a policy which would contrast with that taken by the British government against irregular armed forces[149].

Why, then did the king not punish the Cardinal's insubordinate behaviour? A plausible answer is to be found in Hamilton's dispatch of 5 August 1799, in which, after openly stating that he and Nelson both regretted that Ruffo had been appointed Captain General despite signing the infamous capitulation and negotiating with the rebels, Hamilton wrote that Acton had admitted in a letter to Nelson that the king, as well as fearing the Cardinal's six thousand troops, badly needed them to restore law and order in the capital city.

As for the accusations made against Hamilton, they appear to be groundless. Hamilton always showed devotion and admiration for Nelson, was proud of being on intimate terms with the hero of Aboukir Bay and could have nothing to gain from deceiving and exposing him to infamy and disgrace. Giglioli was so biased against Hamilton as to claim he did not know Naples[150]. But Hamilton did know Naples like a book through his passion for archaeology, volcanology and observation of nature and people as a member of the Royal Society and a personal friend of Joseph Banks. He knew Naples so well as to prefer the *lazzaroni* to Neapolitan nobility and express his wish to end his life in the Kingdom of Naples. Had Giglioli read Hamilton's two private letters to his nephew, Charles Greville, she would have hesitated to pass such a disgraceful sentence on Hamilton. Hamilton certainly harboured a grudge against the British government as they had showed no appreciation and gratitude of his job as a diplomat in Naples. Yet Hamilton had managed to persuade the Neapolitan government to be an ally of Great Britain and open its ports to the His Majesty's ships, of which Nelson had certainly taken advantage in pursuing the French Fleet and destroying it at Aboukir Bay. Hamilton can be charged of something else instead, that is of his perfidious role in persuading Ferdinand IV to wage war on the French although he was well aware of the inadequacy and manifold shortcomings of the Neapolitan army. A change of perspective is therefore necessary and that reckless resolution might be seen to have been the trigger for the whole affair of the Revolution.

To sum up, the documents reveal the following incontrovertible evidence:

1) Ferdinand IV sent Cardinal Ruffo his orders about the armistice in good time and insisted on ratification.

2) The Cardinal knew both about Nelson's imminent arrival and similarity of views between him and the king.

3) The Cardinal first tried to force Nelson's hand but, faced with the king's instruction, could not help leaving the patriots to their fate.

4) Nelson acted as befitted a naval officer and out of a sense of duty

5) Nelson did not deceive the patriots, but followed the king's instructions for Ruffo to the letter.

6) It is absolutely fanciful to try to treat Nelson and Hamilton as separate actors. They shared the same views and attitudes, and their successive *ménage a trois* leaves no room for doubt about it. The very ferocity of Bourbon reaction amply showed that Ferdinand IV did not need anyone's instigation to take his revenge on the rebels. Indeed, Hamilton went so far as to regret that there had been so many executions after the restoration of the monarchy (see Hamilton's dispatch of 19 September 1799).

7) The Neapolitan Jacobins had no alternative but to embark on the trans-ports because the city of Naples was firmly in the hands of both the Cardi-nal's troops and the *lazzaroni*. On the other hand, the armistice and capitu-lation had been signed mainly because Ruffo, Micheroux and Foote were afraid the enemy's fleet would soon be appearing in the bay of Naples. Had Méjean, for instance, wanted to save the patriots, he would not have waited as many as two days to ratify the treaty, thus allowing Nelson to arrive in the bay on 24 June 1799.

The 'Great Question', of which Giglioli speaks in the 15th chapter of *Naples in 1799*, is actually a question of who really cared about the Jacobins' fate. In the light of facts and documents, the answer is bound to be a melan-choly one, i. e. that their fate was no-one's concern. The only way out for them was the sea since the Franco-Spanish fleet would never arrive, the city was controlled by the Sanfedists and Lazzaroni and Méjean inspired no trust at all. So the British fleet was the lesser evil as compared with the violence raging in the city. If a trick was played, one must conclude that the author was the Cardinal himself who cunningly managed to respect the treaty and obey the king's orders at the same time by sending Micheroux with two British officers to the Castle of St Elmo in order to persuade the patriots to evacuate the castle and get on board the transports. But he knew only too well that they would never set sail for Toulon.

Finally, as far as the accusations of Foote and Southey are concererned, one can simply point out that while the former had a guilty conscience or con-flict of interest, the latter was justly lampooned by Byron as a turncoat.

Therefore it comes as no surprise that in 1819, two decades after these events, Lord Byron, who was to fight and die for Greece's freedom, dedicated the second stanza of the first Canto of his *Don Juan* to Lord Nelson with an implicit judgment:

> *Nelson was once Britannia's god of war,*
> *And still should be so, but the tide is turn'd;*
> *There's no more to be said of Trafalgar,*
> *'Tis with our hero quietly inurn'd;*
> *Because the army' s grown more popular,*
> *At which the naval people are concern'd;*
> *Besides, the prince is all for the land- service,*
> *Forgetting Duncan, Nelson, Howe, and Jervis.*[151]

Giovanni Capuano

NOTES

INTRODUCTION

1 For a fuller account see my *Naples and Napoleon. Southern Italy in the Age of the European Revolutions (1780-186?)* (Oxford University Press, Oxford 2006).

2 See the excellent biographies of Sir William by Brian Fothergill *Sir William Hamilton* (London 1969) and David Constantine *Fields of Fire. A Life of Sir William Hamilton* (Weidenfeld & Nicholson London 2001)².

3 Hence the name 'Sanfedists' for the volunteers who responded to Cardinal Ruffo's appeals in the provinces for support to destroy the Republic and its supporters in Naples: see Davis (2006) 87-9, 107-26.

4 The term that came to be used almost universally in the eighteenth century to describe the poorest classes in Naples.

5 *Captain Foote's Vindication of His Conduct in the Bay of Naples in the Summer of 1799* (2ⁿᵈ edition, Hatchard, London 1810) pp. 154-5.

6 See also: John A Davis 'L'Inghilterra, Nelson e la Repubblica Napoletana del 1799' in A.M. Rao (edi) *Napoli 1799. Fra Storia e Storiografia* (Istituto Italiano per gli Studi Filosofici, Vivarium. Napoli 2002) pp. 393-427.

7 For detailed descriptions of these and other individuals mentioned in the Introduction see Giovanni Capuano's notes to the dispatches in the second part of this volume.

8 The vessels that were to carry the patriots under safe-conduct by sea from Naples to France.

9 Nelson to Lord Keith 27 June 1799 – see below Doc. 28.

10 For the most recent general accounts of these events see: A.M. Rao 'La Repubblica Napoletana del 1799' and 'La prima restaurazione borbonica', in A.M. Rao & P. Villani *Napoli 1799-1815. Dalla Repubblica alla Monarchia Amministrativa* (ESI, Napoli 1994); M. Battaglini, *La Repubblica Napoletana. Origini, nascita, struttura* (Bonacci, Roma 1992); Id., *Atti, leggi, proclami ed altre carte della Repubblica Napoletana 1798-1799* (Salerno 1983, 3 vols); in English see Davis (2006) Chapters 4-7.

11 See Battaglini (1983) 2108-9, 2110-2114: these figures are also analysed in Carlo Knight 'Gli "Imbarcati" del 1799', in *Rendiconti dell'Academia di Archeologia, Lettre e Belle Arti*, Vol lxvii 1997-8 (Napoli 1997-8) pp. 469-515.

12 Maria Carolina to Ruffo, Palermo April 5 1799 in H.C. Gutteridge *Nelson and the Neapolitan Jacobins. Documents relating to the Suppression of the Jacobin Revolution at Naples in June 1799* (Navy Record Society 1903) p. 36

13 Maria Carolina to Ruffo, Palermo May 17 1799 in *Ibid* p. 56. Federici was a Neapolitan officer who had served under Frederick the Great and had accepted the rank of general in the Republican army – he was executed in October 1799.

14 Acton to Hamilton, Palermo June 26 1799, in *Ibid* p. 242.

15 See Appendix below.

16 These are vividly described in the recent novel by Barry Unsworth *Losing Nelson* (Hamish Hamilton, London 1999) which offers a brilliant contemporary exploration of the links between cults of heroism and national identities. On the mythologizing of the Republic see: A.M. Rao, 'Dalle elites al popolo: cultura e politica a Napoli nell'età dei lumi e della rivoluzione', in *Napoli 1799* ed. R. De Simone (Napoli 1999, Franco De Mauro Editore).

17 Captain A. Mahan, *The Life of Nelson. Embodiment of the Sea Power of Great Britain*, London, Little Brown & Co 2 Vols: Vol II, p. 1 – in the months following the Restoration Nelson repeatedly failed to obey Keith's orders to leave Sicily.

18 See Anna Maria Rao's comments on the debates amongst the Neapolitian exiles in Paris over the conduct of the Neapolitan army in the campaign of 1798, Mack's denunciation of the Neapolitan officers for treachery, the behaviour of the French military commanders – especially MacDonald and Méjan – following the Directory's decision to dismiss Championnet on account of his willingness to support the protests of the provisional government against the punitive policies imposed by Paris (Rao 1994, pp. 407-19). On the links between the cult of the hero, concepts of military honour and national identity in Britain in the Napeoleonic period, see L. Colley, *Britons. Forging the Nation 1707-1837* (Yale University Press, New Haven and London, 1992).

19 See eg V. Cuoco, 'La politica inglese in Italia' (4-8 gennaio 1806), in *Scritti Vari*, ed. N. Cortese & F. Nicolini (Laterza, Bari 1942) pp. 201-213; P. Colletta, *Storia del Reame di Napoli* (Firenze 1848) Vol 1, p. 171.

20 B. Croce, *Storia del Regno di Napoli* (Laterza, Bari 1945).

21 House of Commons: Hansard 3 February 1800.

22 Cited in: Captain Foote's, *Vindication of His Conduct in the Bay of Naples in the Summer of 1799* (2nd edition, Hatchard, London 1810) p. 9.

23 Foote to Rev. S.J. Clarke, March 11 1807, in *Ibid*, p. 39.

24 Cf A.M. Rao, *Esuli. L'Emigrazione Politica Italiana in Francia (1792-1802)* (Guida, Napoli 1992) pp. 448-452.

25 Helen Maria Williams, *Sketches of the State of Manners and Opinions in the French Republic towards the Close of the Eighteenth Century* (London 1801, 2 Vols) Vol 1 p. 179. The text of the Capitulations is included in Appendix 4. On Helen Maria Williams see: A.M. Rao, 'Tra civiltà e barbarie: storie inglesi della Repubblica napoletana del 1799', in R. De Lorenzo (ed) *Risorgimento, Democrazia, Mezzogiorno d'Italia. Studi in onore di Alfonso Scirocco* (Franco Angeli, Milano 2003) pp. 708-739 and Id, *Esuli* (1994) pp. 452.

26 R. Southey, *Life of Nelson* (John Murray, London 1813, 2 Vols: reprinted W.P. Nimmo, Hay & Mitchell, Edinburgh 1898 1 Vol) p. 170.

27 Jeafferson Miles, *Vindication of Admiral Lord Nelson's Proceedings in the Bay of Naples* (Bailly, London 1843; reprinted Marine Books, Cheshire 1991).

28 Sir Nicholas Harris Nicolas, *The Despatches and Letters of Vice Admiral Lord Viscount Nelson* (London 1844-7: reprinted Chatham Publishing, London 1997) Vol III: Nicolas had served in the Royal Navy in the Mediterranean under Admiral Duckworth and Lord Exmouth between 1808 and 1816.

29 Reprinted as F.P. Bradham, *Nelson at Naples. A Journal of June 10-30 1799* (David Nutt, London 1900).

30 Captain A..Mahan, *The Life of Nelson. Embodiment of the Sea Power of Great Britain*, London, Little Brown & Co, Vol 1, p. 441

31 H.C. Gutteridge, *Nelson and the Neapolitan Jacobins. Documents relating to the Suppression of the Jacobin Revolution at Naples in June 1799* (Navy Record Society 1903) p. xxx1.

32 Constance H.D. Giglioli (née Stocker), *Naples in 1799. An Account of the Revolutions of 1799 and the Rise and fall of the Parthenopean Republic*. New York, Dutton. London John Murray 1903.

33 David Vincent, *Nelson, Love and Fame* (Yale University Press, New Haven 2003) pp. 327-335.

34 C. Knight, 'Sir William Hamilton e il mancato rispetto da parte di Lord Nelson della "Capitolazione" del 1799', in *Atti del'Accademia Pontiana* n.s xlvii, 198 (Napoli 1999) pp. 373-397.

35 Barry Unsworth, *Losing Naples*, Hamish Hamilton, London 1999).

36 Susan Sontag, *The Volcano Lover* (Farrar Straus Giroux, New York 1992).

37 See Fothergill (1969) & Constantine (2001). On Sir William as a collector and connoisseur see Jenkins, Ian & Sloan, Kim, *Vases and Volcanoes. Sir William Hamilton and his Collection* (British Museum Press 1996). On the Grand Tour: Cesare de Seta, *L'Italia del Grand Tour da Montaigne a Goethe* (Electra, Milano 1996); Edward Chaney, *The Evolution of the Grand Tour* (Frank Cass London, Portland Oregon 1998); Barbara Naddeo, 'Cultural capitals and cosmopolitanism in eighteenth century Italy: the historiography and Italy in the Grand Tour', in *Journal of Modern Italian Studies* 10 (2) June 2003 pp. 183-99.

38 See Jenkins & Sloan cit: see also Maxine Berg, *Luxury and Pleasure in Eighteenth Century Britain* (Oxford University Press 2005).

39 Davis (2006) pp. 1-70.

40 See also John Roberston, *The Case for the Enlightenment. Scotland and Naples (1680-1760)* (Cambridge University Press 2005).

41 G. Pagano de Divitis, *Il Commercio inglese nel Mediterraneo dal Cinquecento al Settecento* (Guida, Napoli 1984); G. Pagano de Divitiis & V. Giura, *L'Italia del secondo Settcento nelle realzioni segrete di Wiliam Hamilton, Horace Mann e John Murray* (ESI, Napoli 1997). See also Biagio Salvemini, ' The arrogance of the market; the economy of the Kingdom between the Mediterranean and Europe', in G. Imbruglia (ed.), *Naples in the Eighteenth Century* (Cambridge University Press, Cambridge UK 2000) pp. 70-94.

42 See e.g G. Rousseau, 'The sources of Priapus: Anti-clericalism, homosocial desire and Richard Payne Knight', in G. Rousseau & R. Porter (eds), *Sexual Underworlds of the Enlightenment* (Manchester University Press 1987) pp. 101-42.

43 Doc 24 (Palermo 31 August 1797).

44 *Ibid.*

45 Davis (2006) 55-6.

46 On European international relations in this period see: Paul W Schroeder, *The Transformation of European Politics 1763-1848* (Clarendon Press, Oxford 1994).

47 E.g S. Engerman & P.K. O'Brien, 'The Industrial Revolution in Global Perspective', in R. Floud & P. Johnson (eds) *Cambridge Economic History of Modern Europe* (Cambridge University Press 2004).

48 See: Piers Mackesy, *The War in the Mediterranean 1803-1810* (Cambridge University Press, Cambridge 1971).

49 On the history of the conspiracy and the origins of the republican experiment see: A.M. Rao, 'La Repubblica napoletana del 1799 e la prima restaurazione borbonica' in A.M. Rao and P. Villani, *Napoli 1799-1815. Dalla Repubblica alla Monarchia amministrativa* (Edizioni del Sole, Napoli 1995); M. Battaglini, *La Repubblica Napoletana. Origini, nascita, strutture* (Barocci, Roma 1992); M. Battaglini & A. Placanica, *Atti, leggi, proclami ed altre carte della Repubblica napoletana 1798-1799* (Istituto Italiano per gli Studi Filosofici, Di Mauro Editore, Cava dei Tirenni, 4 vols s.d.).

50 Davis (2006) pp. 72-5.

51 See below Doc 6: Naples 6 March 1798.

52 Sir John Clapham, *Cambridge Diplomatic History of Europe* (1922) p. 236. On Bonaparte's policies see also A. Grab, *Napoleon and the Transformation of Europe* (Palgrave, London 2003).

53 Mahan, Vol. I, p. 363.

54 Schroeder (1994) pp. 177-182.

55 Doc 1798/43: Caserta 6 Nov 1798.

56 Nelson to Earl Spencer November 1798, in Nicholas Vol 3, p. 170.

57 *Ibid* p. 171.

58 Davis (2006) 74-5.

509 V. Cuoco, 'La politica inglese in Italia' (4-8 gennaio 1806) in *Scritti Vari* ed N. Cortese & F. Nicolini (Laterza, Bari 1942) pp. 201-213.

60 P. Colletta, *Storia del Reame di Napoli* (Firenze 1848) Vol 1, p. 171.

61 For the most recent bibliography on the counter-revolution see: A.M. Rao (ed.), *Folle Contro-Rivoluzionarie. Le insorgenze popolari nell'Italia Giacobina e Napoleonica* (Carocci, Roma 1999) Introduzione, pp. 9-36.

62 Nicolas Vol 2 p. 264 (Nelson to Earl St Vincent, Feb 3 1799).

63 *Ibid.*

64 *Ibid.* p. 275 (Nelson to Earl St Vincent, Palermo, March 2 1799.)

65 *Public Record Office*, London; *Foreign Office* (FO) Vol 12 Hamilton to Lord Grenville, 17 Jan 1799.

66 Nelson to the Duke of Clarence, April 11 1799, in Nicholas Vol 3, p. 324.

67 See, for example, the three letters to Troubridge (7 April 1799), Earl St Vincent (6 May 1799) and to Foote (6 May 1799) (in Nicholas, Vol 3 pp. 318, 347, 376) expressing delight at news of the execution of Jacobin rebels: cited in Knight (1998) p. 393 and 393 n72. See also Giglioli p. 70 & p. 309.

68 H.T. Dickinson (ed.) *Britain and the French Revolution* (London 1989); C. Crossley & I Small, *The French Revolution and British Culture* (Oxford 1989).

69 Schroeder (1994) pp. 162-3.

70 Cf. especially Rao (1994) pp. 448-452.

71 Cf. Coley (1994) pp. 88-98.

72 On the Irish rebellion see: M. Elliott *Partners in Revolution. The United Irishmen and France* (Yale University Press, New Haven, 1982)

73 The instructions are well known: 'To treat with such rebels is impossible, it must be put an end to. The rebel patriots must lay down their arms and surrender at the discretion of the King. Then in my opinion an example should be made of the leaders. Finally, I recommend to Lord Nelson to treat Naples as if it were a rebellious Irish town... I recommend... the greatest firmness, vigour and severity; our future tranquillity and positions depend upon it'. Maria Carolina to Lady Hamilton (Palermo, June 25, 1799) in Gutteridge p. 213

74 A detailed account of the French withdrawal is given in *Souvenirs du Maréchal MacDonald, Duc de Tarente* (Paris 1892) pp. 72 et seq: MacDonald was the French born son of Neil MacDonald, a Scottish Jacobite who accompanied the Pretender to France after the '45.

75 The Vicaria was the main criminal court and prison in Naples.

76 Guttridge, p. xxxvi (3rd April 1799).

77 *Ibid.* p. xxxvii

78 *Ibid.* pp. xliv-xiv

79 Foote (1810) pp. 24-25: 'from all the Intelligence I received I had much more reason to expect the French than the British fleet in the Bay of Naples'.

80 Foote to Nelson May 24, June 2nd and June 4th 1799 – Foote pp. 116-124.

81 Foote to Nelson June 16th: Foote 132-133.

82 Foote to Nelson, June 4th 1799: Foote p. 124

83 Knight (1999) p. 396: the letter was published in A. Dumas *I Borboni di Napoli* (Napoli 1862) vol IV, pp. 87-89 and then republished in Giglioli pp. 301-2 and Guttridge p. 271.

THE DISPATCHES

1 The National Archives, FO 70/10-14.
2 Davis (1999) p. 5.
3 See his two letters to his nephew, Charles Greville, dated 4 August 1799 and 22 September 1799, respectively.
4 In Hamilton's case, that happened more than once causing the Foreign Office to warn him and, eventually, in all likelihood, to dismiss him.
5 Most of the biographical information about Hamilton comes from Constantine's *Fields of Fire.*
6 Sir James Gray (1708-1773) was Envoy Extraordinary in Naples from December 1753 to October 1764. Within a few months of his arrival in Naples he was already involved in discussions with young Ferdinand IV about the plans of the new Royal Palace of Caserta. He took an interest in the Herculaneum excavations and actively promoted the Amateur Society, supporting many young travellers. In 1759 he was appointed Envoy Extraordinary Plenipotentiary. He finally returned to England in 1765, leaving two illegitimate children in Naples.
7 Venturi (1987) pp. 298-99.
8 De Divitis, Giura (1997) pp. 14-15.
9 Constantine (2001) p.16.
10 Hamilton would repeatedly complain about it.
11 Constantine (2001) p. 24.
12 Constantine (2001) p. 16, pp. 23-24.
13 Davis (1999) p. 7.
14 Constantine (2001) p. 213.
15 Manuel de Godoy (1767-1851) was a Spanish statesman. An army officer, he won the favour of Queen Maria Luisa of Spain and rose rapidly at the court of Charles IV. The king made him chief minister in 1792, and, except for a brief period, Godoy ruled continuously until 1806. Godoy joined the First Coalition (1793) against France, but in 1795 he made peace and was awarded the title of *principe de la paz*. His alliance with France involved Spain in a long war with England. The unpopularity of Godoy's government became acute after he concluded the Convention of Fontainebleau (1807) with Napoleon. Prince Ferdinand VII led the opposition and in 1808 was proclaimed king. Godoy was captured but was then rescued by the French and sent to Paris.
16 John Francis Edward Acton (1736-1811). Descended from Shropshire baronets, he was born a French Catholic in Besançon, where his father was a physician. Acton came to Florence in 1755 to join his uncle, John Acton, whom he succeeded as commander of the Tuscan Fleet in 1766. In August 1788 the Grand Duke, at the insistence of his sister, Queen Maria Carolina of Naples, promoted Acton to General and sent him to Naples to help reorganize the Neapolitan navy. By 1790 he was Chief Minister and worked closely with Sir William Hamilton during the French wars. In 1800 he married, with Papal dispensation, his brother Joseph's young daughter, Mary Anne; she bore him two sons and a daugher. Acton died in Palermo on 11 August 1811.
17 Captain Thomas Francis Freemantle (1765-1819). Third son of John Fremantle, he was made captain in 1791 and was with the Mediterranean Fleet from 1793 to 1797.In 1810 he became admiral. He died in Naples in 1819.
18 Gilbert Elliot-Murray-Kynynmond, 1st Earl of Minto (born Edinburgh, Scotland, 23 April 1751- died Stevenage, England,21 June, 1814) was a Scottish politician and diplomat. About 1763 Gilbert Elliot and his brother Hugh were sent to Paris, where their studies were supervised by the renowned Scottish philosopher David Hume, and where they became intimate with Honorè Mirabeau. Having passed the winters of 1766 and 1767 at the University of Edinburgh, Gilbert entered Christ Church, Oxford, and

on quitting the university he was called to the bar. In 1776 he entered parliament as an independent Whig MP for Morpeth. He became very friendly with Edmund Burke, and on two occasions was an unsuccessful candidate for the office of Speaker. In 1794 Elliot was appointed to govern Corsica, and in 1797 he assumed the additional names of Murray-Kynynmond and was created Baron Minto. From 1799 to 1801 he was envoy-extraordinary to Vienna, and having been for a few months president of the board of control he was appointed governor-general of India at the end of 1806. He governed with great success until 1813, during which he expanded the British presence in the area to the Moluccas, Java, and other Dutch possessions in the East Indies during the Napoleonic Wars. He was then created Viscount Melgund and Earl of Minto. He died at Stevenage on 21 June 1814 and was buried in Westminster Abbey.

19   Fabrizio Ruffo (1755-1832), Prince of Castelcicala, was born in Naples and joined the diplomatic service rather late. At the outbreak of the French Revolution, he was Neapolitan ambassador to St. James's court and was asked to represent his own government at Paris, but, in the face of danger, chose to stay in London. After his return to Naples, he became foreign minister and was a member of the junta responsible for the trial of political prisoners. According to Colletta, he was among those who advocated the most tyrannical measures. When Ferdinand IV was forced to leave Naples, he helped the king embark and sailed with him to Palermo. In 1815 he was appointed ambassador to Paris and the next year returned to London where he signed a trade treaty. In 1820 he refused to recognize the constitution proclaimed in Naples, so he lost his post. In 1829, after managing to get the French government to extradite a political refugee, named Galioti, he was violently attacked by French newspapers for his involvement in the notorious juntas of 1795 and 1799. He brought an action for libel against them but the journalists were acquitted. The 1830 revolution did not see him change his political opinions. He died of cholera in Paris in 1832.

20   Francis Drake (1764-1821). Drake arrived in Genoa as British Minister Plenipotentiary on 15 August 1793. From September 1795 to May 1796 Drake was also acting as commissioner with the Austrian army in Italy. Lady Berwick described an incident in which the Drakes had been surrounded in a country house near Genoa and had only escaped through Austrian intervention with a 'price' remaining on Drake's head

21   Thomas Graham (1748-1843). As a young man, Graham spent a year in France and then proceeded to Italy and Germany in order to complete his education. Following his wife's death in 1792, Graham pursued a distinguished military career. He was in Northern Italy from May 1796. In December he was trapped with the Austrian forces in Mantua, but succeeded in escaping through the French lines to report their plight to the Imperial commander.

22   Tommaso Maria di Somma, ninth Marquis of Circello (1737-1826) joined the Royal Company of Lifeguards. He was then appointed ambassador to Copenhagen by Tanucci in 1775 and was minister in Vienna from 1777 to 1786. On 12 July 1793 he signed the treaty of alliance between Britain and Naples. In September 1793 he was nominated ambassador to Great Britain and remained in England until 1804. After his return to Naples in 1804, he became foreign minister and in 1806 fled with the king to Sicily. He returned to Naples in 1815 and was appointed foreign minister once again. He died in Naples in 1823.

23   Prince Augustus Frederick (1773-1843) was the sixth son of George III. He spent nearly ten years in Naples, primarily for his health, but, after his illicit marriage with Lady Augusta Murray in 1793, he was also a disconsolate wanderer, rejected by his father George III. In June 1796, on receiving the news of the occupation of Bologna by French troops, the Prince went to Naples where he formed the Royal Neapolitan Club, composed of all the English noblemen and gentlemen who were travelling in Italy and resident some time in Naples. In March 1798 a Mr Livingston, a dour Scot, arrived from London to join the Prince's retinue, settle his finances and get him away from Naples.

Livingston considered Italy an immoral country and told the King that the Prince had constant dinners and suppers with very bad society. The Prince's last visit to Italy was made in 1799. He finally returned to England in May 1800.

24 This dispatch can be considered an epitome of all of Hamilton's subsequent letters. From his 'remote situation', where he could hardly give the Foreign Office any important information on international affairs, all he could do was tell Lord Grenville about what little took place at the Bourbon Court: the King was engrossed in his 'shooting parties' and the looming threats to his kingdom did not seem to worry him enough. Such lethargical ataraxy, which is traditionally associated with the mentality of Latin people, could not fail to upset an Englishman's pragmatically-oriented mind, ending up by being a cliché in Hamilton's following dispatches.

25 Epidemic diseases occurred very frequently in armies because pathogens need high density populations to reproduce. Infectious diseases such as flu, smallpox, etc., have played a major role in shaping history. Until World War Two, more victims of war died of war-borne microbes than of battle wounds. The winners of the past were not always the armies with the best generals and weapons, but were often merely those bearing the nastiest germs to transmit to their enemies. A case in point is represented by the European conquest of the Americas that began with Columbus's voyage of 1492. See Diamond (1998) pp. 196-201.

26 Reading between the lines, one might be under the impression that Hamilton did not think well of the King's indulging in his passion for hunting at a very critical moment for the Kingdom of Naples; besides, the king's way of hunting was, so to say, a passive one with beaters pushing game towards a place where he and his company were lying in wait to slaughter it in comfort and safety.

27 In Hamilton's time, the origin of viral diseases was not known: influenza, for instance, was attributed to 'the flowing in of ethereal fluid' badly affecting people's health. The term was applied to the influenza epidemic which began in Italy in 1743 to be soon after adopted as the standard English term for the disease.

28 The first part of the dispatch where Hamilton mentions the faulty organization of the Neapolitan army and the demotion of three officers appears to be significantly relevant in the light of the dramatic events that were to take place at the end of the following year. It clearly shows that Hamilton must have been well aware of the inadequacy of the Kingdom's armed forces by the time he eventually managed to talk the Bourbon court into waging war on the French in December 1798.

29 Charles Goddard acted as British consul in Naples in 1796 in the absence of Sir James Douglas. Lord Grenville had obtained the post for him, as he was in a bad state of health.

30 Joseph Denham, born in 1751, began trading in Civitavecchia early in 1771. In 1783 he was living with his family on the first floor of the Bottega del Sarmiento, Scalinata di Trinità dei Monti. On 5 February 1794 he was writing to Lady Hamilton in Naples concerning the 4th Earl of Bristol's intention of asking Sir William to resign as British Envoy in favour of his own nephew.

31 Adelaide and Victoria were King Louis XVI's old aunts. They were living in Rome under the Pope's protection.

32 Lady Berwick, a widow, set out from England with her three daughters. In October 1792 they were in Venice and by July 1796 she had settled with two of her three daughters in Naples where other English travellers were gathering as the French advanced. The following March, on her way back to England, she died and was buried at Manfredonia. Sir William Hamilton took her two daughters under his protection until the arrival of their brother Lord Berwick. Emily and Anne were both to die unmarried in England.

33 Thomas Jenkins (1722-1798) was a painter, dealer, antiquary and banker. Born in Rome, he became the richest and most influential figure of the English colony in the latter half of the 18th century. He was a sort of mentor to British travellers residing in Rome, where,

there being no British ambassador, he may have been said to have done the honour of the
nation. The French invasion led to his final departure in 1798 and his valuable collections
were left behind to the French. He died at Yarmouth just after he landed.

34   The treaty contained very onerous terms for the Pope's State: in particular, according to
articles 12 and 13, by the 5th of March the Pope was to deliver over to the French army's
treasurer at Foligno 15 million lire *tornesi* as payment of the balance of the debt from the
Bologna armistice and another fifteem million lire in cash, diamonds and other valuables
in two instalments by March and April, respectively.

35   A small sailing ship commonly used in the 17th and 18th centuries.

36   At the tip of the south-western coast of Portugal.

37   Of course, Hamilton believed that England was a crucial factor in maintaining order and
peace in Europe whose balance was being threatened by revolutionary France. "Perfidious"
is his strong term of abuse for the enemy but, actually, the phrase "perfidious Albion", an
English rendering of French "la perfide Albion", had already been used by the Marquis de
Ximenès to refer to England's alleged treacherous policy towards foreigners. Ironically
enough, Hamilton's later cajoling Ferdinand IV into waging war may be said to
substantiate that charge to a great extent. Hamilton invariably spells "french" with a small
letter, most probably to point out his contempt for the enemy.

38   Hamilton never uses the progressive passive which is not to be found in the English
language until the late years of the 18th century. The earliest instance is from the year
1769. See Baugh and Cable (1993) pp. 286-88.

39   This clearly shows that the Queen of Naples, as well as leaning politically towards
England, was Hamilton's main source of information at the Bourbon court

40   Marzio Mastrilli, first Marquis, then Duke of Gallo. Born in Palermo, he took up a career
as a diplomat at a very early age. In 1795 he left for Vienna where he escorted Ferdinand
IV's daughter, who was destined to be Emperor Francis II's bride. He remained at Vienna
as ambassador, earning great respect at the Austrian court. He negotiated with Napoleon
and took an active part in the Capoformio treaty as minister plenipotentiary of the
kingdom of Naples. Having returned to Naples, he succeeded Acton and, after the king
fled to Palemo, was sent to Vienna not to return to Naples until the end of 1799. Later
on, he was Giuseppe Bonaparte's foreign minister and, in Murat's time, was made duke
and was head of government until 1814. On 20 May he signed the terms of surrender
and saved himself from the people's fury thanks to the intervention of the Austrians. On
his return to Naples, he was given a cold reception by King Ferdinand IV and retired to
a villa at Capodimonte. In 1820 he became a member of the new government and went
to Vienna as ambassador in lieu of prince Ruffo. He was then appointed lieutenant-
general of the kingdom and foreign minister. Finally, he retired to private life once and
for all to die very old.

41   As later dispatches will show, the same thing was to happen to Hamilton, who, though
in possession of the king's permission, kept putting off his departure for over two years.

42   This dispatch, which is interesting in many respects, appears to be built on a marked
contrast between the confusion reigning at the Borbon court and Hamilton's self-
proclaimed ability to influence the kingdom's foreign policy. The Neapolitan ruling
triad consisting of general Acton, who, though feeling the cold even in the southern
climate, was yet prompted by vaulting ambition, of the king completely absorbed in his
pastimes, and of the queen, endowed with an outstanding political talent but prone to
dangerously perturbing fits of passionate love, did not seem to guarantee a foreign policy
consistently favourable for England. In spite of all this, the thirty years Hamilton had
spent at the Neapolitan court had not passed in vain in that he had managed to rescue
the Kingdom from its subjection to Spain orienting it towards Britain. Lady Hamilton
too had done her part by conquering the queen's heart and becoming her confidante.
Clearly, it is not by chance that the British minister's application for permission to leave
Naples to look after his own interests at home was placed between his boasting of his

political cleverness and another precious service he had been rendering to the king himself, namely the protection from the French afforded to prince Augustus who had been living in Naples for some time. In his recent biography, Constantine maintains that Hamilton's apparently noble refusal to avail himself of the king's permission actually concealed his fear of losing his much-sought-for job and quotes two letters in support of his claim. In the former, privately written to the Secretary of State, Hamilton, though confessing that he was not enjoying good health owing to a bilious disorder, having even received money offers to leave his job to other applicants – the blameworthy phenomenon of jobbing, i.e. people's search for vacant jobs – however averred he was equal to his task since, if it were not the case, he would himself ask the King to pension him off. In the latter, addressed to his nephew, Hamilton complained about his straitened circumstances, felt the need to have some rest, but refused to do so unless he was given an assurance he would get a pension large enough to allow him to continue to lead a comfortable life in Naples as a reward for his long, fruitful service rendered to the British nation (see Constantine 2001, pp. 206-7). If it is true that Hamilton's main worry in life was his chronical lack of money which would often cause him to sell his valuable art collections, on the other hand, one might also think that Hamilton was looking forward to playing a major role in forthcoming momentous events.

43 This is the first of a number of mentions of the imminent death of Pope Pius VI (Giovanni Angelo Braschi), who would not actually die until two full years later. It was under his pontificate that the reclamation of the Pontine Marshes, the improvement of the Ancona harbour, the completion of St. Peter's and the foundation of the Vatican Museums were all carried out. After French general Berthier occupied Rome to avenge the assassination of a member of the French embassy, the Pope was requested to give up his temporal sovereignty. On his refusal, he was imprisoned and taken first to Siena, then to Grenoble and eventually to Valence, where he died. Later on, his body was brought back to Rome.

44 Jean-Baptiste Camille count of Canclaux, French general, was born in Paris in 1740. He became field-marshal in 1791 and lieutenant-general in 1792. In 1795 he was made commander-in-chief of the army of the Brest coast. He held no office until Robespierre's fall when he was given command of the Western Army. His talent in diplomatic negotiations earned him his appointment as ambassador to Spain, but he had to give up owing to his bad health. In 1796 he was appointed ambassador to Naples where he gained general respect. Replaced by Garat, he returned to Paris and offered Napoleon his services. He died in Paris in 1817.

45 Coded letter.

46 The Hereditary Prince of the Two Sicilies, Francis, born on 19 August 1779, had, since 1790, been engaged to Archduchess Clementina, daughter of Leopold II, first Granduke of Tuscany, then Emperor of Austria. The wedding was celebrated in Foggia.

47 In the last sentence of the dispatch Hamilton seems to contradict himself. He has mentioned all the problems and threats facing Italy, yet thinks the French are unlikely to invade the kingdom of Naples. One might surmise that what Hamilton actually wanted to communicate to to Lord Grenville is that the Neapolitan Court might have reached a secret agreement with French, in which case the Kingdom's harbours would hardly be accessible to the British ships.

48 Here, Hamilton's final condemnation of the French – not accidentally spelled with a small letter – is conveyed through fashion. The way the members of the French legation are dressed is a metaphor for the disorder and bad taste which the excesses of the French Revolution have brought with them. Hamiton's use of climax is particularly effective: he begins with Madame de Canclaux's partially naked arm, goes on to Mademoiselle de Canclaux's objectionable hat and reaches a climax with the First Secretary's clothes, a real eyesore. The minister's description moves from top to bottom as if to express contempt for the French Secretary's overall appearance: his hair cut short like that of Cromwell's followers, the roundheads, his large spectacles and indiscrete gaze, his coat and boots and

the final touch of a huge scimitar, which does not fit in with a gala dinner at all. It is as if the British minister is looking down on the enemy, who, though lacking good taste, is yet becoming so powerful as to be likely to challenge British naval superiority. In the end, Hamilton sets against the uncouth, perfidious enemy, the good breeding of prince Augustus who embodies the harmonious, reassuring continuity of British tradition.

49 A report written by the English Consul, James Tough, to Lord Grenville on the general conditions of Sicily.

50 Italian for "subjects".

51 Impure alkali made by burning dried plants, especially of *Salsola soda*.

52 Probably a misspelling for sumaco, sumac or sumach: a preparation of the dried and chopped leaves and shoots of plants of the genus *Rhus* used in tanning and dyeing, and formerly as an astringent.

53 A preparation of dried beetles with toxic and vescicant properties, sometimes taken as an aphrodisiac.

54 François Cacault was born in Nantes in 1743. In 1764 he became a mathematics teacher at the Ecole Militaire but five years later had to leave his job after killing his adversary in a duel. Overwork having caused him health problems, doctors advised him to go on a long journey on foot so he travelled all over Italy. He took up Italian and made observations about the inhabitants of Italy. After his return to France he became embassy secretary to Naples. He remained there as minister plenipotentiary until 1792. However he did not cease to live in Italy, as an agent of France, without a fixed residence, and was involved in all the events. Deputy of the Lower Loire in the Council of Five Hundred on 16 April 1798, he approved the coup of 18 Brumaire, and was nominated a deputy of the Corps Legislatif on 24 December 1799. Ambassador to Rome from 1801 to 1803, he was became senator in 1804, a year before he died.

55 As in the 18 July dispatch above, Hamilton persists in his destructive criticism and demonization of French Jacobinism embodied by the secretaries of the French Legation, the most ideologized and politicized members of the French embassy at Naples. Jacobin radicalims finds expression in a refusal of the rules of etiquette which Canclaux knows and respects, thus arousing suspicions on his political correctness.

56 An official recognition of a consul by a foreign government, authorizing him or her to exercise office.

57 The Congress of the German Princes who met to reach an agreement on the terms of peace with France, represented by the plenipotentiary Bonaparte. On 9 March 1798 it was resolved that the left bank of the Rhine be annexed to France, as already agreed on the year before.

58 Coded letter.

59 Being placed at the beginning of a sentence, the word "French" is necessarily spelled with a capital letter, which clearly shows that Hamilton deliberately spelled it with a small letter out of contempt whenever it was in other places in a sentence.

60 Karl Mack von Leiberich (1752-1828), one of the most famous Austrian generals, joined an Austrian cavalry regiment in 1770, becoming an officer seven years later. He distinguished himself in the Turkish war and in 1797 was promoted to lieutenant field marshal. In the following year he accepted, at the personal request of the emperor, the command of the Neapolitan army. He captured Rome in November 1798 but soon after had to flee his own troops who mutinied. He took refuge in a French camp and Napoleon ordered he should be sent to France as a prisoner of war. Two years later he escaped from Paris in disguise and was not employed for some years. He was then made commander of the army which opposed Napoleon in Bavaria but, much to the disgust of Austria's allies, surrendered an almost intact Austrian army at Ulm in 1805 with very little resistance. Condemned to death for his cowardly act, he was imprisoned instead and eventually pardoned. He was never again to hold a command.

61 General Acton.

62 Hamlet, 1 iv 43. On saying these words, Hamlet does not know yet whether the ghost is a good or a bad one. Horatio relates the ghost's apparition to something extraordinary, as happened in Rome on the asssination of Caesar. In Hamilton's case, "questionable" had undoubtedly negative connotations: he probably wanted to point out that not all the members of the Neapolitan government regarded the French as actual enemies and that the king and Acton were not definitely in favour of Great Britain.

63 Once again, Hamilton is hinting at the contrasting views about the French at the Bourbon Court and in the government.

64 The structural and stylistic features of the dispatch clearly show that it was written in a hurry. Of the three paragraphs of which the dispatch consists, the second one, the most important, seems to have been written in one go and in a paratactic mode, its juxtaposed sentences suggesting a sort of verbal outpouring at a very critical moment. Hamilton probably did not have enough time to revise the text, which accounts for the inconsistency in the use of tenses.

The dispatch is entirely built on the emotive function. In the first part Hamiltons boasted of his insight and ability to foresee future poltical events. In the second, after stating the hard terms of the peace signed by the Pope, he tried to emphasize the dangerous state of affairs at Naples. He mentioned the risk prince Augustus was running but at the same time was implicitly asking to be credited with rendering the king an essential service. In the last paragraph it is evident that Hamilton, by refusing to take a decision, aimed at providing proof of his own correctness and discipline. However, as we shall see later on, there would be occasions on which Hamilton did not refrain from taking the initiative, coming in for muted criticism from the Foreign Office.

65 British Minister at Vienna.

66 This section of the dispatch has aroused the curiosity of Constantine, Hamilton's biographer, who finds it difficult to read into the reason why Hamilton offered to carry out a diplomatic mission at the Russian court (see Constantine 2000, p. 214). In the light of Hamilton's later secret dispatch of 17 April, one might even think that the British minister was actually considering leaving the Kingdom since the French army was rapidly advancing and the British government had not yet resolved to send a fleet into the Mediterranean.

67 Coded dispatch.

68 The protection of Naples.

69 British military power essentially consisted in its navy.

70 Lord Grenville seemed to be worried that his instructions might be disregarded or misconstrued: he had sent a very detailed dispatch about what the British governments intended to do in the Mediterranean, had instructed Marquis Circello's messenger to tell Hamilton personally again every detail of the talks he had had with the Neapolian minister in London, yet felt compelled to stress once again the importance of Hamilton's complying with the resolution passed by the British government. That Lord Grenville's worry was well-founded was to be proved by later events: the remoteness of Naples allowed Hamilton to enjoy some freedom of action and, at times, to make his own decisions in contrast to the resolutions passed in his country.

71 In this dispatch, too, Hamilton does not fail to draw attention to another precious service he was rendering to his own King by looking after the French and Corsican Emigrants under the protection of, and subsidized by, His Britannic Majesty. He was getting ready to leave Naples since prince Augustus was no longer in Naples, the French were looming large menacingly and George III had not yet resolved to send a fleet into the Mediterranean.

In the last paragragh Hamilton expresses his own opinion on Naples, with which many a traveller would have agreed, namely a fine country characterized by fatalism and indolence, and which only trusts to luck: an attitude affecting the whole population which obviously sounds unacceptable to a fellow countryman of that literary prototype of a capitalist, Robinson Crusoe.

72 France.

73 The Kingdom of Naples.

74 James Harris, first earl of Malmesbury (1746-1820) was an English diplomat who served at Madrid, Belin, Petersburgh, The Hague. In 1795 he negotiated the marriage between the prince of Wales and Caroline of Brunswick. His *Diaries and Correspondence* were published in 1845.

75 Prizes, i.e. ships or other items of property captured in naval warfare, are often mentioned in Hamilton's dispatches. Their estimated value was shared out among officers and sailors. For example, Nelson's total prize money fom the Nile ships came to £ 2,358 4s 6d.

76 Wenzel Anton, prince of Kaunitz, (1711-1794) was an Austrian statesman, who distinguished himself in 1748 at the Congress of Aix-la-Chapelle and as ambassador to the French court from 1752 to 1752. He was appointed Chancellor in 1753 and directed Austrian policies for almost 40 years.

77 General Acton.

78 See last paragraph of next dispatch.

79 In this dispatch form and content are inextricably interwoven. Hamilton's embarassment in dealing with the delicate topic of prince Augustus' debts is mirrored in the rough, uneven syntax. Prince Augustus was a heavy load for Hamilton to bear since he had been instructed to keep an eye on him: he had married unlawfully and was arousing supiscion of a possible conversion to Catholicism because of his strange way of crossing himself at table. See Constantine (2000) p.205.

80 Sir Thomas Troubridge, 1st Baronet (1758-1807), English admiral, entered the navy in 1773 and, together with Nelson, served in the West Indies in the frigate Seahorse. In 1785 he returned to England in the Sultan as flag-captain to Admiral Sir Edward Hughes. Appointed to command the frigate *Castor* in May 1794, he and his ship were captured by the French while escorting a convoy, but he was liberated soon afterwards. On his return he was appointed to command the *Culloden*, in which he led the line at the Battle of Cape St Vincent, being commended for his courage and initiative by Admiral Sir John Jervis. In the following July he assisted Nelson in the unsuccessful attack on Santa Cruz, and in August 1798, when getting into position for the attack on the French fleet, the Culloden ran aground on a shoal near the entrance to Aboukir Bay and was consequently unable to take any part in the Battle of the Nile. At Nelson's request, however, he was awarded the gold medal commemorating the victory. He then served in the Mediterranean and was created a baronet in 1799; from 1801 to 1804 he was a Lord of the Admiralty, being made a Rear-Admiral just before his retirement. In 1805 Troubridge was appointed to command the eastern half of the East Indies Station and went out in the *Blenheim*. On his arrival the area of command was changed to that of the Cape Station. He left Madras in January 1807 for the Cape of Good Hope, but off the coast of Madagascar the *Blenheim*, an old and damaged ship, foundered in a cyclone and the admiral and all others on board perished.

81 A variable measure of distance, usually estimated at about five kilometres or three miles.

82 Above all, his valuable collection of vases.

83 In his proclamation, Ferdinand IV ordered all the male subjects of the Kingdom, aged 8 to 45, to report to the various corps: he then invited all the authorities and intellectuals of the kingdom to make every effort to persuade the above subjects to train themselves.
    This dispatch marks the beginning of Hamilton's interventionist campaign, consisting of his continuous efforts to persuade the Neapolitan Court and government to wage war on the French, Pontano's lines being his war cry. The arrival of Nelson's fleet in the Mediterranea seemed to have given him renewed vigour to Hamiltom who had been on

the point of leaving Naples in order not to be involved, with his personal property, in the general ruin of the Kingdom.

84 A ship loaded with combustibles and set adrift among enemy ships to ignite and destroy them.

85 In a letter sent to Hamilton from the *Vanguard* off Syracuse, Nelson mentioned a code of the course he would be following. See The National Archives, FO 70/11: 189.

86 The governor of a district or province in the Ottoman Empire.

87 The Ottoman Court at Constantinople (from French *la Sublime Porte*, i.e. the exalted gate).

88 The *Colossus*, which had been in service in the Mediterranean and at Aboukir as a store ship, came back to Naples with Nelson's *Vanguard* after the battle of the Nile. Soon afterwards, she sailed from Naples, carrying spoils from Aboukir Bay, French and English wounded and also Hamilton's vases. She reached Lisbon in November and St Mary's harbour, Isles of Scilly, in bad weather on 7 December. The next day she was driven by the gale out of the roads and ran aground on a reef just south of Samson. All but one of the crew and all the passengers were rescued before the ship broke up. Four large boxes containing all the best vases un Hamilton's collection went down with the ship. See Constantine (2000) p. 244.

89 Jean Paul LaCombe Saint-Michel (1740-1812) was a captain in the 7th artillery regiment on the breaking out of the French Revolution, of which he was a fervent supporter. In November 1789 he was elected to the legislative assembly and joined the radical wing. He voted for the immediate death sentence without appeal for the French King. In 1798 he was sent to Naples as ambassador from the French Republic and, on leaving Naples in February 1799 he was arrested by the English to be released soon afterwards. He returned to Paris and resumed his military career, becoming first brigadier, then field-marshal and finally artillery general inspector. In 1806 he behaved brilliantly in the so-called "campaign of Italy" and against the Prussians. He went into retirement owing to bad health and died in his castle of St Michel in 1812.

90 A malapropism: *tenure* for *tenor*.

91 The dispatch contains peremptory instructions: Hamilton was ordered to tell the Neapolitan court and government exactly what Lord Grenville had already told Marquis Circello in London. There was not the remotest possibility to obtain a financial aid from Great Britain even though the King of Naples was in great need for it for the reasons given in later dispatches.

92 Coded dispatch. The dispatch appears to have been handwritten by someone else except for the ritual complimentary clause. The adjective French is here written with a capital letter, which is further evidence of Hamilton's deliberate use of a small letter in writing it elsewhere.

93 The dispatch bears witness to Hamilton's jingoism and to how facts can be turned into pure propaganda in wartime. The British minister described the enemy's making the most of the British ship's running out of gun-powder as treachery; moreover, it comes as no surprise that the enemy should have suffered heavier losses.

94 One of the three invasion attempts made by the French; their force was commanded by general Humbert, who campaigned for two weeks until defeated.

95 Jean Etienne Championnet (1762-1800) was a French general in the French Revolutionary Wars. Placed in command of the Army of Rome in 1798, which was protecting the infant Roman Republic against the Neapolitan court and the British Fleet, he captured Naples in 1799 from the Second Coalition and set up the Neapolitan Republic. However, he got into trouble with the Directory by denouncing the malpractices of one of its agents in Naples; moreover, his harsh rule caused popular discontent, and he was recalled in disgrace. Later acquitted, he commanded the Army of the Alps, but the campaign was unsuccessful and he had to resign. He fell ill with typhus and died at Antibes in 1800.

96 John Thomas Duckworth (1748-1817), English naval commanding officer, joined the navy as a volunteer and served in the American Reolutionary War and in the French Revolutionary Wars. He was commander-in-chief in Jamaica from 1803 to 1812.

97 Jacques Etienne Joseph Alexandre Macdonald (1765-1840), Duke of Taranto and Marshal of France, was born at Sedan. His father came of an old Jacobite family, which had followed James II to France, and was a near relative of the celebrated Flora Macdonald. On the breaking out of the Revolution he joined the revolutionaries and was appointed aide-de-camp to general Dumoriez. Promoted colonel in 1793, he refused to desert to the Austrians with Dumoriez and as a reward was made brigadier. In 1797 he served first in the army of the Rhine and then in that of Italy. When he reached Italy after the peace of Campo Formio, he first occupied Rome, of which he was made governor, and then, in conjunction with Championnet, he defeated general Mack, and revolutioned the kingdom of Naples under the title of the Parthenopean Republic. Later on, he distinguished himself in various military campaigns and was made Marshal of France and created Duke of Taranto by Napoleon to whom he remained faithful to the last. At the Restoration Macdonald was made a peer of France and given the Grand Cross of the Order of St. Louis. He spent his later years in retirement at his country-place where he died.

98 It allowed the King of Naples to withdraw from the war against France and remain neutral in case the Emperor should make peace with the French.

99 This dispatch, which is highly significant if read in the context of Lord Grenville's instructions of 3 October 1798, marks the climax of Hamilton's persistent attempts to persuade the Neapolitan court and government to wage war on the French. Hamilton slyly deceived the Queen of Naples and Marquis Gallo by making them believe that the chances, if any, of obtaining the indispensable financial aid from Great Britain were ultimately linked to the king's continuing his military operations against the French. The fact that the Queen and Marquis Gallo's insisted on asking for a secret clause concerning a loan is irrefutable evidence that Hamilton had let them hope for it in contrast to the Foreign Office'instructions received.

100 Hamilton told Emma he wasn't going to die with the "guggle-guggle-guggle" of salt-water in his throat (Constantine 2000: 223).

101 See note 41.

102 Francesco Pignatelli (1732-1812), born of a noble family, took up a military career at a very early age. After killing his adversary in a duel, he had to leave Naples, being not allowed to return until Ferdinand IV became king of Naples. Sent by Queen Carolina to the court of Spain to plead Acton's case, he was not successful but, in spite of this, he won favour with both the Queen and Acton by concealing the failure of his mission from Ferdinand IV. When a spate of earthquakes hit the Calabrian region, he was appointed chief administrator; though charged with embezzlement, he continued to enjoy an untarnished reputation at Court. He was then appointed marshall of the Kingdom, and, when the king fled to Palermo in December 1798, he became vicar general. As a result of his armistice with general Championnet, he had to face up to the people's violent reaction, so he, too, fled to Palermo. Arrested and imprisoned in the Girgenti castle, he returned to Naples after the French were driven out of the capital city. Sentenced to death for his involvement in a Bourbon plot in 1806, he was pardoned and sent into exile. He returned to Naples again at the time of Murat's rule and died in 1812.

103 The paragraph summarises, as it were, the conservative politics of the civil servant Hamilton, who abhorred revolutionary chaos and subversion of traditional order. To him, monarchy was obviously the best form of government because it brought with it justice, order and welfare, and consequently inspired a true patriotic spirit, which instead was nowhere to be found in the kingdom of Naples ruled by the Bourbons. Hamilton could not ignore the manifold problems that plagued the kingdom where popular discontent was widespread, and where Jacobin revolutionary ideas might easily

take root and be disguised as a remedy to century-long evils. Intense though his loathing of all things french was, he was, however, well aware of the abysmal gap existing between the absolute rule of the Bourbons and the constitutional monarchy of Great Britain born out of the Glorious Revolution of 1688. Here was the main reason for the shameful defeat of the Neapolitan army, in which he probably couldn't help feeling involved.

104 An edict by the Palermo Senate of 7 January 1799 forbidding any person, whether noble or of low birth, to hunt in the Mondello swamp near Palermo, right of hunting being reserved to Ferdinand IV only.

105 It might be objected that no patriotic spirit would have existed in Britain either if the common people there had been starving to death.

106 Fabrizio Ruffo (1744-1827), cardinal, soldier and politician, was born at San Lucido in Calabria. Placed by Pope Pius VI among the "chierici di camera" who formed the papal civil and financial service, he was later promoted to be treasurer-general, a post which carried with it the ministry of war. In 1791 he was removed from the treasurership to be created cardinal though he never became a priest. In December 1798 he fled to Palermo with the royal family and was chosen to head a royalist movement in Calabria where his family exercised large feudal powers. He succeed in upsetting the Republican government and by June had advanced to Naples. He lost favour with the king by showing a tendency to spare the republicans, so he resigned his vicar-generalship to the Prince of Cassaro. During the revolutionary troubles of 1822 he was consulted by the king and was even in office for a very short time as a loyalist minister.

107 A small three-masted vessel with lateen and usually some square sails, formerly much used in in the Mediterranean especially by pirates and merchants.

108 Hamilton does not pass a wholly negative judgment on Mack's behaviour; in fact, he seems to be making allowances for it. This is in agreement with Nelson's fluctuating opinion of Mack as a commanding officer: see Vincent (2003) p. 307.

109 According to the new treaty, partly modified as compared with the 1793 Convention, Great Britain would be obliged to obtain the restitution of the whole Kingdom of Naples on account of its commitment not being limited to naval protection only.

110 This dispatch is interesting in many respects, but, above all, supports what has already been said about the old systems of communication and transport. At the end of the 18th century, means of communication and transport were essentially the same as in previous times, except for the greater size and cruising speed of sailing ships. At a time when there was no steam engine, telegraph, radio and so on, information was transmitted by land on horses and by sea in ships. It is therefore not surprising that the news of the Nelson's victory at Aboukir of the 1st August should not reach Naples until September and that a treaty take ages to be concluded and ratified. Consequently, these lengthy time intervals gave Hamilton, too, broad opportunities to make his own decisions, and the Foreign Office felt the need to draw Hamilton's attention to the damage caused to Great Britain by his condescending to an apparently negligible alteration in the phrasing of an article of the treaty. Lord Grenville, of course, blamed it all on an unintentional mistake made by Marquis Circello, nor could he have done otherwise, but, doubtless, Hamilton was negligent in conducting the negotiations for which he had been given full powers, unless one prefers to think he deliberately wanted to play into the King of Naples's hands. Lord Grenville thought it necessary to say again that the financial aid for the kingdom of the Two Sicilies had been kindly donated by George III and was to be used for a regular army. The British Government did not trust an irregular army which was not led by a career soldier and Ruffo's army did not seem to have the necessary requirements. Yet, in spite of British deep concern, Ruffo's army was to be successful and reconquer Naples.

Lord Grenville's final remark on the correct use of the money does not seem to be a credit to the Neapolitan Court and government.

111 Edward James Foote (1767-1833), was admitted to the Naval Academy of Portsmouth
     in 1799 and then served in the Mediterranean under Sir John Jervis. In March 1799, he
     was sent, together with Captain Troubridge into the Bay of Naples and after
     Troubridges's departure, he signed, as senior commanding officer, an agreemen with the
     Neapolitan Jacobins and the French for the surrender of Castle dell'Ovo and Nuovo,
     which Nelson however refused to respect because he thought it was not valid. Nelson
     did not find fault with him for his behaviour, so Foote showed his appreciation to him.
     It was not until 1807, after Nelson's death, that Foote published a vindication of his
     behaviour with an attack on Nelson. The fact that Foote had read in Nelson's biography
     by Harrison that the great admiral had termed the 1799 treaty "infamous", although
     Nelson had only been referring to Cardinal Ruffo. After his return to England Foote
     continued to command the *Seahorse* for a while and, later on, became the commander of
     the King's yacht *Princess Augusta*. Appointed to the rank of vice-admiral in 1821, he died
     in Southampton in 1833.
112 Here, Hamilton obviously meant "Fra' Diavolo" because "Gran Diavolo" was the
     nickname given to Giovanni delle Bande Nere, a famous mercenary captain in the
     employ of the pope Leo X who died in 1526, as well as Giuseppe Musso, a brigand who
     committed robberies and murders across the Genoa hinterland at the turn of the XVIII
     century.
     Fra Diavolo (lit. Brother Devil; April 7, 1771–November 11,1806), is the popular name
     given to Michele Pezza, a famous Italian brigand leader who resisted the French
     occupation of Naples and is remembered in folk legends and in the novels of the French
     writer Alexandre Dumas as a popular guerilla leader. The nickname "Fra Diavolo" was
     given to him by his school teacher, because of his excessively lively character and because
     of the monk's habit he always wore; the reason behind this was that when he was five he
     fell ill, and his mother swore an oath to always dress him in such a habit if he survived.
     He was born of low parentage at Itri. Little is known with certainty of his early life,
     though he apparently was known for committing murders and robberies. When the
     Kingdom of Naples was overrun by the French and the Parthenopaean Republic
     established in 1799, Cardinal Fabrizio Ruffo, acting on behalf of the Bourbon king
     Ferdinand IV, who had fled to Sicily, undertook the reconquest of the country. For this
     purpose he raised bands of peasants, prisoners, bandits and other lazzaroni (the lowest
     class of the people) under the name of Sanfedisti or bande della Santa Fede (bands of the
     Holy Faith). Ruffo pardoned Pezza for murders and made him a leader of one of these
     bands. Pezza, like his fellow-bandit warriors under Ruffo, styled himself the faithful
     servant and subject of Ferdinand, wore a military uniform and held military rank, and
     was even created duke of Cassano. Despite this, Pezza became known for committing
     many atrocities. His excesses were such that the Neapolitan general Naselli had him
     arrested and imprisoned in the castle of St Angelo, but he was liberated soon after. When
     Joseph Bonaparte was made king of Naples, tribunals were established to control
     banditry, and a price was put on Fra Diavolo's head. After spreading terror in Calabria
     and Sicily, he returned to the mainland at the head of 200 convicts. For two months he
     evaded his French pursuers, but at length, hungry and ill, he went in disguise to the
     village of Baronissi, where he was recognized, tried and hanged in the public
     marketplace.
113 Hamilton's statement was certainly not true since, in his dispatch to Lord Grenville of
     the 2nd of December, he had admitted to giving the Neapolitan court some grounds for
     hope on condition that the King of Naples would carry on his war on the French.
114 Near Alassio.
115 It must have been one of those popular anti-Semitic revolts which broke out in the
     regions occupied by the French following the granting of civil rights to the Jews: see
     Storia d'Italia (1973) III, pp. 42, 58, 187, 217.
116 Small sailing warships carrying guns on the upper deck only.

117 Modern Torre Annunziata.

118 Foote's vindication of his own behaviour was essentially based on the fact that he had been obliged to make the crucial decision on his own since he was a long way away from both his own superiors and homeland and had no instructions. At a time when systems of communication were still in their infancy, a commanding officer would at times be also required to act as a politician.

119 Taking this dispatch at its face value, one is led to think that the drastic measures taken against the Jacobins were the sole responsibility of Nelson and the British government. Ferdinand IV was too busy hunting game in the Montello swamp to take any initiative, limiting himself to giving his consent instead.

120 The letter is addressed to Hamilton's nephew, Charles Francis Greville, who featured prominently in the British minister's life by introducing him to Emma and looking after his estate in South Wales.

121 It is a slip of the pen for 10 July.

122 Hamilton's banker in London.

123 Hamilton's estate near Pembroke, in Wales, where he had been authorized by an Act of Parliament passed in 1790 to build quays, docks, piers and to establish a market. See Constantine (2000) p. 201.

124 Alexsandr Vasilyevic Suvorov (1729-1800) was one of the few great generals who never lost a battle. He was famed for his manual *The Science of Victory* and noted for the sayings 'Train hard, fight easy', 'The bullet is a fool', the bayonet a fine chap'. He entered the army as a boy and became a colonel in 1796. The scourge of the Poles and the Turks, he was dismissed by the Emperor Paul I, who summoned him to take the field again in 1799, this time again the French Revolutionary armies in Italy. The campaign opened with a series of Suvorov's victories but, betrayed by the Austrians, he was forced to an extraordinary strategic retreat which earned him the rank of *generalissimo*. He was promised to be given the military triumph but the court intrigues led Paul I to cancel the ceremony. Worn out and ill, Suvorov died a few days later on 18 May 1800, at St Peterburgh.

125 A Spanish or Sicilian coin of varying value.

126 A spray of gems worn on the head in the shape of an egret's plume.

127 A warship serving as a transport, with part of her armament removed.

128 The high-flown words and elaborate syntax of the dispatch have no other use than that of sweetening the pill of dismissal; moreover, they sound highly ironical compared with Hamilton's bitter words of resentment for the British government in his letter to his nephew of 22 September 1799. The *dispositio* or layout of the dispatch serves a well-defined stategy: eulogy for Hamilton is cleverly placed between the permission to return home and the notice of final, irrevocable dismissal.

129 See The National Archives, FO 70/14.

130 Constantine (2001) pp. 262-65.

131 The most frequent terms which appear in his dispatches are "accounts" and "reports" – almost always in need of final confirmation – and general informatiom obtained from hearsay.

132 Constantine (2001) pp. 98-99; 162-63.

133 Constantine (2001) pp. 4-5.

134 Constantine (2001) p. 193; Acton (1974) pp. 260-61.

135 Diamond (1998) pp. 67-81.

136 Vincent (2003) p. 330.

137 Constantine (2001) p. 230.

138 The National Archives, FO 43, ff. 22-25. See the appendix.

139 The three famous *f*'s that are usually said to have been the basis of Bourbon rule in Southern Italy.: *feste, farina, forca* (festivals, flour and gallows)

140 Diamond maintains that, besides justifying the transfer of wealth to kleptocrats, institutionalised religion brings two other benefits: a) a bond not based in kinship; b) a motive for sacrificing one's life on behalf of others. Well, it would seem that those two extra benefits have never applied to Naples.

141 In this regard, what Putnam writes about the lack of civic spirit in Southern Italy could also apply to the refusal of an industrial lifestyle. Like failure to cooperate, lack of industrialization does not necessarily signal ignorance or irrationality. Both of them might simply be rational when viewed from another perspective. Just as the agricultural revolution of 11,000 years ago brough with it advantages but also disadvantages, so industrialization might not appeal to people who rationally choose to stick to an older lifestyle for a number of reasons. It is therefore not a case that the king's silk factory at S. Leucio was run according to principles that were unknown to Adam Smith and which he certainly would not have approved of, and that the people who worked there together with their whole families used to call the King "Papà". See Putnam (1993) pp. 163-64; Diamond (1998) 85 ff.; Capuano (1999).

142 Hamillton's paradigmatic career was: soldier, equerry, MP and finally diplomat.

143 The assemblies of the nobles.

144 The National Archives, FO 43, ff. 22-25.

145 Sacchinelli (1836) p. 255; Giglioli (1903), p. 304.

146 Vincent (2003) p. 330.

147 'This is the only allusion to a precise law given to Ruffo, and considering that Ruffo was advocating clemency and pardon up to the last moment, one may suppose the question was in fact open, and only closed when the Court saw that Nelson would pull them through'. See Giglioli (1903) p. 310.

148 The phrase, which was first used by Lady Hamilton, was the motto of the Order of Bath, of which both Nelson and Hamilton were members.

149 Pitt's so-called reign of terror got rid of many radical groups who were invoking peace and solidarity with France. Repression by Lord Braxfield was rather fierce in Scotland. See *The Oxford Illustrated History of Britain* p. 434

150 Giglioli (1893) p. 311.

151 Byron (ed. by Quiller-Couch and Smith), London 1962, p. 76Q.

BIBLIOGRAPHY

INTRODUCTION

Published documents and original sources

M. Battaglini, *La Repubblica Napoletana. Origini, nascita, struttura* (Bonacci, Roma 1992).

Id., *Atti, leggi,proclami ed altre carte della Repubblica Napoletana 1798-1799* (Salerno 1983, 3 vols).

M. Battaglini & A. Placanica; *Atti, leggi, proclami ed altre carte della Repubblica napoletana 1798-1799* (Istituto Italiano per gli Studi Filosofici, Di Mauro Editore, Cava dei Tirenni, 4 vols s.d).

F.P. Bradham, *Nelson at Naples. A Journal of June 10-30 1799* (David Nutt, London 1900).

P. Colletta, *Storia del Reame di Napoli* (Firenze 1848).

B. Croce (ed.), *La Riconquista del Regno di Napoli nel 1799* (Laterza, Bari 1943).

V. Cuoco, 'La politica inglese in Italia' (4-8 gennaio 1806), in *Scritti Vari*, ed. N. Cortese & F. Nicolini (Laterza, Bari 1942) pp201-213.

A. Dumas, *I Borboni di Napoli* (Napoli 1862).

Captain Foote's Vindication of His Conduct in the Bay of Naples in the Summer of 1799 (2nd edition, Hatchard, London 1810).

Constance H.D. Giglioli (née Stocker), *Naples in 1799. An Account of the Revolutions of 1799 and the Rise and fall of the Parthenopean Republic.* New York, Dutton. London John Murray 1903).

H.C.Gutteridge *Nelson and the Neapolitan Jacobins. Documents relating to the Suppression of the Jacobin Revolution at Naples in June 1799* (Navy Record Society 1903).

Captain A. T. Mahan, *The Life of Nelson. Embodiment of the Sea Power of Great Britain* London, Little Brown & Co, 2 vols, Boston 1899).

Jeafferson Miles, *Vindication of Admiral Lord Nelson's Proceedings in the Bay of Naples* (London, Bailly 1843; reprinted Marine Books, Cheshire 1991).

Sir Nicholas Harris Nicolas, *The Despatches and Letters of Vice Admiral Lord Viscount Nelson* (London 1844-7: reprinted Chatham Publishing, London 1997).

R. Southey, *Life of Nelson* (John Murray, London 1813, 2 Vols: reprinted W.P. Nimmo, Hay & Mitchell, Edinburgh 1898).

Helen Maria Williams, *Sketches of the State of Manners and Opinions in the French Republic towards the Close of the Eighteenth Century* (London 1801, 2 Vols).

Souvenirs du Maréchal MacDonald, Duc de Tarente (Paris 1892).

Secondary Sources

Maxine Berg, *Luxury and Pleasure in Eighteenth Century Britain* (Oxford Unibersity Press 2005).

Edward Chaney, *The Evolution of the Grand Tour* (Frank Cass London, Portland Oregon 1998).

Sir John Clapham, *Cambridge Diplomatic History of Europe* (1922).

L. Colley, *Britons. Forging the Nation 1707-1837* (Yale University Press, New Haven and London, 1992).

David Constantine, *Fields* of Fire. A Life of Sir William Hamilton (Weidenfeld & Nicholson, London 2001).

B. Croce, *Storia del Regno di Napoli* (Laterza, Bari 1945).

C. Crossley & I. Small, *The French Revolution and British Culture* (Oxford 1989).

John A. Davis, *Naples and Napoleon. Southern Italy in the Age of the European Revolutions (1780-186?)* (Oxford University Press, Oxford 2006).

John A Davis, 'L'Inghilterra, Nelson e la Repubblica Napoletana del 1799', in A.M.Rao (ed.) *Napoli 1799. Fra Storia e Storiografia* (Istituto Italiano per gli Studi Filosofici, Vivarium. Napoli 2002) pp393-427.

H.T. Dickinson (ed.), *Britain and the French Revolution* (London 1989).

S. Engerman & P.K. O'Brien, 'The Industrial Revolution in Global Perspective' in R. Floud & P. Johnson (eds), *Cambridge Economic History of Modern Europe* (Cambridge University Press 2004).

G. Pagano de Divitis, *Il Commercio inglese nel Mediterraneo dal Cinquecento al Settecento* (Guida, Napoli 1984).

G. Pagano de Divitiis & V. Giura, *L'Italia del secondo Settcento nelle relazioni segrete di William Hamilton, Horace Mann e John Murray* (ESI, Napoli 1997).

Cesare de Seta, *L'Italia del Grand Tour da Montaigne a Goethe* (Electa, Milano 1996).

M. Elliott, *Partners in Revolution. The United Irishmen and France* (Yale University Press, New Haven 1982).

Brian Fothergill, *Sir William Hamilton* (London 1969).

A. Grab, *Napoleon and the Transformation of Europe* (Palgrave, London 2003).

Jenkins, Ian & Sloan, Kim Vases and Volcanoes. Sir William Hamilton and his Collection (British Museum Press 1996).

C. Knight, 'Sir William Hamilton e il mancato rispetto da parte di Lord Nelson della "Capitolazione" del 1799', in *Atti dell'Accademia Pontiana*, n.s. xlvii, 198 (Napoli 1999) pp373-397.

Carlo Knight, 'Gli "Imbarcati" del 1799', in *Rendiconti dell'Academia di Archeologia, Lettre e Belle Arti*, Vol lxvii 1997-8 (Napoli 1997-8) pp469-515.

G. Imbruglia (ed.), *Naples in the Eighteenth Century* (Cambridge University Press, Cambridge UK 2000).

Piers Mackesy, *The War in the Mediterranean 1803-1810* (Cambridge University Press, Cambridge 1971).

Barbara Naddeo, 'Cultural capitals and cosmopolitanism in eighteenth century Italy: the historiography and Italy in the Grand Tour', in *Journal of Modern Italian Studies* 10 (2) June 2003, pp183-99.

A.M. Rao, 'Tra civiltà e barbarie: storie inglesi della Repubblica napoletana del 1799', in R. De Lorenzo (ed.), *Risorgimento, Democrazia, Mezzogiorno d'Italia. Studi in onore di Alfonso Scirocco* (Franco Angeli, Milano 2003) pp708-739.

A.M. Rao (ed.), *Napoli 1799. Fra Storia e Storiografia* (Istituto Italiano per gli Studi Filosofici, Vivarium. Napoli 2002).

A.M. Rao (ed.), *Folle Contro-Rivoluzionarie. Le insorgenze popolari nell'Italia Giacobina e Napoleonica* (Carocci, Roma 1999).

A.M.Rao, 'Dalle elites al popolo: cultura e politica a Napoli nell'età dei lumi e della rivoluzione', in *Napoli 1799*, ed. R. De Simone (Napoli 1999, Franco De Mauro Editore).

A.M. Rao, 'La Repubblica napoletana del 1799 e la prima restaurazione borbonica', in A.M. Rao and P. Villani, *Napoli 1799-1815. Dalla Repubblica alla Monarchia amministrativa* (Edizioni del Sole, Napoli 1995).

A.M. Rao, 'La Repubblica Napoletana del 1799' and 'La prima restaurazione borbonica', in A.M. Rao & P. Villani, *Napoli 1799-1815. Dalla Repubblica alla Monarchia Amministrativa* (ESI, Napoli 1994).

A.M. Rao, *Esuli. L'Emigrazione Politica Italiana in Francia (1792-1802)* (Guida, Napoli 1992).

John Roberston, *The Case for the Enlightenment. Scotland and Naples (1680-1760)* (Cambridge University Press 2005).

G. Rousseau, 'The sources of Priapus: Anti-clericalism, homosocial desire and Richard Payne Knight', in G. Rousseau & R.Porter (eds), *Sexual Underworlds of the Enlightenment* (Manchester University Press 1987).

Biagio Salvemini, 'The arrogance of the market; the economy of the Kingdom between the Mediterranean and Europe', in G. Imbruglia (ed.), *Naples in the Eighteenth Century* (Cambridge University Press, Cambridge 2000).

Paul W. Schroeder, *The Transformation of European Politics 1763-1848* (Clarendon Press, Oxford 1994).

Susan Sontag, *The Volcano Lover* (Farrar Straus Giroux, New York 1992) Barry Unsworth *Losing Nelson* (Hamish Hamilton, London 1999).

David Vincent, *Nelson, Love and Fame* (Yale University Press, New Haven 2003).

THE DISPATCHES

Manuscripts

The National Archives, Kew, London: Foreign Office 70/10-14.
The National Archives, Kew, London: Foreign Office 43, ff. 22-25.

Printed sources

A.A.V.V, *Napoli 1799. La Rivoluzione Napoletana del 1799* (Napoli, 1999).
H. Acton, *The Bourbons of Naples* (London, 1974).
M. Baratta, I *terremoti d'Italia* (Bologna, 1979).
*Byron (*edited by Quiller-Couch and Smith) (London 1962).
G. Capuano, *Viaggiatori britannici a Napoli nel '700* (Napoli, 1999).
D. Constantine, *Fields of Fire* (London, 2001).
P. Colletta, *Storia del Regno di Napoli dal 1754 al 1825* (Firenze, 1848).
B. Croce, *La Riconquista* (Bari, 1943).
B. Croce, *La Rivoluzione napoletana* (Bari, 1912).
B. Croce, *Storia del Regno di Napoli* (Bari, 1965).
V. Cuoco, *Saggio storico sulla Rivoluzione di Napoli* (Manduria, 1998).
J. A. Davis, *L'Inghilterra e la Rivoluzione Napoletana del 1799* (Napoli, 1999).
De Divitiis - Giura (a cura di), *L'Italia del Secondo Settecento* (Napoli, 1997).
J. Diamond, *Guns, Gems and Steel,* (New York, 1998).
A. Dumas, *I Borboni di Napoli* (Napoli, 1969-71).
C. Giglioli, *Naples in 1799* (London, 1903).
R. Jakobson, *Language in Literature* (Cambridge, Mass., 1987).
R. D. Putnam, *Making democracy work* (Princeton, 1993).
A. M. Rao, P. Villani, *Napoli 1799-1815* (Napoli, 1995).
A. M. Rao (a cura di), *Napoli 1799 - Fra Storia e Storiografia* (Napoli, 2002).
Storia d'Italia, (Torino, 1973).
The Oxford History of Britain (ed. by Kenneth O. Morgan) (Oxford, 1986).
F. Venturi, *Settecento Riformatore,* vol. V, t. 1 (Torino, 1987).
E. Vincent, *Nelson* (New Haven & London, 2003).

INDEX OF NAMES

Acmet (Commodore) 2

Acton, John (General) 3, 4, 5, 8, 13, 14, 15, 19, 20, 22, 23, 28, 31, 34, 37, 45, 46, 47, 48, 51, 56, 59, 65, 91, 92, 93, 94, 95, 96, 97, 98, 101, 102, 106, 107, 112, 116, 117, 118, 126, 128, 132, 139, 142, 146, 151, 155, 157, 172, 173, 180, 181, 182, 193, 194, 195, 196, 198, 199, 200, 214, 215, 216, 217, 218, 222, 224, 225, 234, 237, 241, 244, 247, 248, 250, 252, 258

Albert (Prince) 144

Andria (Duke of) 69, 159, 207

Anfuso, Pietro 39

Angri (Duke of) 159

Ascoli (Duke of) 139, 201

August Frederick (Prince) 37, 43, 48, 52, 54, 56, 59, 60, 62, 68, 74, 76, 80, 88, 92, 96, 99, 134, 145, 197, 224, 242, 245, 246, 247, 248, 252

Azar (Cardinal) 51

Baillie (Commander) 2

Ball (Captain) 3, 25, 59, 65, 117, 129, 133, 145, 156, 160, 169, 172, 177, 182, 183, 215

Barlow, Catherine 1, 32

Bashaw (Captain) 213

Battaglini, Mario 4, 237, 239, 255

Belmonte Pignatelli (Prince) 46, 65, 69, 90, 93, 105, 115, 142, 217

Berthier (General) 73, 74, 76, 77, 127, 154, 214, 245

Berwick (Lord - Lady) 41, 44, 62, 66, 242, 243

Blanquet (Admiral) 118

Bomeester, Daniel 36, 38, 39, 57, 64

Bomeester, John 57, 64

Bouligny 62, 146

Bowen (Captain) 101, 110, 113

Bradham, F. P. 8, 238

Braschi (Cardinal) 72, 245

Bridport (Admiral) 26

Bristol (Lord) 72, 91, 243

B(u)onaparte, Luigi 138

B(u)onaparte, Napoleone (General) 15, 16, 17, 18, 19, 25, 39, 40, 41, 45, 49, 50, 54, 58, 62, 68, 70, 91, 101, 103, 104, 106, 110, 111, 112, 114, 127, 138, 149, 155, 160, 167, 168, 202, 210, 211, 214, 239, 244, 246, 252

Burke, Edmund 24, 34, 242

Busca (Cardinal) 109

Cacault (Monsieur) 62, 246

Caracciolo (Ragusian agent) 109

Caracciolo, Francesco (Captain) 3, 4, 5, 7, 9, 20, 124, 192

Caracciolo, Lucio 5

Carlo (Archduke) 41

Carlo III (King) 14, 29

Cassano (Duke of) 207, 252

Cassaro (Prince of) 213, 216, 251

Castelcicala (Prince of) 46, 60, 64, 68, 74, 242

Castelcicala (Princess of) 142

Cavelos 37

Championet (General) 135, 136, 150, 151, 152, 156, 158, 159

Circello (Marquis of) 19, 37, 46, 76, 83, 96, 90, 92, 94, 100, 105, 107, 120, 122, 131, 137, 164, 165, 173, 178, 194, 195, 207, 215, 242, 247, 249, 251

Cirillo, Domenico 213

Clarence (Duke of) 24, 240
Clementina (Archduchess) 50, 51, 53, 245
Colletta, Pietro 61, 62, 238, 240, 242, 255, 258
Constantine, David 10, 31, 237, 241, 245, 250, 253, 256, 258
Croce, Benedetto 6, 238, 255, 256, 258
Cuoco Vincenzo 6, 20, 22, 238, 240, 255, 258
Cuttò (Prince) 139

Darby (Captain) 168
Davanzati, Forges (Bishop) 7
Davenport, Andrew (Proconsul) 93
De Burgh (General) 40, 42, 43, 44
De Canclaux 51, 54, 55, 56, 58, 63, 72, 245, 246
De Curtis, Michele (Judge) 26
De la Chaise 105, 109
Della Torre, Giuseppe (Don) 106
Denham 40, 70, 243
Diamond, Jared 161, 168, 179, 201, 202, 213, 243, 253, 254
Di Filippis, Costantino 183
Dixon (Captain) 110, 112, 176
Drake 37, 242
Duberly 62
Duckworth (Commodore) 26, 136, 238, 250
Dufort (General) 71, 72, 73
Duns (Captain) 204

Eden, Morton (Sir) 79, 82, 90, 92, 96, 113, 116, 126, 166, 171, 176
Elliot, Gilbert (Sir) 37, 38, 40, 42, 87, 96, 152, 240, 241, 242
Elphiston (Captain)
England (Consul) 210
England, William (Consul) 208
Erskine, James (Sir) 212

Federici (General) 5, 237
Ferdinand IV (King) 2, 13, 14, 18, 19, 20, 21, 26, 29, 32, 226, 227, 229, 232, 233, 234, 235, 241, 242, 244, 248, 250, 251, 252, 253
Foley (Captain) 205
Foote (Captain) 2, 6, 7, 25, 26, 27, 28, 169, 182, 183, 186, 234, 236, 237, 238, 240, 252, 253

Forresti, Spiridion (Consul) 161, 162
Fortiguerri (Mareshal) 43
Fothergill, Brian 10, 237, 239
Fox, James Charles 6, 38, 146, 212
Freemantle (Captain) 37, 241

Galeppi (Monsieur) 72
Gallo (Marquis of) 16, 19, 20, 45, 65, 74, 87, 92, 93, 94, 95, 100, 102, 105, 107, 126, 136, 137, 138, 140, 147, 163, 173, 194, 195, 213, 244, 250
Garrat 88, 89, 90, 104, 105, 119
Gardiner, Alan (Sir) 181
Gesso (Duke of) 149
Ghillini (Count) 66
Gibbs, Abraham (Banker) 99, 110, 129, 134, 152, 208
Giglioli, H. D. 9, 28, 238, 240, 254, 255, 258
Gillray, James 10, 25
Girardon (General) 198
Goddard 40, 42, 44, 93, 243
Graham (Colonel) 37, 174, 180, 210, 215, 218, 242
Gran Diavolo 170, 171, 174, 179, 252
Gregory (Lieutenant) 136
Grenville (Lord) 24, 31, 32, 148, 197, 240, 243, 245, 247, 249, 250, 251, 252
Gunning (General) 62
Gutteridge, H. C. 9, 255

Hamilton, Emma (Lady) 7, 9, 17, 25, 34, 250, 253
Hardy (Captain) 102, 167, 201, 209, 214
Hock (General) 25
Holwell (Captain) 126, 127, 162, 174, 192
Hood (Captain) 126, 127, 162, 174, 192
Hope (Captain) 105, 143, 152, 154, 183, 184, 248
Horse (Captain) 156

Jenkins 41, 71, 239, 243
Jervis, John (Sir) 43, 46, 96, 97, 236, 248, 252
Joubert (General)

Keith (Lord) 5, 6, 27, 28, 180, 181, 182, 196, 237, 238
Knight, Carlo 9, 18, 28, 102, 104, 237, 239, 240, 256, 257

La Combe St. Michel 119, 124, 125, 136, 138, 140, 249
La Tonella (Prince) 207
Latouche-Tréville, Louis (Admiral) 14
Leopold (Prince) 124, 206
Lewis (Captain) 198, 207, 209, 212
Livingston 79, 82, 88, 99, 134, 242, 243
Lloyd (Captain) 168
Lock, Charles 146, 160
Lorenzana (Cardinal) 51
Lucas (Consul) 197
Ludolaf (Minister) 161
Louis XVI (King of France) 24, 34, 89, 243
Luigi XI (King di Francia)
Luzzi (Prince) 69, 201, 215

Macdonald (General) 136, 170, 250
Mack (General) 20, 21, 49, 73, 124, 125, 128, 132, 135, 136, 138, 139, 141, 144, 145, 146, 147, 150, 153, 156, 158, 238, 246, 250, 251
Magra (Consul) 109, 115
Mahan, A. T. 8, 9, 238, 239
Mahony (Colonel) 212, 218
Maria Carolina (Queen) 3, 4, 13, 14, 22, 24, 26, 237, 240, 241
Maria Theresa (Empress) 13, 47
Marie Antoinette (Queen) 13, 14, 34
Maresca, Antonio 8
Market 93
Mattei (Cardinal) 51
Metternich 30
Micheroux (General) 3, 4, 9, 27, 139, 162, 181, 185
Migliano (Prince of) 149
Miles, Jefferson 8, 66, 179, 238
Minto (Lord) 144, 241, 242
Mitchel (Commodore) 148, 149, 238
Moliterno (Prince) 5, 154, 156, 159
Moore, Hannah 25
Moreau (General) 200, 202
Munster (Count) 59, 60, 99
Murray (Captain) 119, 239
Muschin, Puschin (Count) 55

Naselli (General) 135, 154, 210, 213, 252
Nelson, Horatio (Lord) 1, 2, 3, 4, 5, 6, 7, 8, 9, 17, 18, 19, 20, 21, 23, 24, 25, 26, 27, 28, 29, 32, 34, 40, 62, 101, 102, 103, 104, 105, 106, 107, 108, 109, 110, 111, 112, 113, 114, 115, 116, 117, 118, 119, 124, 125, 126, 127, 128, 129, 130, 131, 132, 133, 134, 135, 136, 138, 139, 140, 141, 142, 143, 144, 146, 147, 149, 151, 152, 155, 156, 157, 158, 159, 160, 161, 162, 166, 167, 168, 169, 171, 174, 175, 176, 177, 179, 180, 181, 182, 183, 187, 188, 189, 190, 191, 192, 193, 194, 195, 196, 197, 198, 199, 200, 201, 202, 204, 205, 206, 207, 208, 209, 210, 211, 212, 213, 214, 215, 216, 222, 224, 225, 226, 227, 231, 233, 234, 235, 236, 237, 238, 239, 240, 248, 249, 251, 252, 253, 254, 255, 256, 257, 258
Niza (Marquis of) 214, 215
North 40
Novelli (Mareshall)

O' Brien, Patrick 14, 239, 256
O' Hara (General) 216
Oswald (Captain) 184, 196, 199

Paget, Arthur 31, 219
Parkinson (Lieutenant) 189
Pembroke (Lord) 47, 253
Pignatelli, Francesco (Mareshall) 65, 69, 90, 92, 146, 150, 151, 153, 154, 250
Pitt, the Younger 24, 25, 134, 254
Pontano, 97, 107, 196, 223, 224, 248
Proby (Lord) 43

Ragland 45, 48, 93
Riario (Duke of)
Ricciardi, Omodeo 7
Roccaromana, (Duke of) 5
Ross (Banker) 197, 206
Ross (General) 202
Ruffo, Fabrizio (Cardinal) 2, 3, 4, 5, 8, 9, 23, 24, 26, 27, 28, 154, 157, 159, 162, 167, 170, 171, 174, 179, 187, 189, 190, 191, 196, 199, 202, 204, 207, 213, 222, 226, 227, 231, 234, 235, 236

Salandra (Duke of) 153, 156
Saumerez, James (Admiral) 119, 120
Saxe (Prince of) 47, 139
Scott (Merchant) 115
Smith, Sydney (Sir) 112, 145, 154, 161, 162, 176, 202, 203, 210, 211, 254
Sontag, Susan 239

Southey, Robert 7, 9, 236, 238, 255
Spencer (Lord) 7, 106, 112, 152, 154, 161, 189, 240
Stigliano (Prince) 46, 207
Stuart (Cardinal) 109
Stuart, Charles (Sir) 162, 166, 167
Stuart, William (Lord) 169
St. Vincent (Lord) 32, 83, 95, 97, 98, 100, 101, 103, 106, 108, 110, 129, 155, 162, 172, 189
Suvorov (Mareshall) 253
Sylvester (Messenger) 189

Tanucci, Bernardo 14, 242
Tatter 68, 88, 89
Thompson (Captain) 129
Thurn (Count de) 4, 184, 185
Torre (Duke of) 106, 156
Tough, James, (Consul) 36, 62, 64, 71, 246
Troubridge (Captain) 3, 24, 26, 102, 103,

117, 127, 129, 138, 160, 167, 169, 170, 171, 174, 175, 181, 182, 193, 194, 196, 198, 207, 208, 210, 224, 240, 248, 252
Trouvet 56, 63

Usacon (Admiral) 204, 207, 208, 209, 211, 212
Unsworth, Baron 9, 238, 239

Vernon 62, 66
Vincent, David 17

Wellesley, Arthur (Later Duke of Wellington) 17
Williams, Helen Maria 7, 238, 255
Wyndham 49, 139, 147, 149, 168, 173, 174, 175, 208

Zurlo (Cardinal) 143